Cultural Tourism
Second edition

Cultural Tourism remains the only book to bridge the gap between cultural tourism and cultural and heritage management. The first edition illustrated how heritage and tourism goals can be integrated in a management and marketing framework to produce sustainable cultural tourism. The current edition takes this idea further to base the discussion of cultural tourism in the theory and practice of cultural and heritage management, under the understanding that for tourism to thrive, a balanced approach to the resource base it uses must be maintained. An 'umbrella approach' to cultural tourism represents a unique feature of the book, proposing solutions to achieve an optimal outcome for all sectors.

Reflecting the many important developments in the field, this new edition has been completely revised and updated in the following ways:

- new sections added on tangible and intangible cultural heritage and World Heritage sites;
- expanded material on cultural tourism product development, the cultural tourism market and consumer behaviour, planning and delivery of exceptional experiences;
- new case studies throughout drawn from cultural attractions in developing countries such as Southeast Asia, China, South Africa and the Pacific as well as from the developed world, particularly the United States, Britain, Japan, Singapore, Australia and Canada.

Written by experts in both tourism and cultural heritage management, this book will enable professionals and students to gain a better understanding of their own and each other's roles in achieving sustainable cultural tourism. It provides a blueprint for producing top-quality, long-term cultural tourism products.

Hilary du Cros is an Honorary Research Fellow at the University of New Brunswick, Canada with a PhD from Monash University, Melbourne. She has a unique perspective on tourism, heritage and arts management after 30 years as an academic and consultant in the Asia-Pacific Region. Books include *The Arts and Events* with Lee Jolliffe (Routledge 2014) and *Cultural Heritage Management in China* with Y.S.F. Lee (Routledge 2007).

Bob McKercher is a Professor of Tourism at the Hong Kong Polytechnic University. He has wide ranging research interests focused around special interest tourism markets, product development and consumer behaviour. He received his PhD from the University of Melbourne, Australia, a Masters degree from Carleton University in Ottawa, Canada, and his undergraduate degree from York University in Toronto, Canada. Prior to entering academia, he worked in a variety of operational and advocacy positions in the Canadian tourism industry.

Who would have thought it could be done? Well they did it! The authors have taken an already well-written, informative, and insightful volume to higher heights. du Cros and McKercher have expanded this new version of *Cultural Tourism* to be more inclusive and updated in its content and coverage. This erudite book is a must read for scholars and practitioners who are interested in the enormity and pervasiveness of culture as a resource for tourism!

Dallen J. Timothy, Professor, School of Community Resources and Development, Arizona State University

Cultural Tourism

Second edition

Hilary du Cros and Bob McKercher

Routledge
Taylor & Francis Group

LONDON AND NEW YORK

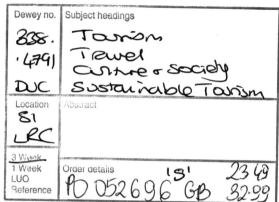
First published 2002

Second Edition Published 2015
by Routledge
2 Park Square, Milton Park, Abingdon, Oxon OX14 4RN

And by Routledge
711 Third Avenue, New York, NY 10017

Routledge is an imprint of the Taylor & Francis Group, an informa business

© 2002 and 2015 Hilary du Cros and Bob McKercher

The right of Hilary du Cros and Bob McKercher to be identified as the authors of this work has been asserted by them in accordance with sections 77 and 78 of the Copyright, Designs and Patents Act 1988.

British Library Cataloguing in Publication Data
A catalogue record for this book is available from the British Library

Library of Congress Cataloging in Publication Data
Cultural tourism / Hilary du Cros and Bob McKercher.—2nd Edition.
pages cm
Includes bibliographical references and index.
G156.5.H47M35 2014
910—dc23
2014021328

ISBN: 978-0-415-83396-7 (hbk)
ISBN: 978-0-415-83397-4 (pbk)
ISBN: 978-0-203-79060-1 (ebk)

Typeset in Times New Roman
by GreenGate Publishing Services, Tonbridge, Kent

MIX
Paper from responsible sources
FSC www.fsc.org FSC® C013604

Printed and bound by CPI Group (UK) Ltd, Croydon, CR0 4YY

To Eve

Contents

List of plates

List of figures

List of tables

List of boxes

Preface

A lot has changed since the first edition of this book was published in 2002. To reflect that there has been much water under the bridge, this second edition of *Cultural Tourism* includes new sections on the creative arts, tangible and intangible cultural heritage, and World Heritage sites. It also has expanded sections on cultural tourism product development, the cultural tourism market and consumer behaviour, planning and delivery of exceptional experiences.

The authors have tried to include a broad cross-section of cultural assets and tourism attractions of every scale from around the world to show not only the cultural diversity of assets available, but also the issues associated with developing them for tourism for the long term. This development should also include relating cultural attractions and products more closely to the communities in which they are anchored. Although this approach is becoming more widely accepted in some places, it needs to be spelt out for others where short-term gains still seem to be the order of the day.

Accordingly, this book highlights the key issues about building partnerships, strategic marketing, and ongoing management for cultural tourism. It also provides a theoretical and operational context for understanding cultural tourism, so that these issues can be understood more readily. Finally, some suggestions have been made for future improvements and research, in light of emerging cultural tourism markets and possible new sustainable tourism products that may be developed in the next 12 years or longer.

Acknowledgements

A number of tourism, heritage and arts management professionals and others have contributed to this book. They have helped by talking to us about their situations, providing photos or by giving advice generally. In particular, the authors would like to thank: Lee Jolliffe, Angie McGowan, Barry Hiern, Chin Ee Ong, Sammie Liu and Shelby Harrison who were extremely helpful with their comments. Finally, from Taylor & Francis, Emma Travis and Philippa Mullins deserve a special mention.

We would also like to express our thanks to the University of New Brunswick, the Hong Kong Polytechnic University, and the National University of Singapore for providing institutional support in the course of preparing the manuscript.

Abbreviations

AM	arts management
AMO	Antiquities and Monuments Office
BBC	British Broadcasting Corporation
CHM	cultural heritage management
CM	cultural management
DEA	Department of Environment Australia
DMO	destination marketing organization
EIA	environmental impact assessments
HKIEd	Hong Kong Institute of Education
HUL	historic urban landscape
IATF	Inter-Agency Task Force
ICCROM	International Centre for the Study of the Preservation and Restoration of Cultural Property
ICH	intangible cultural heritage
ICOM	International Council of Museums
ICOMOS	International Council on Monuments and Sites
IFACCA	International Federation of Arts Councils and Cultural Agencies
IFT	Institute for Tourism Studies
IGO	intergovernmental organization
IUCN	International Union for the Conservation of Cultural and Natural Resources (also known as the World Conservation Union)
IVE	immersive virtual environment
MOS	Museum of Sydney
NEA	National Endowment for the Arts
NGO	non-governmental organization
NHA	National Heritage Area
NOHJF	New Orleans Heritage and Jazz Festival
SAR	special administrative region
SCA	sustainable creative advantage
UNESCO	United Nations Educational, Scientific and Cultural Organization
UNWTO	United Nations World Tourism Organization
WHC	World Heritage Centre
WHC	World Heritage Committee
WHS	World Heritage site
WKCD	West Kowloon Cultural District
WTTC	World Travel and Tourism Council

Part A
Setting the context

⬤1 Introduction
Defining cultural tourism

Cultural tourism has changed dramatically since it was first recognized as part of the array of available tourism experiences in the late 1970s and early 1980s. It was recognized as a distinct product category only in the late 1970s when tourism marketers and tourism researchers realized that some people travelled specifically to gain a deeper understanding of the culture or heritage of a destination (Tighe 1986). Initially, it was regarded as a specialist, niche activity that was thought to be pursued by a small number of better educated, more affluent tourists who were looking for something other than the standard sand, sun, and sea holiday. It has grown from those humble beginnings to become a mainstream, mass product. Depending on the source and the destination, research, often using a questionable method, indicates between 35 percent and 80 percent of all tourists are cultural tourists (Mandala 2009; Molle and Deckert 2009; Richards 1996; TV 2013).

It is not surprising then that destinations are clamoring to get onto the preverbal cultural tourism bandwagon, for the opportunity to engage in a community's diverse tangible and intangible cultural heritage assets creates the potential to provide peak experiences for tourists. Destination management organizations (DMOs) now appreciate that cultural tourism, in its broadest sense, provides an opportunity to position communities uniquely and, in doing so, gain a sustainable competitive advantage. The role of the cultural heritage management community has expanded as well, from managers and custodians of cultural assets, to providers of products. Academics, consultants, and government agencies have also embraced this topic as an exciting research field. As a consequence, our understanding of what cultural tourism is, who cultural tourists are, and what is required to provide quality experiences has become much more sophisticated.

Yet, while the field has grown, much also remains unchanged, as many misconceptions about the nature of this activity, the level of interest by tourists and factors leading to successful product development still persist. Most importantly, the growth of the field has created new management challenges relating to how to achieve true, triple bottom line sustainability. Most DMOs are interested primarily in increasing the volume of arrivals and yield of visitors by promoting their attractions, activities and unique cultures. But, promotion often occurs without due consideration for the impact increased visitation may have on the assets, the local residents who use them and, indeed, whether local stakeholders want increased visitation. Unique and place-based culture is already under increasing pressure from globalization, standardization and internationalization, with tourism often seen as a key threat (Jansen-Verbeke and Russo 2008; Smith 2003; UNESCO 2003).

How to create sustainable cultural tourism is the critical issue facing this sector, for its special nature requires both an understanding of tourism and cultural management. It cannot be achieved if one is pursued at the expense of the other. This task is even more challenging given the diversity of cultural items and assets that form the foundation of this activity, the need to address the legitimate interests of different stakeholders, often with opposing agendas, and the need to provide an enjoyable and rewarding experience for tourists.

This book, hopefully, will help smooth that path. This chapter focuses on defining what cultural tourism is and how to distinguish it from other forms of tourism. The next two chapters examine sustainability and review some of the benefits and risks associated with pursuing culture as a tourism product.

What is cultural tourism?

Cultural tourism is one of the oldest forms of special interest tourism, and yet, remains one of the more misunderstood types. People have been travelling for what we now call cultural tourism reasons since the days of the ancient Romans visiting Greece and Egypt (Perrottet 2002) or Chinese scholars making journeys to beautiful landscapes (Yan and McKercher 2013). At the same time, places and activities that we now label as representing cultural tourism products were not identified as such until recently. Instead, visiting historic sites, cultural landmarks, attending special events and festivals, watching street performances, or visiting museums were seen as part of a broader lexicon of sightseeing activities that formed part of the total tourism experience.

In fact, there is still much debate about what cultural tourism is and who cultural tourists are, for all travel involves some cultural element caused by leaving one's own home and travelling to different places. Doing so forces one from a comfortable home culture into a somewhat alien culture, even if it is only to a nearby domestic destination. Many people have the mistaken belief that experiencing cultural difference is equivalent to cultural tourism, and therefore argue that anything and everything can fall under its umbrella. But such a conceptualization serves little purpose, other than to conflate ideas, confuse terms and mislabel both tourists and attractions.

In fact, the seemingly fundamental questions of what cultural tourism is and who cultural tourists are have proven to be difficult to answer definitively, for there are almost as many variations of definitions as there are tourists. The inability to establish a clear conceptual foundation of what it is we are looking at and who the participants are has resulted in misuse of the term and confusion over who its core stakeholders are, leading ultimately to people defining the term to suit their own narrow interests. This issue was recognized almost 20 years ago by the American Chapter of ICOMOS (the International Council on Monuments and Sites), which observed that "cultural tourism as a name means many things to many people and herein lies its strength and its weakness" (US ICOMOS 1996: 17). More recently Smith (2003) adds that confusion over what constitutes 'culture', the sector's basic building block, adds an extra layer of confusion.

Over the years, a number of definitions have been proposed that embrace some element of this activity, but do not encapsulate it fully. Early tourism-related definitions place cultural tourism within a broader framework of tourism and tourism management theory (Zeppel and Hall 1991) or as a form of special interest tourism (Zeppel 1992; Ap 1999). For example, the United Nations World Tourism Organization (UNWTO) defines cultural tourism as:

> the movement of persons to cultural attractions in cities in countries other than their normal place of residence, with the intention to gather new information and experiences to satisfy their cultural needs and all movements of persons to specific cultural attractions, such as heritage sites, artistic and cultural manifestations, arts and drama to cities outside their normal country of residence.
>
> (Whyte, Hood and White 2012: 10)

A second group of motivation-related definitions focuses on the belief that cultural tourists are motivated to travel for different reasons than other tourists. Organizations such as the UNWTO (2006a) and the Canadian Tourism Commission (Whyte, Hood and White 2012) describe cultural tourism on the basis of the desire to learn about a destination's cultural heritage as a significant travel motive. Building on this idea, a third group of definitions adopts an experiential approach that argues motivation alone does not encapsulate the full magnitude of this sector. Instead, cultural tourism involves some meaningful experience with the unique social fabric, heritage and special character of places (Blackwell 1997; Schweitzer 1999), or as a quest or search for greater understanding (Bachleitner and Zins 1999; Hannabuss 1999). The US National Endowment for the Arts, for example, defines it as "travel directed toward experiencing the arts, heritage, and special character of a place" (Whyte, Hood and White 2012: 8).

Almost all definitions, though, are circular in nature, for most of the tourism motivational and experiential definitions also include an operational component, often to illustrate the point being made. The UNWTO (2006a) suggests cultural tourism represents movements of people motivated by cultural intents such as study tours, performing arts, festivals, cultural events, visits to sites and monuments, as well as travel for pilgrimages. Whyte, Hood and White (2012), for example, indicate the Canadian Tourism Commission definition includes performing arts (theatre, dance, music), visual arts and crafts, festivals, museums and cultural centres, and historic sites and interpretive centres, while the US National Endowment for the Arts specifies museums, historic sites, dance, music, theatre, book and other festivals, historic buildings, arts and crafts fairs, neighbourhoods, and landscapes. Indeed, it is common to define cultural tourism by activity, using definitions that read something like 'cultural tourism includes visits to …'. The Australian State of Victoria, for example, defines cultural tourists as "those who attended a theatre performance, a concert or other performing arts, a cultural festival, fair or event; or visited a museum, art gallery, art or craft workshop or studios, and/or a history or heritage site while on their trip to Australia" (TV 2013). Richards (2011) has adopted a hybrid definition linking motivation to behaviour, when he suggests cultural tourism essentially involves visits to cultural attractions and events by culturally motivated people.

Cultural tourism: an umbrella term that defines a product category

Each of the approaches has some merits, but each is also limited in scope. The main benefit of tourism-related definitions is that they identify cultural tourism as a form of tourism and not a form of cultural heritage management. But they are too generic to be used in a meaningful manner. Motivational and experiential definitions recognize that the reasons for travel, and thus experiences sought by cultural tourists differ from those of other tourists. They may be conceptually robust but also make it difficult to define the types of products they use. Operational definitions resolve the product dilemma, and also indicate that many cultural tourism products are places of local cultural significance used by local stakeholders. But these definitions are the weakest of all, for they assume that anyone who visits a place or has an experience that may or may not reflect a destination's cultural heritage must be, by definition, a deep cultural tourist according to the motivational and experiential definitions. In doing so, they fail to appreciate that people visit places for many reasons and that the application of a singular, deep motive runs the risk of misrepresenting the importance of the attraction in the overall trip decision-making process. In fact, the use of this overly simplistic definition has been responsible for most of the bad research published documenting the size and importance of the market.

The challenge then becomes one of how to define cultural tourism in a manner that captures the essence of the experience, can be used by DMOs as a marketing tool, can be used to identify potential products and, most importantly, also can be used to identify and proscribe management actions that reflect the legitimate needs of all stakeholders. This book adopts a more marketing oriented approach by defining cultural tourism as a product class that is defined by four interrelated factors.

Cultural tourism is defined as:

> A form of tourism that relies on a destination's cultural heritage assets and transforms them into products that can be consumed by tourists.
>
> (McKercher and du Cros 2005: 211–212)

This definition recognizes that cultural tourism involves four elements:

- tourism;
- use of cultural assets;
- consumption of experiences and products;
- the tourist.

Tourism

To state that cultural tourism is a form of tourism may seem self-evident and rather tautological. The word 'tourism' is a noun and the word 'cultural' is an adjective used to modify it. As such, it is vital to recognize that, above all else, cultural tourism is a form of tourism and not a form of cultural management. The decision to embark on cultural tourism must be based on sound tourism reasons first and cultural management reasons second. And, equally as important, cultural tourism products must be managed as products. This point needs to be appreciated more by some members of the cultural management community, particularly those who resist the tourismification of cultural assets that are already attracting tourists.

The use of cultural assets

While recognizing this activity is a form of tourism, one can never forget that its principal building blocks are a community's or a nation's cultural heritage assets. ICOMOS defines heritage as a broad concept that includes tangible assets, such as natural and cultural environments, the encompassing of landscapes, historic places, sites and built environments, as well as intangible assets such as collections, past and continuing cultural practices and knowledge and living experiences (ICOMOS 1999). In recent years, the concept has also been expanded to include a wide array of contemporary and heritage arts that express something unique about a group's or an individual's world view. These assets are identified, performed, safeguarded, handed down and/or conserved for their intrinsic values or significance to a community rather than for their extrinsic use values as tourism attractions. In fact, the tourism potential of assets is rarely considered when they are first identified as significant to a community.

One of the paradoxes of cultural tourism is that, while the decision to enter this sector must be driven by tourism considerations, the assets it utilizes are managed by the principles of cultural management (CM) within which arts management (AM) and cultural heritage management (CHM) are subcategories. That is, contemporary arts, tangible and intangible heritage from which cultural assets spring can be subject to the professional management principles and practices of heritage site managers, arts administrators, gallery and museum curators, and more. In addition, many cultural assets may serve a multitude of user groups, including tourists but also including local schoolchildren, traditional owners and other local residents. These groups may value the asset for different reasons and seek different benefits from its use, making the presentation task more difficult. These competing approaches can be a source of friction between tourism, arts and CHM interests. Part B introduces the reader to the key principles of CM and how they are applied to tangible and intangible cultural assets, with the inclusion of contemporary arts.

Throughout the book, a distinction is made between a cultural asset/item and a cultural tourism product. A cultural asset/item represents the uncommodified or raw asset that is identified for its intrinsic values. A cultural tourism product, on the other hand, represents an asset that has been transformed or commodified specifically for tourism consumption.

Plate 1.1 Welcome Tourist! Vigan WHS, Philippines

Welcome tourist! While many communities feel this way, it not always a given. Employing long-term integrated planning and management that is inclusive of local communities will keep signs like this up on the wall.

Consumption of experiences and products

All tourism involves the consumption of products and experiences (Richards 1996; Urry 2002). Cultural tourism is no different. The use of the term 'consumption' is controversial to some, for they see the production of waste as an inevitable outcome of consuming something, and moreover, see consumption as an act of destruction. In this case, though, consumption is used to identify the essential process of experiencing attractions at a wide variety of levels, but can also be used in the connotation of risk. Cultural tourists want to consume experiences, but not everyone is capable of having the same depth or quality of experience. Some want or can only have a superficial experience, while others want a deeper experience. In order to facilitate this consumption, cultural heritage assets must be transformed into products. The transformation process actualizes the potential of the asset by converting it into something that the tourist can understand more readily and enjoy. There is a risk, though, that the transformation can lead to destruction if not managed carefully. The issue of how it should be managed responsibly and with respect to cultural value is discussed in more detail in Part D.

The tourist

The tourist is the final element to be considered. Tourists are non-local residents travelling primarily for fun, recreation, escape or to spend time with family and friends (Pearce and Lee 2005). They have limited and, usually, fixed time budgets. Most are looking to be entertained, while only a small number are looking for deeper learning experiences. Most also have a limited knowledge of a destination's cultural heritage and living culture. As such, they are a fundamentally different user group than local residents, with completely different needs and wants. Products that suit their needs may be inimical with the needs of local residents.

The type, quality and veracity of information received prior to arrival will shape their expectations and also their expected behaviour while visiting (see Plate 1.1). A vast array of information gatekeepers will set expectations, a task that has become more complicated with the social media revolution (du Cros and Liu 2013; Sharda and Ponnada 2008). Some of these sources are reliable, but many others may not be, and instead promote behaviours that are incompatible with the desires of asset managers. While most tourists want to do the right thing, in the absence of clear guidance of appropriate behaviour they will either follow the actions of other visitors, or revert to accepted norms of behaviour from their home culture. Successful cultural tourism products must be shaped with this type of visitor in mind, as they are likely to be the majority.

An umbrella product class: overview

The maturation of the field has also seen the fracturing of the cultural tourism concept into a series of increasingly small sub-genres of allegedly discrete activities or product types. Each is identified as being unique and each is then positioned as having special management challenges and opportunities. Whereas once we talked about cultural tourism, today attempts have been made to disaggregate many products, activities and experiences that fall under the broad umbrella of cultural tourism, such as arts and crafts workshops, fringe festivals, purchasing souvenirs of folk arts, gastronomy tours, industrial heritage museums, agricultural heritage parks, cultural activities that are part of mega events (e.g. the London Cultural Olympiad), and many more (Goodrich 1997; Miller 1997; Richards 1996; Smith 2003; Thorne 2012; TV 2013).

Has this level of disaggregation helped or hindered our understanding of cultural tourism? On the one hand, the identification of many constituent elements highlights the diversity of the field. On the other hand, it has served to confuse the issue. Franklin and Crang (2001:6) argue, in general, that tourism studies have been prey to coping with an expanding field through developing ever more refined sub-divisions and more elaborate typologies. The merits of defining sub-genres must be questioned, especially if the broad array of cultural tourism products and experiences faces common product development, management and sustainable use challenges. Indeed, the disaggregation of cultural tourism into a series of component parts may be doing more damage than good, by masking common issues and creating unneeded complexities. Kirshenblatt-Gimblett (2004) argues that establishing even a most basic distinction between tangible and intangible heritage is arbitrary and sometimes counterproductive, for the two are intimately linked. She writes,

> Increasingly, those dealing with natural heritage argue that most of the sites on the world natural heritage list are what they are by virtue of human interaction with the environment. Similarly, tangible heritage, without intangible heritage, is a mere husk or inert matter. As for intangible heritage, it is not only embodied, but also inseparable from the material and social worlds of persons.
>
> (Kirshenblatt-Gimblett 2004: 58)

Cultural tourism is treated as an umbrella term in this book that is best understood as representing a product class of experiences and activities that embodies a destination's cultural heritage assets. A product class is defined as a group of products that share some common characteristic or characteristics that distinguish them from other product classes. The building blocks of a community's cultural assets and the need to convert them into tourism products represent the key features that differentiate cultural from other tourism products classes, for these features raise unique managerial and product development considerations. Separate product categories can be identified within each product class. A product category is a group of related products that are distinguished from other products in the same class by one or more significant features. Within each category, smaller sub-units can be found. The adoption of a product class approach enables us to address issues that are common to all forms of cultural tourism and also focus on some issues that are unique to individual types of experiences, without getting bogged down in minutiae.

The product class approach has been used to great effect in many business-related taxonomic systems. For example, it is possible to identify clearly defined product classes of beverages (alcoholic, juice, milk or dairy, carbonated waters, and non-carbonated waters), and within each to identify product categories (e.g. within carbonated drinks, sugar and sugar-free, etc.). It is more challenging in tourism, for no clear classification system exists, partly because tourism is fundamentally an experiential activity, where products are consumed to satisfy the person's need and wants. Products may represent the platform whereby different experiences can be enjoyed. The same product may satisfy different needs, and therefore, could be classified as belonging to different product classes. Scale complicates the issue further, for cultural tourism products can range in scale from single small objects, to transnational cultural landscapes. Ultimately, then, the identification of product classes and product categories will be somewhat arbitrary.

Various attempts have been made to classify the array of cultural tourism products over the last 20 years, since Prentice (1993) indentified 23 different types of cultural tourism experiences, ranging from science-based attractions (science museums, technology centres), through to attractions associated with primary production and industrial heritage to sports, religion and gardens. Scale also ranged from villages and hamlets through to countryside and entire regions. Yale (1998) identified 12 types of attractions, including festivals and events and an amorphous 'miscellaneous' category. A few years later Leask and Yeoman (1999) classified attractions into one of three categories of built, natural, and living heritage and then added a scale dimension (nation/region, area, and site) to distinguish different types. Richards (2011) developed a matrix based on Form (past to present) and Function (education to entertainment). Tweed (2005) has arguably made the most ambitious attempt to develop a taxonomy of cultural tourism products. He identified four broad categories: objects, places, events, and sites. A number of sub-categories were then grouped under each broad theme. Objects were the primary focus of this system, with only indicative examples offered for places, events, and sites. The objects category was further sub-divided into monuments, buildings, and infrastructure, with further sub-divisions made under each heading. For example, the buildings sub-group included housing (with four further sub-divisions), industrial heritage, military attachments, and 14 other types.

Table 1.1 represents an alternate categorization of the cultural tourism product class. A total of 11 product categories constitute the cultural tourism product class. A few features must be appreciated when considering this classification. Products have been grouped according to key themes (see Plate 1.2). The groupings reflect key features that distinguish one product category from another, and in doing so, present different management and product development challenges that will be discussed throughout this test. For example, far greater flexibility exists in purpose-built or adaptive re-use sites than in built sites that have not been transformed for tourist use. Second, the product categories are not mutually exclusive. In fact, there is much overlap, for example, natural heritage and extant ethnic communities are intimately linked. The key differences, though, relate to how the product is identified. Third, a difference is noted between the product and the

Plate 1.2 Art tourists in China

Particular product categories for assets will need to be acknowledged in the planning and management for tourism. For instance, arts tourism of the kind shown above where artists travel to more aesthetically pleasing cultural assets to practise their skills falls under the creative industries category in Table 1.1.

Table 1.1 Classification of cultural tourism product categories

Product Category	Built: non touristic	Touristic purpose: built or modified	Economic	Transport	Cultural landscapes	Creative industries	Religious	Diaspora ethnic	Extant ethnic (extant)	Intangible heritage	Dark	Natural heritage (mixed values)
Descriptor	Prehistoric, historic and contemporary built heritage not transformed for touristic use	Purpose built attractions, including adaptive reuse of extant facilities	Tangible and intangible heritage associated with Agriculture, Industry, etc.	Transport, Infrastructure or Super-structure	Combined tangible and intangible features	Arts, performance, etc.	Tangible and intangible artifacts and practices	Tangible and intangible focusing largely on migrant communities	Tangible and intangible heritage associated with extant ethnic communities	Features (combined with some tangible) that reflect living cultures	Sites of human suffering	Cultural tourism associated with and defined by natural landscapes
Examples	Archeological sites Ruins Listed historic sites and buildings Other historic structures Artifacts Forts Castles Historic houses Iconic contemporary architecture Cemeteries Vernacular architecture	Theme parks Museums Cultural centres Conversion of historic sites to tourist attractions	Industrial heritage Attractions based on primary productions (mining, forestry, etc.) Farms and farm museums Agricultural practices Rare breeds (livestock and plants) Vineyards Distilleries, breweries, wineries, etc.	Canals Maritime structures (lighthouses, etc.) Ships Cars Railways Dams Bridges Roads	Historic towns Seaside resorts Neighbourhoods Industrial zones Linear or circular touring routes Precincts	Low to high culture Dance Performance Popular culture Theatre Literature Film Events and festivals focusing on the creative industries	Religious sites (churches, temples, mosques, etc.) Sacred sites Relics Religious practices Religious festivals and events	Diaspora Urban ethnic precincts Immigration festivals and events Ethnic festivals in migrant countries Homecoming festivals in source countries Slum tours Poverty tours Ethnic foods	Minority cultures Handicrafts Agricultural practices and associated traditions, lifestyles, etc. Clothing Foods Traditions Customs Folklore Oral traditions Voices Ceremonies Values	Traditions Customs Folklore Oral traditions Voices Ceremonies Values Famous people Food, wine, Local markets Sports	War sites Battlefields War graves War memorials Slavery Concentration camps Genocide sites Prisons	Conservation areas Botanic gardens Agricultural practices (e.g. terraced farming) Historic recreational use Wildlife and associated cultural practices Zoos

'platform' that can be used to offer the product. For instance, festivals have been identified as exemplars of product types in different categories, due to the fact that the festival represents a means to an end and not necessarily an end in itself. Finally, the classification associates cultural heritage with place, especially when considering the natural heritage product category. Natural heritage can also be associated with nature-based tourism in all its forms. Natural heritage as a cultural tourism product, though, must have some association with human use of meaning.

A note on cultural tourists

The cultural tourism market is described in detail in Chapter 8. It is often assumed, erroneously, that the market is homogeneous. However, as discussed in Chapter 8, great diversity of cultural tourists exists, based on the importance this activity has in the overall trip decision-making process and the depth of experience sought or had. Five cultural tourist market segments are referred to throughout the book. They are the:

- purposeful cultural tourist: cultural tourism is the primary motive for visiting a destination and the individual has a deep cultural experience;
- sightseeing cultural tourist: cultural tourism is a primary or major reason for visiting a destination, but the experience is more shallow;
- serendipitous cultural tourist: a tourist who does not travel for cultural tourism reasons, but who, after participating, ends up having a deep cultural tourism experience;
- casual cultural tourist: cultural tourism is a weak motive for visiting a destination and the resultant experience is shallow;
- incidental cultural tourist: who does not travel for cultural tourism reasons, but who nonetheless participates in some activities and has a shallow experience.

Key learning outcomes

- Cultural tourism is a form of tourism and not CM.
- A cultural asset represents the uncommodified or raw asset that has intrinsic value foremost.
- A cultural tourism product represents an asset that has been transformed or commodified specifically for tourism consumption.
- Cultural tourism consists of four elements:
  - tourism;
  - cultural assets as a building block;
  - consumption;
  - the tourist.
- Cultural tourism can be considered as a discrete product class with diverse sub-categories to appeal to a diversity of potential users.

---

② Challenges in achieving sustainable cultural tourism

Introduction

The emergence of cultural tourism as a popular tourism activity presents both opportunities and threats to its sustainable management. On the one hand, increased demand by tourists provides a powerful political and economic justification to expand conservation and safeguard activities. On the other hand, increased visitation, over-use, inappropriate use, and the commodification of assets without regard for their cultural values pose a real threat to their physical integrity, and in extreme cases to their very survival. It is for this reason that international CHM advocates began to promote a charter of principles almost 40 years ago to protect cultural values from inappropriate tourism uses (ICOMOS 1976). More recently, museum professionals also proposed an additional charter, over concerns about many of the same issues, plus tourism's role in the illicit traffic of movable cultural objects (ICOM 2014a).

The potential risks associated with tourism are greater than ever as demand increases, particularly in and from the developing world (Arlt 2006; Winter, et al. 2009) due to a lack of suitable management structures and because some tourists from emerging economies have different standards of accepted behaviour. Pressure is also being placed on many assets, particularly cultural festivals and arts events, to perform in a more business-like manner in order to secure funding (McNicholas 2004; du Cros and Jolliffe 2014). The challenge is how to find a balance between tourism and CM and between the consumption of extrinsic values by tourists and conservation/safeguarding of the intrinsic values by cultural managers, for, at times, conflicts have emerged between the two sectors as they vie to use the same foundation for their activities (Bowes 1994; Jamieson 1995, France 2011; Bandarin and van Oers 2012).

Sustainable cultural tourism is or should involve a partnership that satisfies both tourism and arts/CHM objectives. The potential mutual benefits of such a partnership are well understood (Robinson 1999). ICOMOS, in its second tourism charter, for example, states 'tourism can capture the economic characteristics of heritage and harness these for conservation by generating funding, educating the community and influencing policy (ICOMOS 1999).' The UNWTO (2006a and b) suggests cultural tourism can help reduce poverty through employment, local enterprise development, crafts, infrastructure development, voluntourism, and tax revenues. Elsewhere it (UNWTO 2006c) identifies increased community pride, an economic motive to conserve heritage and improved governance as possible benefits.

In practice, though, the relationship is often uneasy, for tourism and CM stakeholders often do not understand each other's interests, do not share a common language or goals, and are confronted with limited and incomplete data to inform decisions (Boniface 1998;

Jansen-Verbeke 1998; Garrod and Fyall 2000; Baxter 2010). Cohen and Cohen (2012: 2191) identify a further issue when they write:

> while conservation, preservation and restoration of heritage sites are allegedly based on sound scientific principles, these processes are in fact profoundly suffused by ideological and political considerations, as national and other authorities exploit them to strengthen the identity of their collectives or their own legitimating. Such considerations influence decisions regarding the choice of sites destined for preservation and the manner of their restoration.
>
> (Cohen and Cohen 2012: 2191)

The main stumbling blocks seem to be the continued operation of tourism and CM in parallel rather than in partnership. Even though both sectors have been increasingly holding conferences and seminars that include at least one session on issues related to the other stakeholder, full appreciation of each other's needs and motives is still a work in progress. Integration and partnerships can only be achieved if each side develops a stronger and more comprehensive understanding of how the other views the assets, values them and seeks to have them used. This chapter begins with a review of the sustainability challenge facing the tourism sector and then discusses the role of the tourism and the CM sectors in relation to sustainability. It concludes with a discussion of the types of relationships that can exist between tourism and cultural heritage.

The challenge of triple bottom line sustainability

While sustainable use of cultural assets is a given, caution must be used when the term 'sustainability' is introduced, for it is a much abused word that has been used by different groups to promote completely different agendas. To some stakeholders, sustainability means economic viability, where the intrinsic values of an asset can be compromised and local residents' needs ignored as long as wealth is generated. To other stakeholders, sustainability can be used as an excuse to oppose most uses, arguing that any use will invariably lead to a site's destruction.

The issue has become even more complicated with the popularization of triple bottom line sustainability in recent years. The term triple bottom line was introduced initially in a commercial context to argue that enterprises needed to integrate economic, social and environmental objectives into their core business strategy (Elkington 2004). The need for such a change grew out of the broader recognition for businesses to function in a manner that is more in line with current notions of corporate soaial responsibility (Elkington 2004). In essence, it was designed to reflect a holistic management philosophy (Stoddard et al. 2012). Such a management approach provides many benefits for the tourism sector, including the ability to tap into previously unrecognized markets, enhance connection with stakeholders and minimize adverse social and environmental impacts (Dwyer and Edwards 2013).

However, it is often difficult to apply in practice. A risk exists that it can be used for cynical purposes as a form of reputation management with little commitment to its principles (Stoddard et al. 2012; Dwyer and Edwards 2013). In addition, integration may be challenging as different departments with different roles may develop different practices, resulting in parallel activities, rather than an integrated approach to sustainability (Elkington 2004). Stoddard et al. (2012) also note many organizations use such an approach rigidly as an accounting method and have overlooked the need to establish and follow a corporate philosophy in keeping with the idea's initial intentions.

The greatest operational challenge, though, is how to measure 'sustainability' (Stoddard et al. 2012). Economic performance is easy to measure precisely and quickly, while social and ecological performance is both difficult to measure and must be assessed over a long time frame that falls well outside of normal accounting periods. A further issue lies in what to measure. The complexity of measuring 'sustainability' is reflected in the UNWTO (2004a) publication *Indicators of Sustainable Development for Tourism Destinations: A Guidebook*. The guide, which was initially intended to be a practical handbook, is 507 pages long and identifies 47 key sustainability indicators under 13 broad themes covering such topics as the well-being of host communities, tourist satisfaction and controlling tourist activities. Specific indicators range from sex tourism to solid waste management.

Working towards a sustainable cultural tourism sector creates a number of challenges. The first is the diversity of products available. The previous chapter identified 11 product categories that constitute cultural tourism (see Table 1.1). Some measures of sustainability are common to all, but each also has its unique challenges. Each also necessitates the development of slightly different approaches and different sets of indicators to manage for a true triple bottom line. Generic sustainable development policies may provide a broad framework, but they may be too vague to be operationalized in the range of spatial, social and cultural contexts that embody cultural tourism. How to determine which sector leads, and how to translate ideas into a working management plan or strategy is the topic of Part E.

In addition, as will be discussed, not all assets have the same tourism potential, and not all places with strong tourism potential have the ability to cope with large numbers of tourists. Thus, sustainability must be interpreted differently depending on the asset in question. For some assets, optimizing economic return may represent suitable management strategies. For others, though, a more preservationist-oriented approach might be suitable whereby use is controlled and, in some cases, actively limited. For others still, a mix of both is desirable.

The achievement of the three ideals may be mutually exclusive, as the pursuit of one objective has often been regarded as being inimical to the attainment of others (Jacobs and Gale 1994; Boniface 1998; France 2011; Popp 2012; Xu et al. 2013). Kerr (1994) noted that what is good for conservation is not necessarily good for tourism, and what is good for tourism is rarely good for conservation. This statement is still relevant today. Tourism values have been compromised to ensure the cultural integrity of assets is maintained, especially when a management attitude exists that any tourismification is considered to be a corrupting influence or largely unwelcome (Hovinen 1995; Fyall and Garrod 1996). Lowenthal (1998) observes that managers of historic places sometimes take their stewardship so seriously that they can become overly possessive or selfish in their treatment of such assets when challenged by other stakeholders whose requirements for using such assets may differ. Alternatively, cultural values have been compromised for tourism gain (Urry 2002, Stocks 1996, McKercher and du Cros 1998; Yang 2011).

Finally, the parallel roles played by different stakeholders in product development, promotion and product management further complicate the issue. Tourism stakeholders are largely responsible for attracting tourists and, understandably, their primary focus is on economic sustainability. The arts and cultural heritage communities, on the other hand, are primarily responsible for management and conservation of the range of places visited and associated experiences. Understandably, as well, their focus is more on the social and ecological components of the triple bottom line.

Parallel evolution of tourism and cultural management

The differing roles identified above highlight a deep divide between the tourism and CM sectors, for they share little in common apart from the resource base. Each evolved independently with different core ideologies and values to serve different sets of stakeholders, different political masters, achieve different objectives and to perform significantly different roles in society. Tourism industry professionals value cultural assets as raw materials for its products to generate tourism activity and wealth. Arts/heritage management professionals value the same assets for their intrinsic merits. To a large extent, practitioners of both sectors still operate in parallel, with little real evidence of the collaboration and camaraderie needed to form true partnerships between the two sectors.

Table 2.1 summarizes the extent of the differences between CHM, AM and tourism. CHM evolved to conserve and protect a representative sample of our heritage for the future. Its goal is to serve the broader public good. AM evolved as a medium to administer and encourage creativity that also can have an obvious economic value, hence the numerous creative industries that abound today. CM is largely structured around public sector or not-for-profit organizations though it does take into account the role of the private sector that services visual and performing arts markets. CM's stakeholders tend to be community groups, arts/heritage professionals or representatives of minority or ethnic groups, and public administrators tend to value cultural assets for their intrinsic worth first and extrinsic or use values later. Importantly CM professionals tend to come from a social science or arts background foremost rather than a business management one.

Conversely tourism is essentially a commercial activity that is dominated by the private sector and is driven by profit or by the desire of governments to achieve economic objectives. Its stakeholders tend to represent the commercial sector objectives. Because of this focus, tourism is much more interested in the use value of assets rather than in their existence value. Tourism industry professionals tend to come from the commercial world and increasingly are receiving business educations focusing either on the business of tourism or marketing.

Collaborators or competitors?

Historically, the relationship between tourism and CHM has been seen as one that invariably must result in conflict. In some cases, conflict may be beneficial for it focuses attention on something that needs to change for the benefit of all concerned (Bennett et al. 2001). While it is one possible outcome, conflict does not always have to occur. There are many examples where successful partnerships are formed, especially in many community-based tourism initiatives where concerns of local residents play a key role in the development process (Goodwin and Santili 2009). Partnerships are also likely to occur when stakeholders have respect for each other, have a direct interest in the issue under debate, and seek pragmatic compromise solutions. Many more instances exist where the two sectors operate in parallel, each respecting the other's role and neither interfering in it.

Conflict has been defined as goal interference, where the actions of one set of stakeholders interfere with the achievement of another group's goals (Jacob and Schreyer 1980). Goal interference can occur directly, where the actions of others affect one's enjoyment, or indirectly, where a general and more pervasive feeling of dislike or an unwillingness to appreciate the other's views exists (Jackson and Wong 1982). It is most likely to emerge

Table 2.1 *Comparing arts/cultural heritage management and tourism*

	Cultural heritage management	Arts management	Tourism
Structure	Public sector oriented Not for profit	Both public and private sector orientated Not for profit/profit making	Private sector oriented Profit making
Goals	Social goals	Social goals/ Commercial goals	Commercial goals
Key stakeholders	Community groups Heritage groups Minority/ethnic/ indigenous groups Local residents Organizations for heritage professionals/ religious leaders	Public/community arts organizations and creative industry groups Art collectors, consumers, critics and curators Artists/performers and local residents Organizations for arts professionals/critics	Business groups Non-local residents Tourism trade associations and destination marketers Local residents Tourism industry bodies
Economic attitude to assets	Existence value Conserve for their intrinsic values	Existence and/or use value Consume for their intrinsic or extrinsic appeal	Use value Consume for their extrinsic appeal
Key user groups	Local residents	Either local or non-local residents	Non-local residents
Employment background	Social science/arts degrees	Social science/Arts degrees	Business/marketing degrees
Use of asset	Value to community as a representation of tangible and intangible heritage	Value to community as a form of expression and/ or financial investment	Value to tourist as product or activity that can help brand a destination
International political bodies/NGOs	ICOMOS/ICOM/ UNESCO: promote heritage conservation and safeguard living culture	IFACCA/ICOM/UNESCO: promote value of arts to society and encourage equity of access to arts and arts education	UN/WTO/WTTCUN: promote development of tourism
National/ regional political/ bureaucratic bodies	National, state and local agencies and some museums concerned with heritage management, archives	National, state and local agencies and some museums concerned with AM	National, state, regional tourism bodies

in situations of resource scarcity, where a perception exists that one group will benefit to the detriment of the other (Hensel et al. II 2006), when one party asserts its interests at the expense of another party's interests (Bennett et al. 2001), when a vocal minority attempts to hijack community discussions (Salazar 2012), when new users pose a threat to access or exclusivity (Cheung 1999), where differences in leisure preferences exist (Carpenter 2008a), where differences in participants' desires and motivations for pursuing a specific activity differ (McKercher et al. 2008), and for a variety of other reasons. If not resolved, conflict between users of the cultural asset can move from an essentially intellectual, and therefore distant debate, to one that becomes personal and emotive in nature (Burgess et al. 1988).

The imposition of tourism as a new, powerful and highly competitive stakeholder can upset a long-standing status quo throwing otherwise stable systems into turmoil until a new, but highly altered form of stability re-emerges. Demands by tourism can create or exacerbate unresolved issues at contested or dissonant heritage sites, where the entire debate about the meaning and resultant use of the site is unresolved (David and Oliver 2006). It has been our experience that stakeholders have allowed tourism interests to dominate during the initial stages of development, even though they often have little knowledge of, or regard for, the impacts it can have on the cultural assets they are promoting. Arts and heritage managers are then forced to react to these changes, leading them to question the benefits of tourism (Jamieson 1995).

Relationships between tourism and cultural management

To understand more about the relationship between tourism and CM it is worth looking at tourism's relationship with CHM first for an idea. A complex relationship exists between tourism and CHM that is affected by at least five mitigating factors: the independent evolution of tourism and CHM; the existence of a politically imposed power balance between stakeholders; the diversity of stakeholders with different levels of knowledge; the diversity of heritage assets under consideration; and, the different ways in which assets can be consumed (McKercher et al. 2005). The separation of tourism and CHM may provide some benefits if each has a clearly defined role and sees little need to interfere in the other's role. Problems tend to arise only when one stakeholder transcends the realm of the other, or when the political power balance changes and governments seek to introduce or change heritage management legislation to stimulate tourism.

Generally, as well, relationships work best when fewer stakeholders are involved. Problems are more likely to arise when peripheral stakeholders impose themselves on situations and argue ideological, self-interested positions that may be separate from a real life clash of values at hand. The issue is complicated even further when the range of possible cultural heritage assets is considered, given that each has its own specific group of stakeholders and, therefore, own unique relationship issues. Finally, different consumption patterns create different relationships. Passive visitation, where tourists simply observe, as in the case of wandering through historic streetscapes, is the least intrusive. Active consumption of experiences associated with the asset, through visits to museums, art galleries, religious sites, theme parks, or the consumption of live performances can generally be managed easily. But, active consumption of experiences not normally associated with the intangible cultural values can prove problematic. Restaurants and nightclubs located in renovated historic buildings are typical of assets engendering this type of behaviour.

Six possible relationships have been identified that exist along a conflict/partnership continuum, as shown in Table 2.2. Full partnerships represent one end. They are most likely to occur at purpose-built facilities or in purpose-designed cultural tourism experiences where the desired experiences can be crafted around a desired set of cultural or heritage management objectives. Full conflict represents the other end of the continuum. This situation is likely to occur when tourism is imposed on local communities without consultation or consideration of their needs. It can also occur when existing facilities are suddenly subjected to a massive influx of visitors, overwhelming the site. Partnerships are unlikely to evolve spontaneously, instead they usually require intervention from a dominant management agency, while conflict is most likely to occur in a management vacuum. However, conflict is unlikely to be long lasting, as eventually stakeholders either reach some sort of equilibrium or one stakeholder is excluded.

Full cooperation

It is easiest to achieve full partnership at purpose-built facilities because the number of competing stakeholders is limited, clearly defined financial and CHM objectives have been identified, and a clear power/management hierarchy exists to ensure that both

Table 2.2 *Possible relationships between tourism and cultural management*

Conflict/ Partnership continuum	←———→				
Full cooperation	*Working relationships*	*Peaceful co-existence*	*Mild annoyance*	*Nascent conflict*	*Full conflict*
True partnership for the mutual benefit of both sectors Meaningful and regular dialogue Interests are well balanced	Realization of common needs and interests Begin dialogue Work to ensure that the interests of both are satisfied	Sharing of the same resource Some dialogue, but little cooperation or recognition of the need to cooperate Derive mutual benefits from its use, but still largely separate and independent	Goal interference attributable to one stakeholder Lessened satisfaction as a result of contact One stakeholder exerts adverse effects, lack of understanding between stakeholders but without real hostility	Problems without easy solutions emerge Changing power relationships with emergence of one dominant stakeholder whose needs are detrimental to the other stakeholder	Open conflict and hostility between stakeholders

objectives can be achieved in a balanced manner. Importantly, as well, these types of facilities are located outside of existing neighbourhoods, minimizing the interaction between tourists and local residents. Top down leadership coupled with a shared vision that such facilities serve both tourism and cultural goals ensure that necessary comprises are made to satisfy each other's needs (see Plate 2.1).

Full cooperation is much harder but not impossible to achieve in extant, non-purpose-built facilities. In such cases, there must be mutual agreement among all stakeholders that either tourism or cultural values management interests will dominate the management process and that the others' needs will be modified to serve the needs of the overall management goals. Community-based heritage tours and events that feature actual living spaces and rites of passage include close consideration of the residents' requirements of their culture. In the former case, the facility will be managed in such a way as to facilitate its consumption, while in the latter case, consumption will be permitted, but only to the point that it does not interfere with the cultural values being safeguarded (see Plate 2.2).

Working relationships

Functional working relationships, rather than full partnerships, are more likely to occur in extant assets that are shared by tourism and CM. Both sets of stakeholders appreciate that the other has legitimate interests and both also appreciate that, while they may have their differences, they also share much in common. Over time, a working relationship develops between stakeholders with each set willing to make some accommodations to satisfy the

Plate 2.1 Brand new Buddhist theme park and temple, Vietnam

A local hotelier has developed a religious tourism attraction that would also bring people to his hotels by building this Vietnam Buddhist theme park, pagoda and temple. The local community is highly supportive of the project seeing benefits for both promoting the province of Ninh Bihn to tourists and gaining more followers for the Buddhist religion.

Plate 2.2 Church sign, Philippines

Religious cultural assets are often the most culturally sensitive for host communities. Conflict between different user groups can easily arise if not careful.

needs of the other. Management structures are put in place to retain the relationship that has evolved. This type of parallel relationship works best when each sector assumes a clearly defined role, has little desire for a closer relationship and perceives little benefit in developing one.

This situation works well providing power relationships remain relatively stable and that no new stakeholders claim an interest in the asset. The empowerment of one stakeholder, or the introduction of others, such as the 'discovery' of a cultural asset by a new tour operator who decides to bring large numbers of tourists, can throw this relationship out of balance. Productive working relationships can exist for both high or low visitation cultural tourism products, provided that they are managed for such use levels.

Peaceful coexistence

Peaceful coexistence is likely to occur when both sets of stakeholders share the resource but feel little need to cooperate. This type of situation is most likely to occur when visitation levels are low, or when a large number of tourists consume the product in an unobtrusive manner. Likewise, this type of relationship is most common when CM activity is low, or when management occurs in a manner that does not interfere with tourism use. Examples of peaceful coexistence are the preservation of historic streetscape or heritage buildings. Here large numbers of tourists may consume the streetscape, but otherwise exert little adverse impact on the conserved buildings. Indeed, tourism may be cited as a justification for the continued conservation of such places (see Plate 2.3).

Plate 2.3 Hereford streetscape, UK

Conservation area planning or zoning controls to which no stakeholders seem to object protect Hereford's city centre and streetscape from unsympathetic development that would compromise its cultural values and tourism appeal.

Peaceful coexistence can also be fostered by an informal recognition that different users will visit the same site at different times of the day. Usually this type of behaviour occurs organically as residents learn to modify their behaviour to avoid crowds (Soontayatron 2013). At other times, it can result from overt management practices, where places are closed to tourists at certain times and open to them at others. Such a situation occurs frequently in working basilicas in Europe, where the church is closed to tourists during religious events.

Mild annoyance

Mild annoyance, possibly leading to a later state of conflict occurs when the actions of one set of stakeholders are seen to interfere with the desired goals of another set. It does not stop the individual from participating in an activity but lessens the level of enjoyment. Here, residents and local stakeholders recognize the benefits of tourism, but also have to compromise their own behaviour, actions or activities in order to cater for its needs. Mild annoyance is likely to occur when the stakeholders feel that the current situation is beginning to evolve in an unfavourable direction. It may be that greater numbers of tourists are beginning to visit an asset, reducing the pleasure felt by the existing users. Or, it may be that changing management regimes is a factor affecting the ability of the tourism stakeholders to achieve their sector's goals (see Plate 2.4).

Plate 2.4 Buses park in the centre of a narrow street near St Paul's ruins, Macau

Permanent congestion caused by massive increases in regional tourism to the World Heritage site 'Historic Centre of Macau' has caused problems for traffic control around the key parts of the site, which in turn causes stakeholder conflict.

Nascent conflict

Nascent conflict is the step between mild annoyance and full conflict. The actions of one stakeholder or set of stakeholders are seen to have an adverse effect on the other(s). Moreover the problems that arise defy easy resolution. Nascent conflict will emerge when a stable system is pushed out of stasis due to external factors. It is also likely to emerge when the power relationship between stakeholders changes fundamentally, as in the case of including a cultural heritage asset in a tour itinerary, without consulting the asset managers. Likewise, alterations to a management plan that are seen to benefit one stakeholder at the cost of another could trigger nascent conflict. Ideally, nascent conflict should be resolved before it evolves into full conflict (see Plate 2.5).

Full conflict

Open conflict can emerge between arts/heritage and tourism stakeholders. While conflict has been identified often in the literature, McKercher et al. (2005) note it represents a temporary stage in the relationship between stakeholders. Over time it tends to self-resolve, either by residents adjusting to new users, or one or other group being blocked from using the asset. Conflict can be triggered by a number of factors, with change in power relationships being the most common. The emergence of tourism as the dominant user, coupled with the perception that assets are being managed for tourism use at the cost of their intrinsic values can produce a state of conflict among CHM advocates (see Plate 2.6).

Plate 2.5 Nan Lian Garden, Hong Kong

The Chi Lin Nunnery was promoted heavily as a tourist attraction without consulting the nuns, who soon found visitation interfering with their devotions. After some tense discussions with the government and Hong Kong Tourism Board, funding was raised to construct the Nan Lian Water Garden nearby to take the pressure off the nunnery.

Plate 2.6 Kun Tin Study Hall, Ping Shan Heritage Trail, Hong Kong

Hong Kong's Ping Shan Heritage Trail was opened in 1993. By 1995, some of the heritage buildings in private hands were closed to visitation, due to an unresolved dispute between the Antiquities and Monuments Office (AMO) and local clan leaders regarding visitor management and other issues. In June 1997, the AMO negotiated a special heritage agreement to reopen some of the historic features and convert a historic police station nearby to a visitor centre for the trail after the relocation of the traffic unit currently in residence. Once all animosities were laid to rest, the AMO and the Tang Clan collaborated again in 2007 for the opening of the Tang Clan Gallery cum Heritage Trail Visitors Centre.

The consequences

The failure to appreciate the need to consider both legitimate CM and tourism needs results in the sub-optimal delivery of cultural tourism experiences and the continued unsustainable development of this area. The consequence may mean lowered visitation levels and decreased satisfaction, threatening the commercial viability of the asset. Worse still, the consequence may mean continued high levels of visitation without signalling how the asset is to be used, resulting in tourists defining the experience themselves, at the peril of the asset. A bored tourist can sometimes be a destructive or disrespectful tourist (du Cros 2007a). See Plates 2.7 and 2.8.

Plate 2.7 Tourists clambering on site, Persepolis World Heritage site, Middle East

Plate 2.8 Tourists at a Buddhist temple in Thailand ignore signage asking them not to photograph the temple ritual

The failure by tourism interests to accept that cultural and heritage assets have legitimate intrinsic values of their own and that those values are meaningful to other users means that tourism may overwhelm an asset and damage the very essence of what makes it appealing in the first place. Further, the failure of some elements of the tourism industry to explain the intrinsic values detracts from the quality of the experience provided. Moreover, unethical actions that encourage inappropriate use can lead directly to the destruction of the asset or open conflict with local communities.

Fortunately, an increasing number of asset managers realize that tourism plays an important role in overall management and presentation to visitors. They are working to incorporate tourism needs within their activities and are striving to develop products and experiences that meet the interests of the tourism industry. Furthermore, a number of tourism professionals are now realizing that cultural tourism products must be treated in a somewhat different manner than other tourism products and that they exist to satisfy more than the narrow interests of tourism.

Key learning outcomes

- Sustainable use of cultural tourism products is essential to their survival as cultural assets and a tourism product.
- Triple bottom line sustainability can be hard to achieve, partly because it is difficult to measure when it requires the application of diverse indicators and also because different time scales apply in particular to economic and non-economic indicators.
- In reality, some trade-off usually occurs, whereby cultural values are compromised for tourism use or tourism values are compromised for heritage conservation.
- The parallel development of tourism and cultural heritage lies at the heart of this issue.

3 Issues, benefits, risks and costs

Introduction

Cultural tourism, like all other forms of tourism is potentially a double-edged sword, capable of benefiting host communities, while also having the potential to destroy the cultural heritage assets that create the tourism product. Many people, though, tend to focus on only one element: cultural tourism is beneficial or cultural tourism is detrimental. The former is an optimistic perspective that explains why many local community leaders view pursuing cultural tourism through rose-tinted spectacles (UNESCO 2000). Observed negative impacts also explain why many heritage management organizations have developed conventions, charters and codes of practice to try to control tourism. Cultural tourism is not a value free activity. How one perceives its impacts, good and bad, is often a reflection of a person's underlying values. The challenge is to bring some realism to the debate and show how proper management can optimize benefits and minimize or mitigate adverse impacts. This chapter presents an overview of the potential benefits and costs of cultural tourism to communities. It begins with a discussion of the many communities that can be affected by this activity and then discusses its impacts on quality of life.

Community

It is necessary to understand what is meant by the term 'community', before any discussion of impacts can occur. Most of us think of communities in fairly narrow terms as neighbourhoods, school districts or towns, when, in reality, the definition of a community is far more subtle, complex, and variable in scale (McKercher and Ho 2012). At its heart, a community can be thought of as a group of interacting people who share similar beliefs, values or common characteristics. Members feel a shared sense of place or have a common emotional bond (Montgomery 1998; Mahon 2007) that identifies them as insiders and others as outsiders. Sense of place, in turn, involves three interrelated elements of place: place identity, place dependence, and place attachment (Jorgensen and Stedman 2001). Place identity refers to how the person defines the place in relation to his or her own value set. It includes such dimensions as distinctiveness, continuity, self-esteem, and self-efficacy that enable the uninterrupted continuation of a person's everyday lifestyle (Twigger-Ross and Uzzell 1996). Place dependence relates to the functional roles places play, with a sense of strong place dependence likely to emerge when it best suits their goals (Jorgensen and Stedman 2001). Finally, place attachment reflects the positive bond between groups or individuals and their environment (Low and Altman 1992) that imbues inhabitants with a sense of belonging or meaning (Gustafson 2006).

That definition is all well and good, except that communities are dynamic entities, with fuzzy and overlapping boundaries. Moreover, the level of attachment can vary (Corsane and Bowers 2012), enabling even temporary users, such as tourists, to develop legitimate attachments (Gustafson 2006; Williams and McIntyre 2012). This observation means individuals can belong to many communities simultaneously, while the geographic bounds of a place may also embrace multiple communities. For example, students may belong to a university's community and to their neighbourhood community simultaneously. Likewise, a cultural heritage asset can cater for both local and touristic communities.

Cultural tourism can impact the quality of life at four different levels of community: neighbourhood, local, national, and international (McKercher and Ho 2012). The level of deep personal attachment will diminish as one moves along the continuum from neighbourhood to international communities and the extent of personal impact felt by cultural tourism, both positive and negative, will also vary. Impacts are likely to be direct and highly personal at the neighbourhood or community level, whereas they are more likely to be indirect and more philosophical at the national or international level. However, even though the impacts may be indirect, they are no less legitimate as reflected by the global outrage over the destruction of the two giant Buddha statues located in the Bamiyan Valley in Afghanistan by the Taliban in 2001.

Interestingly, Timothy (1997) also identifies four different communities of cultural tourist (see Plate 3.1). He suggests that tourists have different levels of connectivity to each type of asset and, therefore, by implication, have different depths of experience depending on which type of asset is visited. World heritage attractions may draw large numbers of tourists that invoke feelings of awe, but they probably do not invoke feelings of deep personal attachment. National cultural assets symbolize a society's shared recollections that represent much about how it expresses its identity through valorization of durable national icons that reflect national pride. Domestic tourists may feel a sense of pilgrimage by visiting these places and paying homage to national symbols that represent their shared identity. Local and personal sites engender progressively stronger feelings of connectivity and likely facilitate different depths of experience by the visitor.

Plate 3.1 Pyramids, Egypt

Timothy (1997) addresses the issue of depth of experience from the perspective of the individual's connectivity to an asset. He identifies four levels of heritage tourism attractions: world, national, local, personal, with people having different levels of connectivity. World famous attractions, like the Pyramids, may draw large numbers of tourists from many countries, but most people will not feel a deep sense of personal attachment to them. Local sites, on the other hand, are more likely to invoke deep feeling of connectivity, but will have little relevance to tourists.

Pocock et al. (2010) also came to a similar conclusion when they argue personal connectivity to cultural assets is associative in nature (person + place = memory). They observed,

> it is the personal qualities of memory that make it an appealing exploration for the interpretation of heritage and application to heritage tourism in particular. Tourism research suggests that visitors increasingly wish to experience the local, and create their own experiences of tourist destinations. The recollections of locals can provide the kinds of experiences desired by tourists, and the engagement of visitors through their own experience and memory creates opportunities for this interactive and self-created experience.
>
> (Pocock et al. 2010: 8)

Cultural tourism and enhanced quality of life

Cultural tourism has the potential to enhance the quality of life of residents in any or all of the four levels of community. McKercher and Ho (2012) have reviewed the literature and identified five thematic domains of benefits with more than 30 different types, as summarized in Table 3.1. Each of the themes is discussed briefly below.

Table 3.1 *Community well-being benefits of cultural tourism*

Benefit	Community	Neighbourhood	Local	National	International
Economic benefits					
Job creation			x	x	
Income generation			x	x	
Economic development			x	x	
Training and capacity building			x	x	
Conservation and adaptive reuse					
Conservation	x		x	x	x
Adaptive re-use	x		x		
Developing sense of personal guardianship of heritage	x		x		
Conserve, value ethnic areas	x		x		
Stop the illicit trade in artifacts			x	x	x
Nation building and national myth making					
National image/identity				x	x
National myth making			x	x	x

Continued

Table 3.1 *Community well-being benefits of cultural tourism, continued*

Benefit	Community	Neighbourhood	Local	National	International
Post-colonial identity/re-identification				X	X
Sharing history/living history			X	X	
Addressing, resolving or highlighting contested histories		X	X	X	
Developing a collective identity/history				X	X
Enhancing a national sense of belonging				X	
Community well-being and connection to place					
Partnerships			X		
Improved quality of life			X		
Developing/enhancing community pride and a sense of community/belonging			X	X	X
Linking communities			X		
Building group and place identity			X		
Value minorities/cross-cultural understanding		X	X	X	X
Build sense of nostalgia			X		
Social inclusivity and balance			X		
Maintain/revitalize traditions and local culture		X	X	X	
Enhance local identity/place attachment		X	X	X	X
Enhance ethnic identity		X			X
Highlight popular culture		X	X		
Provision of leisure and recreation opportunities					
Rationale for cultural product development		X	X		
Produce authentic experience			X		
Serve multiple functions and multiple users		X	X		

Source: McKercher and Ho (2012).

Economic benefits

Cultural tourism has been identified as a powerful economic development tool that can create jobs, induce investment and help revitalize communities in the decline (Gordon and Raber, 2000; Xie 2006; Hall and Lew 2009). It is especially important to many small rural, indigenous or ethnic minority communities that have limited economic development options (Altman 1992; UNWTO 2006a, b, and c; Yang and Wall 2009; Piscitelli 2011; Silapacharanan and Dupuy 2011). Local resident involvement can be direct through ownership of attractions, retail outlets, guest houses, bed and breakfasts, food service establishments, local guide services, and the like, or indirect by producing handicrafts, artworks, and souvenirs to be sold to tourists. These types of commercial opportunities are appealing for they have low barriers to entry (Jamieson 2000) and if developed sensitively can provide unique experiences to visitors (see Plate 3.2).

The influx of visitors is recognized as a factor that helps preserve local cultural traditions (Williams and Stewart 1997; UNWTO 2008b) and also aids capacity building (O'Sullivan and Jackson 2002). Mason (2011) shows how building craft traditions can enhance national pride and, in doing so, safeguard traditions for communities associated with them. Marwick's (2001) study of Malta revealed how the tourism crafts sector revitalized the lace-making tradition and created new employment opportunities in the glassblowing and metalworking area. (See Plates 3.3 and 3.4).

Plate 3.2 Shops in Nara, Japan

Some people criticize the sale of souvenirs in or adjacent to historic sites as a reflection of the commodification and trivialization of local culture. However, what they often fail to appreciate is that the operation of shops, such as this one located in the ancient Japanese capital of Nara, Japan, provides one of the few opportunities for small-scale enterprises to benefit commercially from tourism. People who operate these shops do not have the resources to develop large-scale businesses, but can still generate a reasonable family income. Showing some sensitivity to the placement or style of stalls can mitigate concerns about visual intrusiveness for assets considered to have high aesthetic cultural values.

Plate 3.3 Artisans D'Ankgor workshop, Cambodia

Plate 3.4 Reproduction heads carved by Artisans D'Ankgor

Les Artisans D'Angkor is another example of both capacity building and craft revitalization. It began as an initiative of the European Union as a means of helping young Cambodian artisans, many of whom were disabled during the years of civil war, to find work in their home villages, provide them with a trade and role in society (Plate 3.3). These individuals were also trained to make reproductions of Angkor Thom's artifacts, which has the added benefit of offering tourists an alternative to illegally acquired fragments of temples and other archaeological remains, some of which are now used to repair the temples (Plate 3.4). The organization also provides a number of other benefits, including the preservation of traditional Khmer skills in silk making, stone and wood carving, lacquering and painting. In addition, the sale of authentic reproductions may also help stop, or at least slow, the illegal trade of artifacts.

Conservation and adaptive re-use

Cultural tourism has also been identified as providing the economic rationale to conserve both built heritage (Caffyn and Lutz 1999; du Cros et al. 2005; Hankey and Brammah 2005) and the social fabric of ethnic neighbourhoods (Conforti 1996; Santos et al. 2008) through adaptive reuse. Chang and Teo's (2009) examination of the conversion of shop houses in Singapore into boutique hotels, for example, shows how the addition of retail and guest accommodation revitalized a run-down neighbourhood. The buildings' adaptive re-use and restoration of the historic shop houses has created a source of pride for local residents and now function as an expression of local identity. Importantly, owners see themselves as custodians of these heritage assets. (See Plates 3.5 and 3.6).

Another extremely successful example of transformation occurred in Westergasfabriek, a redundant industrial heritage gasworks site in Amsterdam. The City of Amsterdam felt it could not afford to restore and renovate the site, and instead offered the private sector the opportunity to develop the whole complex on condition that any proposal should have creativity, culture, and sustainability as its core principles. The vision was to turn it into a cultural landmark for both the community and tourists. After some false starts a family bought the site and proceeded to develop the vision. Today, Westergasfabriek has been adapted and renovated to allow new cultural spaces with an intimate atmosphere, incorporating local community recreational use, as well as tourist activities. Creative entrepreneurs work in the renovated historic buildings and many high profile events and festivals are held there. In 2010, the complex won the Netherlands European

Plate 3.5 Cave near Teotihuacán, Mexico

Adaptive reuse can take many forms. Here a cave located outside Mexico City near Teotihuacán that was occupied by vagrants has been converted into a restaurant offering a unique dining experience.

Plate 3.6 Prague Castle, Czech Republic

A historic castle was gradually converted into a cultural precinct with museums, performance spaces and galleries. It is now a popular tourist attraction in its own right with constant cultural activity such as the opera that these costumed caste members are promoting.

Union Prize for Cultural Heritage/Europa Nostra Awards. (see Fastforward 17 2007; Best in Heritage 2011.)

Sometimes, though, adaptive reuse may conserve the physical fabric of a building at the expense of the intangible heritage associated with it (McKercher et al. 2005). This situation has been observed, for example, where churches have been converted into restaurants or nightclubs or through 'facadism', the retention of the original building's façade only. The end result is often mixed, providing some use benefits to local residents and tourists, but at a high cost to the asset's cultural significance. Heritage managers generally fight to oppose such approaches.

Nation building and national myth making

The role of cultural tourism in nation building, by using cultural assets to promote national identity and creating a sense of shared belongingness, in many ways is more important than the economic returns generated. National identity is built on cultural identity and expressed by a variety of symbols and discourses (du Cros 2004: 154). Palmer (1999) adds that the promotion of national symbols as tourist attractions helps build or maintain national identity, for places such as museums and historic attractions remind tourists of the core components of nationhood in a playful and exciting setting. Arts festivals too are socially significant cultural practices, which deserve consideration beyond their contributions to economic and tourism development as a product to enliven a destination (Quinn 2006). (See Plate 3.7).

Plate 3.7 Entry to New Orleans Heritage and Jazz Festival, USA

Haiti theme in 2011 supported the local Haiti community in New Orleans and showcased it to tourists.

Diasporic festivals and events allow participants to affirm their cultural identity far from home. The popularity of Caribbean carnival festivals such as the Notting Hill Carnival in London, UK, and the Caribana in Toronto, Canada, for example, deeply involve the migrant diaspora living in those communities. Tourism thus provides a vehicle for ethnic groups to promote themselves to others (Yang and Wall 2009), and in doing so enhance the idea of what it means to live in a community, be part of a community and take pride in that community (Besculides et al. 2002). Festivals and events have the added benefit of creating an opportunity for diverse groups to work collaboratively to achieve common goals and, in doing so, foster greater cross-cultural understanding (MacDonald and Joliffe 2003; Gursoy et al. 2004). Plus, these events have spawned a range of businesses that generate year round employment for artists and cultural entrepreneurs (du Cros and Jolliffe 2014).

The role of tourism in general, and cultural tourism in particular, in creating new national myths in post-colonial and post-Soviet states is well documented (Bossen 2000; Hughes and Allen 2005). The central government of China has attempted to create the myth of Hong Kong as having a 8,000 year long link to China, interrupted by only a minor and insignificant 150 year British colonial past (du Cros 2004). Likewise, in South Africa, Nelson Mandela's cell in Robben Island off the coast of Cape Town, South Africa, has become a secular shrine to represent post-apartheid South Africa (see Plate 3.8).

Plate 3.8 Robben Island, South Africa

The historic significance of some places elevates them almost to the status of sacred sites. This photograph illustrates the late Nelson Mandela's cell on Robben Island where he was imprisoned for more than 20 years. The cell itself is like all other cells in the prison, except for the fact that it was his. A visit is akin to a pilgrimage for many tourists.

Community well-being and provision of leisure and recreation facilities

A variety of direct and indirect benefits may also accrue to communities. At a very basic level, purpose-built cultural attractions, designated heritage precincts and revitalized historic neighbourhoods provide a range of leisure, recreation, dining and shopping opportunities. Knowledge transfer projects keep heritage, arts and cultural practices alive and resistant to pressure from globalization. Whether these principles are a local effort or have trickled down from the activities of intergovernmental organizations, such as the United Nations Educational, Scientific and Cultural Organization (UNESCO), they are important for helping communities manage cultural change. (See Plate 3.9).

Costs associated with cultural tourism

If delivered properly, cultural tourism can provide a wide range of benefits to the four types of communities identified earlier. However, the risks associated with unsustainable, poorly delivered, and poorly managed cultural tourism can outweigh any benefits a community might experience. Six types of impacts have been identified, as shown in Table 3.2.

Plate 3.9 Community stakeholder meeting for a cultural tourism project, Amritsar, India

A community-based conservation and tourism project in a village near Amritsa, India, empowered an extremely poor Hindu community.

Table 3.2 *Adverse impacts of unsustainable cultural tourism development*

Issue	Indicators of negative impacts
Over-use	Congestion: fluctuating and permanent volume Loss of privacy, amenity and, particularly, local services Gentrification and outmigration Competition over resources and space
Under-use	Seasonality or sudden lack of use create economic impacts Inadequate funding to mitigate any negative impacts/conserve or safeguard assets
Misuse	Inappropriate use of sites Vandalism Souveniring, etc.
Cultural commodification, loss of authenticity and diversity	Over-commodification or trivialization of culture Loss of authenticity Alienation from place and/or culture Diversity of culture repressed or ignored (e.g. only one narrative allowed for interpretation to tourists)
Impacts from the glocal nature of tourism	Profit from tourism goes to external agencies/insufficient local benefit Illegal appropriation of cultural property Illegal or uncompensated appropriation of cultural intellectual property Social amnesia as too many external influences absorbed
Short-term goals/flawed or absent planning process	Unbalanced development and badly planned infrastructure Poor stakeholder relationships and communication Power balance against community interests Inappropriate museumification/commodification Tourists' expectations shaped by forces outside the community's influence

Over-use

Too many tourists can overwhelm cultural attractions, leading to degradation of the physical fabric of the asset, damage to cultural values and a diminished visitor experience (Shackley 1998; du Cros 2007a). It is especially problematic in small communities that lack the requisite infrastructure to cope with large numbers of visitors (Vogt et al. 2008). Also, it can be a problem for those communities that have huge influxes of visitors for popular heritage places or arts festivals (du Cros 2006a; du Cros and Jolliffe 2014). Lerkplien et al. (2013) report tourists at many of Thailand's heritage sites were shocked by the state of deterioration of the monuments. Inappropriate land use, construction to aid transportation and traffic communication networks to enter the attractions, air, water and sound pollution, bad smells, overfilled trash cans, and litter were just some of the over-use problems asset managers face. Levi and Kocher (2013) also note how too many tourists, crowding, and too much commercial activity can disrupt the experience at sacred sites.

Over-use is often accompanied by uneven spatial distribution of tourists, leading to crowding and site deterioration in some areas, with other areas of sites experiencing little or no visitors. Personal observations of visits to Pompeii, Teotihuacán and Angkor World Heritage (WHS) sites illustrate this challenge. Icon attractions or possible tour routes delineated in guidebooks and maps are extremely popular, while lesser attractions, or back streets, are often completely empty. The most extreme example is at the Pyramids of Giza in Egypt where literally tens of thousands of tourists and hundreds of tour buses compete at the most popular viewing platforms, and on turning the corner to the back of the Pyramids the visitor finds him or herself alone in an uncrowded desert environment. Shifting demand from high density to low density areas is a significant management challenge, for tourists generally prefer to capture icon sites and attractions.

How much tourism is too much? It is hard to say precisely, but an evaluation of congestion represents a strong indicator. Congestion found in and around popular attractions can affect local amenities, or crowding may force tourists into non-tourism private or local space. It occurs when physical obstructions block the natural flow or narrow passages causing the flow to slow down (UNWTO 2004b: 3). Alternatively, it can result when the planned carrying capacity of a place is exceeded. Congestion can be a continuous or fluctuating problem that occurs during peak periods (either during the day, on certain days, or at certain times of the year). Understanding the dynamic nature of traffic and visitor flows, therefore, is important when developing strategies to manage congestion.

Ultimately, the carrying capacity of the asset must determine use levels. Such a statement is more easily said than done though, for carrying capacity has both absolute and relative connotations. Absolute capacity refers to the maximum number of people that can enter a place before its fabric begins to get damaged. It can be measured by, for example, car parking capacity, toilet sewage capacity, and the physical robustness of the asset. Relative carrying capacity, on the other hand, is a qualitative construct determined when the volume of visitors affects the desired experience. Crowding, noise, and a perception of incompatibility between users are indicators that relative carrying capacity has been exceeded.

However, carrying capacity as a relative term that is often defined by the user's own (sometimes selfish) perspective. McCool and David (2001) note there is no such thing as an innate carrying capacity, for an area may have multiple capacities, depending upon what objective is planned and implemented for the area. A temple may have a very low capacity if it is purpose-built to provide opportunities for contemplation and solitude in a pristine setting, or a higher capacity if the objective is to provide opportunities that are more social in character and where there are fewer constraints on the impacts caused by tourists. They caution against specifying numerical carrying capacities as these will fail to control, reduce or mitigate impacts, because "impacts are largely a function of tourist behaviour, developer practices and other variables" (McCool and David 2001: 388). It is for this reason that the UNWTO, in conjunction with ICOMOS, produced a manual outlining a range of options and a clear assessment process (UNWTO 2004b).

Under-use

Under-use is less well documented, but can prove to be just as great a threat, especially if asset managers have invested heavily in developing the tourism potential of an asset (McKercher 2001). Low visitation levels may not produce the necessary revenue for needed conservation work, interpretation and ongoing research. More importantly, under-utilization may cause a loss of local support, especially if scarce public sector funds are required to keep it operational (Getz 1994; McKercher 2001). Deacon (2006) points out that tourism has to be economically viable to be sustained. Her study on rock art sites in South Africa reveals tourism revenue is required to generate sufficient income for conservation either directly through entrance fees or associated activities, or indirectly through boosting the economy of the neighbouring region. In addition, she argues that the social benefits of tourism can only accrue if sufficient income is also generated to remunerate indigenous people and local communities for their services as custodians and guides.

Some places have instances of over-use right next to those of under-use. For instance, Macau's icon heritage attraction, St Paul's ruins, is subject to daily overcrowding, while the adjacent visitor centre and city museum attract scarcely one-tenth the number of visitors. Marketing and promotional activities can prove successful to induce tourists to move from more to less popular sites, especially if they are in close proximity to each other. It is more challenging though to shift tourists from popular places to more remote attractions. In the Macau case, recommendations were made to offer free access to the museum and more temporary exhibitions in the museum to induce visitation (du Cros and Kong 2006), while the visitor centre was moved into a restored Portuguese style heritage building and more ancillary activities and shops added to make it more appealing (du Cros 2013). (See Plate 3.10).

Misuse

In other instances, adverse impacts can be noted even when visitor levels are otherwise sustainable, but the tourists engage in inappropriate activities on-site. Brooks (2003) notes "visitors who show little respect for the sanctity of spiritual places, practices and traditions can have an adverse impact on those places and communities". Inappropriate behaviour can range from something as simple as littering or taking photographs when asked not to do so, to more significant impacts, such as souveniring of artifacts from ancient sites or showing little respect for local cultures and traditions (Deacon 2006).

Inappropriate uses are caused by one of two factors, either attracting tourists whose expectations differ from those of the asset managers, or through a failure to educate those tourists about appropriate/expected behaviour (McKercher and Ho 2006). Attracting the wrong type of tourist is most likely to occur if the asset is positioned vaguely in the marketplace, or if the tourist is unaware of the positioning strategy used. The failure to specify the message clearly may result in attracting tourists whose needs are incompatible with the experienced offered (see Plate 3.11).

Plate 3.10 Cumberoona paddle steamer, Australia

Plate 3.11 Tourists climbing, Uluru, Australia

A good idea does not always translate into a successful product. The PS Cumberoona was an Australian bicentennial project initiated by a number of key local stakeholders to create a primary attraction for the regional city of Albury, NSW. However, it has never been commercially successful and is now in dry dock. This project failed for three main reasons. First, the reconstructed paddle steamer was too authentic. It was powered by a wood-fired engine that proved to be highly costly to maintain, requiring additional staff, and raising the ship's fixed costs. Second, it suffered from 'me-tooism'. Other communities along the Murray River that were located closer to main markets had developed highly successful heritage tourism sectors based on their own paddle steamer heritage. The Albury attraction was not seen as being unique. Further, it suffered from weak-market access, as more and better quality experiences were available closer to core markets. Finally, the volume of water on the Murray River is regulated by a series of dams. Water is released to coincide with the irrigation needs of farmers, meaning that for many months of the year the river is essentially turned off. This paddle steamer was located on the downstream side of a major dam, while other communities with successful paddle steamer operations were located upstream of dams. Its location meant that for many months on end, insufficient water was released to permit safe sailing. Even during supposedly high water periods, the flow could be turned off and on. The net result was a reduced and unpredictable operating season meaning few tour operators were willing to include it on their itineraries.

Messages about desired tourist behaviour must be clear and succinct. Here at Uluru, in central Australia, the traditional Aboriginal custodians request tourists not to climb. Yet, more than 100,000 visitors climb each year. There are many reasons why tourists ignore this request, including overt encouragement from the travel trade, and the belief that because others are climbing, this activity is appropriate. A further reason, though, comes from mixed messages about the climb. One message conveys the idea that the climb is culturally inappropriate and not something that is in line with 'Tjukurpa' or traditional aboriginal knowledge. The second message, though, is that the Anangu, or traditional landowners, are distressed at the number of tourists who are injured or die. This mixed message creates confusion among potential climbers as to the real reason behind the request not to climb. In doing so, it also gives them the freedom to choose which message they want to adhere to: cultural inappropriateness or health risk. A number of tourists are initially reluctant to climb out of the belief that it is a sacred site, but once the message is conveyed that people are not encouraged to climb because of the physical risk to their life and limb, they can choose to ignore the first option. Indeed, the risk factor heightens the appeal of the climb for many. In this case, a simple 'please do not climb' message with no further elaboration would be much more effective.

Alternately, many of the social impacts arise from well meaning, but largely ignorant tourists seeking to have their personal needs satisfied in a manner that impinges adversely on the host community. This situation occurs frequently at contested sites where different stakeholders with different value sets compete for supremacy, while simultaneously being forced to share the same physical space until one eventually dominates and displaces the others. As noted by McKercher et al. (2008), a certain level of moral ambiguity exists in these places due to the transmission of mixed signals. The net result is confusion about what is and is not acceptable behaviour. In the absence of clear directions, visitors will rely on the actions of other tourists to inform their behaviour, may revert to accepted cultural norms from their home community, or may feel free to behave in an anarchic manner, often using the excuse of 'I am a tourist' to justify their actions. (See Plates 3.12, 3.13 and 3.14).

Presentation, authenticity and storytelling can also result in the misuse of assets. Cultural sites are not value free. As much as some people would like to believe absolute histories exist, in reality multiple, contested histories often share the same physical locale. Whose story to tell and how to tell that story becomes an important element in presenting sites for tourist consumption. The process of tourismification cannot be fully understood without scanning the context and referring to territoriality in developing cultural tourism, for territoriality is the primary expression of social power. In addition, histories tend to be written with overt political overtones that either create and reinforce national myths, or remind individuals of national tragedies that should never be repeated. As such, great care must be taken in the presentation and interpretation of these histories.

Plate 3.12 Tourists at Ankgor Wat, Cambodia

Most tourists want to do the right thing but, in the absence of signage and other site management tools, are often unsure of what appropriate behaviour is. If tourists see other tourists doing something then many will make the assumption the action is acceptable and behave in a similar way. Unfortunately, their behaviours may result in the degradation of fragile cultural relics, as seen in this case at a temple at Angkor World Heritage site, Cambodia. Watching the sun set over the main temple is one of the must do activities when visiting. The viewing area, though, becomes quite crowded, leading some tourists to seek better vantage points. Over time, an eroded path has been created that has also led to the degradation of the ruined temple. Proper signage, and some form of barrier would resolve this problem easily.

Plate 3.13 Tourist souveniring from the Great Pyramid, Giza

Our unique cultural heritage is under threat for many reasons including the illicit trade of artifacts for commercial gain, or simply by unthinking tourists taking souveniring artifacts, as is shown in this photograph taken at the Great Pyramid in Giza, Egypt. Tourism and the commercial benefits of tourism provide both the financial resources and the moral justification to conserve what heritage remains. Unfortunately, we will never be able to stop some people from feeling the need to take home their own souvenir.

Plate 3.14 Inappropriate behaviour at the Great Pyramid, Giza

Our research into inappropriate behavior among tourists identified a number of neutralization techniques used to justify behaviour (McKercher et al. 2008). The sociological concept of neutralization evolves from the realization that many people are aware that their behaviour is inappropriate, and so must come up with some type of verbal rationalization that excuses or justifies their behaviour. So, despite signage requesting that visitors should not climb the pyramid, some tourists still climb. They may justify their behaviour in a number of ways, such as 'I feel entitled to this activity having come so far' or 'those other tourists did it too'.

Cultural commodification, loss of authenticity and diversity

There is a fine line between presenting cultural tourism products in a manner that facilitates easy consumption and over-commodification that results in the trivialization of local culture, alienation of host communities, and loss of any sense of authenticity. The successful provision of cultural experiences must involve an element of standardization, modification and commodification to ensure consistent quality and to cater for tourists who may know little about the culture of the place being visited. But, over-commodification can result in the delivery of tacky or mundane products resulting in embarrassed or bored guests (Ashley et al. 2005). (See Plate 3.15).

Inevitably, then, any discussion of commodification raises the issues of authority and authenticity in relation to what is done with the information and cultural assets to be shared with tourists. Most commodified products and experiences take into account that most people are not professional anthropologists, historians, artists or conservation architects, even though Eller (2009: 23) has observed that "all of us today live 'anthropological lives' in the sense that we will experience and deal with human physical and cultural diversity continuously, both locally and globally". Increasingly, as well, most also appreciate that tourists are looking for an edutainment experience and not a deep learning experience.

Plate 3.15 Invasion of privacy photo of local residents

Sightseeing and purposeful cultural tourists are looking for back of house experiences that provide a chance to encounter local residents going about their daily lives. Increasingly, these tourists wander well beyond traditional tourism nodes to visit lesser-known cultural attractions or enter residential neighbourhoods in the hope of gaining more authentic experiences. In doing so, they risk treating local residents as commodified tourist attractions, without asking their permission. The incursion of well-meaning tourists into non-tourism precincts can create animosity and culture conflict.

Recently, Cohen and Cohen (2012: 1298) studied the politics of authorization or 'authentication' in this context. They propose two kinds, namely 'cool' authentication (declarative acts which authenticate objects) and 'hot' authentication (immanent, reiterative, informal performative processes of creating, preserving, and reinforcing an object's, site's or event's authenticity). Cool authentication is based on some sort of proof or certification of genuineness, while hot authentication is implicit, based on belief and, therefore, not evidence based. Most cultural assets fall into the 'hot' category, unless a sign or some other medium formally identifies them as 'cool' (such as World Heritage designation). As a result, the task of conveying the values of the places visited is left to local tourism and CM stakeholders. Who controls the message and who shapes the product, therefore, may determine whether it is presented in a culturally appropriate manner.

A reduction in cultural diversity, or an increase in standardization and gentrification are also possible impacts resulting from the tourismification of a destination in part or full. Cultural change is one of the hardest processes to plan for because cultures are dynamic and unpredictable. A certain amount of change is healthy to prevent stagnation. However, the speed at which it can happen may mean that certain aspects unique to a community or part of their quality of life may be at risk of completely disappearing. Flawed planning policies that ignore how tourism can be a factor behind the loss of cultural diversity through standardization of cultural and urban spaces and gentrification also can ignore signs of accelerated cultural change.

Impacts from the glocal nature of tourism

Glocalization is the practice of conducting business and/or delivering products according to both local and global considerations. Salazar (2005) indicates tourism is at the forefront of this trend, as it operates on a global scale by promoting the opportunity to experience the local. He notes further the original meaning of glocalization referred to tailoring global products to local circumstances, but, in the case of tourism products, its meaning has been altered to involve tailoring local (and localized) products to multiple global audiences (Salazar 2005: 631). Many tourists, and especially middle-class, mid-market tourists seek global enterprises (theme parks, hotel chains, restaurants, and so on) and yet also want to experience local culture. They are attracted to glocalized tourist nodes where western amenities and what they believe to be authentic local life are offered. Invariably, then, Salazar (2005) suggests glocalization involves the presentation of a commodified and mystic version of the glocal represented and packaged as local for the global market.

Glocalization does provide an opportunity for communities to become involved in tourism and for increased and meaningful cultural exchange. However, as with any form of tourism controlled by outsiders, communities may get few real benefits and instead may have to cope with impacts. The amount of money that actually remains in local communities is one of the foremost concerns, especially if tourism is pursued as a poverty reduction and social development strategy (UNWTO 2006a and b; Theerapappisit 2009). Often little of the price of the tour is actually spent in the community (sometimes a lunch, sometimes even less), unless overnight accommodation is provided, while opportunities to sell souvenirs, arts and crafts may also be tightly controlled.

A larger issue is how much should such communities be forced to adapt to cater for tourists? It has also been noted that balancing local needs with those of tourists at local celebrations, rituals and festivals can become a source of conflict (du Cros and Johnston 2002; Olsen 2006; Griffiths 2011), whether the issue is privacy-related, such as when tour groups insist on attending local festivities without permission, or a function of cultural sensitivity as in the case of independent tourists accessing sacred spaces and rituals without invitation. Griffiths (2011) has explored the latter in relation to churches in Paris and concluded that members of the congregation were generally welcoming towards tourists provided they were not stared at or interrupted during their devotions. A persistent case of such interruption (photos being taken at the altar) was brought to the notice of the authors in regard to one of Macau's churches in Old Taipa village. The priest's solution to preventing this behaviour recurring during mass was to lock the doors once the congregation had arrived to keep out any such tourists. Other impacts may include examples like the isolation young people working in the tourism industry feel from their peers and families, because of constant and sometimes intimate contact with tourists with vastly different value systems (du Cros and du Cros 2003). These instances would seem to be extreme cases of poor visitor management or stakeholder relations, however they are perfectly possible when only short-term goals and/or a flawed planning process are in place.

Short-term goals/flawed or absent planning process

The previous chapter discussed how differing time frames between financial goals and socio-cultural goals represent the single greatest obstacle to the achievement of triple bottom line sustainability. It matters little how socially sustainable an enterprise is if it is not financially viable. As a result, short-term financial objectives can take precedence over long-term social objectives. No problems arise, providing they are broadly compatible. But short-term financial objectives often involve maximizing revenue, either by a pricing structure that encourages visitation, through the over-commodification of assets in an attempt to appeal to a wider market, or through excessive on-site souvenir sales. In short, the volume of visitors seems more important than the quality of visitors, with the result that the experience is compromised and local impacts heightened.

Funding may also be sought for large-scale development projects without having completed the necessary research to determine whether the project is viable. This situation is most likely to occur in developing economies that seek foreign aid to fast track economic development. There are many examples of unbalanced development and badly planned infrastructure that still haunt destinations trying to improve their cultural tourism management. It is an undisguised truth that these problems are better avoided than fixed. They can eventually compromise tourism appeal and cultural significance for tourists and the community. Often they are the result of an unequal power balance among stakeholders and lack of sympathy towards the long-term survival of the asset. Poor communication and rigid mindsets can also make matters worse.

Optimizing benefits and minimizing impacts?

Cultural tourism is indeed a double-edged sword. Adverse impacts are a reflection of the loss of control over the cultural asset. Key use decisions have either not been made, have been made but not communicated well, have been ignored by stakeholders with differing agenda, or poor decisions have been made. Often the cause can be traced to a belief that asset managers have little or no control over either the volume or type of tourist who visits. Yet, in reality, visitation does not occur spontaneously. Instead, it is induced in response to a number of stimuli communicated to the tourist formally and informally by markers about the type of product/experience to be consumed. The failure to set management objectives, develop core and tangible products to reflect those goals, and position the product in the marketplace to send a desired message about the type of experience to be had to a desired audience, creates a vacuum where tourists or the travel trade can shape experiences to suit their own needs.

The key question is how to control the genie of tourism once it has been released? The answer lies at a community level in the development of a holistic master planning approach that defines what type of tourism sector is desired, how many tourists are wanted and what benefits the community wants to gain from tourism. There is an urgent need for all management stakeholders to develop measures in cooperation with communities that attract realistic visitor numbers designed to protect their cultures and ways of life. Another challenge is to ensure that policymakers and site managers develop cultural tourism activities that do not negatively influence the daily lives of the inhabitants.

A somewhat similar answer also applies at a site, community or cultural landscape level. It too begins with finding common ground among stakeholders, adopting a strategic approach to product/experience development, developing longer-term goals, and finally coming up with a method to implement them. This book advocates that adopting a marketing management strategy represents the best approach to work towards true sustainable development. Such a strategy adopts a long-term perspective and involves all stakeholders in the process, by setting financial and non-financial goals. Importantly as well, it establishes protocols to determine whether a cultural asset has the potential to be a viable product, understand what the market's needs are, and how to shape the product to meet both the needs of the market and other stakeholders.

Given the diversity of cultures likely to be involved in cultural tourism development, it is important that planning and development mechanisms respect these differences and in fact celebrate them. Just remember, community-based development processes are not for the impatient. They take time, patience, as well as understanding and commitment from the local community and other stakeholders in order to achieve sustainable development objectives.

Key learning outcomes

- Communities exist at different scales and people can be related to cultural tourism at different degrees of proximity depending on how 'community' is defined.
- Cultural tourism provides a range of well-documented quality of life benefits including job creation, capacity building, and enhanced recreational opportunities.
- The role of cultural tourism in nation building, national myth creation, and national myth reinforcement is often not recognized fully, but may be more important than its economic benefits.
- The wrong type of tourist, or the right type of tourist behaving badly, can threaten both tangible assets and their associated intangible values.
- Adverse impacts on the community and the cultural asset usually reflect a failure to control the site and the overall tourism planning process.
- Over-use impacts are the most noticeable, but under-use is actually a greater issue when the full spectrum of a destination's cultural tourism products is considered.

Part B
Cultural assets

4 Cultural heritage management principles and practice (with special reference to World Heritage)

Introduction

CHM and AM are subcategories of CM. CHM is the systematic care taken to maintain the cultural values of heritage assets for the enjoyment of present and future generations (du Cros and Lee 2007). As such, it is both a management philosophy and a management process. CHM, or cultural resource management, as it is known in North America, is now a global phenomenon, governed by a series of internationally recognized codes and charters. Most countries have embedded these principles into formal heritage protection legislation or accepted heritage management policies. Tourism is recognized increasingly as a user of heritage, placing greater pressure on all stakeholders to collaborate (UNESCO WHC 2014a; ICOMOS ICTC 2014; World Monuments Fund 2014). The following chapters introduce the reader to some of the core concepts behind the principles and practice of CHM.

This chapter presents an overview of CHM and identifies some of the key management challenges. The politics of CHM need to be understood as well. WHSs are also discussed here. Chapters 5 and 6 look at the underlying principles, management practices, and politics of tangible and ICH, respectively.

Cultural heritage management

The term 'cultural heritage management' is used commonly in most jurisdictions, except in the United States, where the terms 'cultural resource management' and sometimes 'heritage resource stewardship' are used (Pearson and Sullivan 1995: 4; NPS 2011). The use of the word 'heritage' instead of 'resources' signifies subtle but important differences in meaning. 'Resources' implies that the asset being considered has an economic, extrinsic or use value that can be exploited. 'Heritage', on the other hand, is a much broader term that recognizes the non-economic, intrinsic and social values of the asset in question. In doing so, it acknowledges further a legacy with certain obligations and responsibilities

The main goal of CHM is to conserve a representative sample of our tangible and intangible heritage for future generations. This issue is important for two reasons. First, the speed with which the world is changing is so fast that much of our heritage is at risk of being lost either through its physical destruction or the loss of knowledge. CHM seeks to establish a formal system to identify and conserve this heritage for the future. Equally important, the use of the term 'representative sample' acknowledges that not everything can or should be conserved, only the best or most representative of all that has gone before.

People have always produced different kinds of traditions and physical remains, each of which is unique to its era and some of which is non-renewable. There will never be another genuine wreck of the *Titanic*, Egyptian pyramid, Angkor Watt, or peat bog Iron Age burial. They were created under a special set of social, cultural, and economic circumstances, which are impossible to replicate. Where a cultural heritage asset is recognized as being of high cultural significance, then it is imperative to maintain it for future generations to observe and understand. While we may not run out of heritage, we may lose certain types altogether or be overwhelmed by others in a way that gives a lop-sided view of a culture or historical period. (See Plate 4.1).

What is to be conserved, though, is broad. The focus is often on conserving iconic cultural assets, but a truly representative sample must also include more mundane examples that represent normal daily life, values or traditions. Here, age is less important than knowing the full story, for that it is vital to conserve a representative sample of contemporary assets that are evocative of early twenty-first century life as it will become tomorrow's heritage (for instance, designer handbags, and the first smart-phones).

Conservation has a different connotation than preservation. While preservation implies keeping something safe from harm or loss, often by hiding it away, conservation implies the wise use of resources. A key element of CHM then is to make conserved heritage accessible physically and intellectually for use, enjoyment and education. As such, cultural heritage managers are expected to plan for a heritage asset's presentation

Plate 4.1 Archaeological excavation, China

Archaeological excavations are important for research but are not always accessible to the general public or tourists.

and interpretation as an important part of its ongoing conservation and management (ICOMOS 1999). English Heritage (2011) argues that making cultural assets accessible is part of a virtuous cycle of heritage management (Figure 4.1). By enabling people to access heritage, they can then understand its meaning, which in turn, helps them to appreciate its value and why it should be cared for, which in turn helps people enjoy it. And the circle continues.

When considering the sustainable use of this heritage asset, we must consider the amount and type of use that is possible before the intrinsic values are threatened (Pearson and Sullivan 1995; English Heritage 2011; Bandarin and van Oers 2012). However, setting use limits is more easily said than achieved, for each asset has its own meaning and cultural significance and exists in a different social or cultural context. In addition, many publicly owned assets have a management mandate that encourages visitation. Thus, while broad guidelines and protocols can be developed, each asset must be considered individually. In the next chapter, we discuss how different cultures have differing views about how much change can occur before an asset ceases to be authentic. Moreover, fragile sites may require more stringent management actions regarding visitation, regardless of their appeal, while more robust sites can withstand heavier visitation. In other instances, the range of permitted uses might need to be limited.

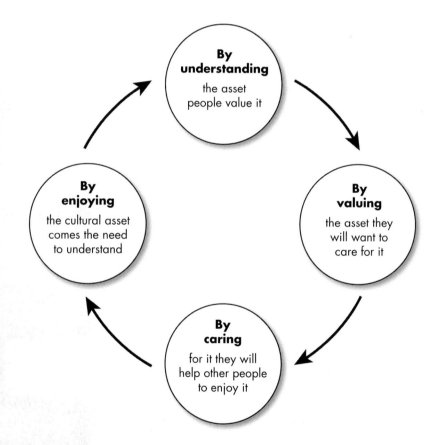

Figure 4.1 The virtuous cycle of cultural heritage management

Source: based on English Heritage (2011).

Good presentation of objects/places means their intrinsic cultural values are interpreted in such a way that all kinds of visitors can understand them. However, two critical caveats must be appreciated. First, making things accessible does not necessarily mean free and open access to all. Access must be managed carefully to ensure that the tangible values of the asset are not damaged or the intangible values compromised. Second, a balance between education and entertainment must be achieved. Museums, for example, are predicated on mainly educational objectives (Ambrose and Paine 1993; Lord and Lord 1999; Best In Heritage 2014; ICOM 2014a), while some heritage theme parks that also see themselves as having a conservation role may focus more on entertainment. (See Plates 4.2 and 4.3).

Plate 4.2 Historic varieties of farm animals become an attraction, Hungary

Unprofitable farms near Lake Balatan in Hungary have been amalgamated into a Historic Agricultural Park. Some older varieties of cattle and other farm animals have been husbanded for current and future generations to enjoy.

Plate 4.3 Weekend fairs and activities, Hungary

Weekend fairs with locally produced products and traditional types of fair games are also a good way to interest tourists in the history of pre-mechanical farming.

Heritage varies in scale, complexity, and management challenges

When most non-heritage professionals think of heritage, they tend to think of heritage places, routes and objects, such as old buildings, historic sites, archeological sites and other physical remains. However, intangible heritage, cultural landscapes, and traditions that embody such things as folklore, storytelling, practices associated with worship, festivals, and other cultural expressions are an equally important element. Different types of cultural tourists want to experience different types of heritage. The casual and incidental cultural tourist and, to a lesser extent, the sightseeing cultural tourist are most interested in consuming tangible heritage experiences. The purposeful and serendipitous cultural tourist, and sometimes the sightseeing cultural tourist, are looking for a more back of house experience and value intangible heritage the most.

Assets can vary in scale and complexity, creating their own unique management challenges. For example, tangible heritage can be as small as a snuffbox collection or near global in scale, as in the case of the Trans-Atlantic Slave Route or the built heritage that comprises the Silk Road. Likewise intangible assets can be as complex as the folklore of 20 ethnic groups in a region or as small as a favourite story told by a storyteller. Importantly as well, the tangible and intangible are intrinsically linked (Kirshenblatt-Gimblett 2004), for the intangible often gives meaning to the tangible, and the tangible often embodies intangible practices.

The conferring of heritage designation represents a form of contemporary recognition of the intrinsic values of these assets and also implies an obligation to manage them for future generations. In some cases, the task is relatively easy, as in the case of museum displays of small items. In other cases, though, the task is incredibly complex, infused with domestic politics and transnational legislation. Whether minority or indigenous cultural heritage is deemed worthy of conserving is an innately political process, while how best to preserve it may lead to conflict between stakeholders. Ideally, tradition bearers should collaborate with archivists, academics, or musicologists to contextualize cultural objects in their care or when documenting 'living' heritage. Custodians, tradition bearers, and local communities should also seek to establish control of the management of particular cultural heritage places and objects, which are closely associated with their intangible heritage by establishing their own site registers, museums and keeping places. How transnational heritage assets are managed may depend on each country's heritage protection legislation, the understanding of the asset's cultural significance, political goodwill, and the way in which human resources can be organized to oversee the implementation of any conservation policy decided upon.

Cultural heritage management: an evolving framework influenced by local conditions

The practice of CHM is still a relatively new phenomenon – its rules, guidelines and protocols are still evolving. It has been observed that jurisdictions tend to follow a five phase development comprising; inventory, development of initial legislation, increased professionalism, emergence of stakeholder consultation and review and integration of prior practices before maturity is established. This is basically a process where public sector agencies gradually implement more principles and practices to enhance CHM in any particular jurisdiction. It coincides often with the community's desire to conserve heritage, followed by a deeper involvement in decision-making and management. These five phases are shown in Table 4.1 along with supporting

Table 4.1 *Cultural heritage management's evolving framework*

Phase	Key features
Inventory	• Growing community interest • Documentation • Evolution from amateurs to professionals conducting work
Initial legislation	• First generation legislation to guide identification and protection of heritage assets • Focus on tangible not intangible heritage • Creation of government heritage agencies • Little integration with other government agencies or laws
Increased professionalism	• Formation of heritage IGOs and NGOs • Formalization of codes of ethics, conservation principles in charters, etc. • Development of related heritage professions (public and private)
Stakeholder consultation	• Emergence of wide array of stakeholders • Areas of conflict identified • More attention paid to community interests
Review	• New understanding of responsibilities • New or revised legislation • More integrated planning and practice • Greater awareness of intangible heritage • Recognition of other users • New paradigm in place • Maturity

sub-indicators of their implementation with the final phase allowing for more integration with other planning and management efforts and a review to enhance particular aspects of the earlier phases.

Jurisdictions first become involved in this activity when academics, community leaders, and politicians begin to recognize the intrinsic value of heritage and see the need to conserve it. This stage often occurs reactively, out of the awareness that important heritage values are being lost. The first step, then, involves nascent attempts to document assets and is often driven by keen amateurs or a small group of heritage professionals. Once the scope of a jurisdiction's assets is recognized, the second stage involves invoking some form of legislation to recognize and conserve them. It may also involve systematically cataloguing the work of enthusiasts and then engaging them further. The creation of formal heritage departments or the establishment of heritage units in other government departments often accompanies this action. Although inventorying of heritage places and cataloguing of objects are important, overemphasis on these actions can mean that long-term conservation objectives are not addressed. Problems can also occur in a heritage planning process when conflicts over use of a cultural asset by different user groups are not anticipated or avoided. CHM must become a process that is both professional and systematic to deal with a diverse range of concerns.

Hence, the next phase reflects increased professionalism in the sector and greater acceptance of this within the local political system. Formal codes of practice and conservation charters are adopted, with countries typically becoming signatories to international charters. Formalizing the management process, rather than just enacting legislation to protect tangible assets, leads to greater professionalism in how assets are identified, how their values are assessed, and how they are managed in the long term. It is at this stage that a wide array of public and private sector heritage professionals, ranging from architects to consulting archaeologists, enter the sector. Similarly, it is often at this stage that universities begin to offer specialist heritage-oriented degree programmes. Much of the expertise in these areas only existed in developed western countries (Byrne 1991; Getty Conservation Institute 2014) until UNESCO and ICCROM (International Centre for the Study of the Preservation and Restoration of Cultural Property) established the Asian Academy Heritage Management Network in 2005 to encourage more courses and training programmes in Asia (UNESCO Bangkok 2014).

The fourth and fifth stages reflect even greater sophistication of the field. In the fourth stage, instead of being imposed by outsiders, an increased awareness of the involvement of key stakeholders as interested parties and managers or co-managers of assets begins to emerge. More attention is paid to community concerns. Existing legislation has to be modified and a more integrative approach to management needs to be adopted. The fifth and last step recognizes the dynamic nature of heritage management where current practice is reviewed and revised as necessary to ensure that a broader societal good is served. The evolution of specific CHM actions, therefore, coincides with the more general societal and political evolution of the value of culture and ways of managing it. As a result, it is almost impossible to impose the final two evolutionary stages successfully in jurisdictions that have just begun to appreciate the need to conserve their heritage and in which CHM has few links with other stakeholders.

A series of international codes, conventions and charters has been developed by a variety of agencies to ensure jurisdictions adhere to similar principles for the identification and management of heritage. These codes define core heritage philosophy and in doing so influence legislation and subsequent management protocols. Some of the agencies involved in heritage management include:

- UNESCO: United Nations Educational, Scientific and Cultural Organization (which began the international focus on heritage with the Convention on the Protection of Cultural Property in the Event of Armed Conflict, 1954);
- ICOMOS: International Council on Monuments and Sites (an international professional organization of heritage professionals concerned mainly with the conservation of tangible heritage assets);
- IUCN: International Union for the Conservation of Cultural and Natural Resources (also known as the World Conservation Union);
- IATF: Inter-Agency Task Force (for improving risk-preparedness for World Heritage places – a more recent development);
- ICCROM: International Centre for the Study of the Preservation and Restoration of Cultural Property (established in Italy by UNESCO in the early 1960s);
- ICOM: International Council of Museums (an international professional organization of heritage professionals concerned mainly with museums).

The use of, or adherence to, international standards and principles is increasing. One example of such a set of standards is *The Venice Charter* (ICOMOS 1976, 1994) devised during the Second Congress of the Architects and Technicians of Historic Monuments in Venice in 1964 and adopted when the International Council on Monuments and Sites formed in 1965. It has not been amended much over the years, although two new principles were added in 2003. (See Plates 4.4 and 4.5). Recently, it has been used in combination with other charters and/or declarations. The key features of *The Venice Charter* spell out the principles behind best practice (as it was understood at the time) and a set of standard definitions of terms for the conservation and restoration of monuments and sites, particularly in relation to:

- historic buildings (extended now to groups of buildings);
- conservation (restrictions on modification);
- restoration with authenticity in mind (no reconstruction);
- archaeological investigation to be professionalized;
- documentation (any action should be documented systematically and a public record kept).

Plate 4.4 Conservation works in Telc, Czech Republic

The Venice Charter initially grew out of the need for conservation principles to guide the conservation of tangible cultural heritage in the face of massive post-war reconstruction and the redevelopment of bombed European cities. This need developed into one for a set of principles to underlie professional practice of restoration internationally. The creation of the Charter was also integral to establishing ICOMOS as an international organization with a reputation for promoting high standards of conservation practice and CHM around the world.

Plate 4.5 Conservation works on wall paintings, Royal Palace, Bangkok

Originally, *The Venice Charter* had a strong focus on historic town centres, historic landscapes and places of artistic and historical importance. Subsequent charters and codes at the regional and more diverse heritage category levels were generated to broaden the focus of the kinds of cultural heritage that should be assessed and conserved (ICOMOS 2004). Accordingly, *The Venice Charter* gave birth to new codes/charters of principles and practices that complement its principles and have influenced not only how tangible heritage is managed, but also intangible heritage.

Even though the Charter is perceived now as having limitations, in some ways it was ahead of its time. For instance, it always held that heritage conservation was not an end in itself, but an activity that should aim at bringing social benefits. The Charter asserted many years before either sustainable development or World Heritage Convention were muted that "the conservation of monuments is always facilitated by making use of them for some socially useful purpose" (Araoz in UNESCO, WHC, ICOMOS, ICCROM and IUCN 2013: 58). Hence, it has always been an instrument that, while anchored in the context of the great cultural and material change of the mid-twentieth century, was trying to look to the future.

Other international organizations besides ICOMOS have charters that form the basis of constitutions (e.g. ICOM's *Code of Ethics* was adopted in 1986; ICOM 2014a). The influence these articles have at the local level can guide the professionalism phase in the development of CHM in each member State (Party) chapter of these international organizations. How well they use these charters and codes in debates over the direction of heritage management and tourism development also varies.

What makes a difference in every jurisdiction is how much general support these codes and charters have from the public sector agencies and how much these documents provide support for the views of professional heritage managers. The phase of increased stakeholder consultation (see table 4.1) is extremely important in the development of every CHM tradition, because this is where heritage professionals first have their views challenged by the community and learn how to share power (if they have any) with them over the cultural assets being managed.

Stakeholders

Defining who stakeholders are and what they expect is important for setting conservation management priorities in mature traditions of CHM (du Cros and Lee 2007). Here, understanding cultural significance and how it relates to the socially constructed meanings of the physical lies at the heart of stakeholder consultation. Key stakeholders therefore include local communities or cultural groups who live near a heritage asset or are attached to it culturally, schools and universities that use it as a resource, government heritage and planning authorities that may be responsible for managing it, and landlords/private owners and commercial users such as the tourism industry. External stakeholders may, in fact, have more power over how the asset is managed and presented to the public than the owners/managers of the asset. The wishes of such international stakeholders as UNESCO or ICOMOS must be addressed in order to secure heritage standing for some places. Alternatively, the tourism sector can be a powerful stakeholder, especially when supported by government which can push for management actions that benefit the sector to the detriment of the asset.

Ostensibly stakeholder consultation seems a rather straightforward process. In reality, most assets have multiple stakeholders with differing degrees of connectivity to the asset, differing levels of legitimacy, and widely differing viewpoints about how assets should be managed. Consequently, the process of consulting stakeholders is one of most political areas of CHM practice and one that puts heritage managers themselves and their decisions under the most scrutiny. CHM in fully democratic societies is usually subject to open media coverage where in very strident public debates it has been observed that without expert opinion it is "just a bullring" (du Cros 2002: 113). Furthermore, the term 'consultation' means different things in different societies. In some cases, the process is so consensual that it feels like a never-ending process which results in lengthy delays. In other cases, it is little more than window dressing, where consultation consists of holding one large public meeting and informing people what will be done (not that that is an approach to be recommended).

Yet, stakeholder consultation plays a defining role in the successful development of management strategies. It is for this reason that it permeates the entire process from initial discussions to ongoing management of assets. However, it is not always done well. Landorf (2009) examined the relationship between heritage tourism and sustainable development at six British sites. Her study concluded that while all management plans identified major stakeholders, only two defined their relationships in detail. She noted that the depth of consultation and the extent to which it influenced the final strategic direction was not particularly evident, leading her to conclude that WHS managers are not actively planning and managing the economic and social sustainability dimensions in the same way they are managing the environmental sustainability dimension.

The National Heritage Area (NHA) model for stakeholder inclusion has been developed over the last 30 years by the US National Park Service and the Alliance of National Heritage Areas. It was originally set up with the goal of providing a "cost effective way of telling America's story and conserving natural and historic resources" (ANHA 2014). As of 2014, 49 Areas have set up internal partnerships of stakeholders from local government agencies, non-profit groups and businesses – all of which has taken the pressure off the National Park Service to facilitate these connections itself. The programme has always to tried to make consultation a priority in developing new attractions within the NHAs. Usually, special non-profits are established after the official government designation of an NHA to specifically encourage cooperation between stakeholders, promote public–private partnerships and find funding. (See Plates 4.6 and 4.7).

Tourism interests represent just one of many possible user groups whose needs must be considered. In some instances, their needs are compatible with local users, while at other times

Plate 4.6 Pittsburgh, USA

The Rivers of Steel NHA has the historic industrial city of Pittsburgh as its heart. Created by Congress in 1996, the NHA's mission includes the management of tangible and intangible heritage associated with the eight counties known for steel production and heavy industry. Dual goals of heritage management and economic development are realized through a series of projects and programmes to encourage mainly domestic self-drive tourism to the area. For this work to be successful, a broad array of stakeholders are involved from each of the counties in relation to particular projects.

Plate 4.7 Sam Tung Uk Museum, Hong Kong

This is a case of potentially incompatible users. Sam Tung Uk Museum is a 200 year old walled village in Hong Kong that has been declared a monument and converted into a small house museum. Its displays are designed primarily for schoolchildren and the residents of the surrounding neighbourhood but it is also promoted by the local DMO as a historic tourist attraction. While visually interesting, much of the interpretation is geared towards primary school aged visitors and is seen by tourists as being too basic.

their needs may be incompatible. The need to address divergent needs is most likely to occur in cases where users have different levels of knowledge about the asset, different interests in it, different cultural backgrounds, and different expectations about what the asset can deliver.

Management challenges

The management of cultural heritage assets can be complicated by a number of exogenous factors. To begin, it is much easier to achieve consensus when there is a single overriding agency responsible for the entire site, but becomes increasingly difficult where there are multiple agencies or where no single formal agency exists. Land tenure arrangements also complicate the management challenge. The Hadrian's Wall WHS in the UK is, perhaps, an exceptional case. Here, the majority of the site is in private ownership, as is most of the buffer zone around it. According to its most recent management plan (UNESCO 2007), a considerable number of bodies own and manage approximately 10 percent of the site specifically for conservation and access, while the rest consists of medium to large estates, owner occupied farms, and residential and commercial lots in urban areas. A number of trusts have some involvement in the site, along with eight local authorities, English Heritage, and other groups. Tourism and economic development roles, plus a large number of central government agencies and departments all share some responsibility for site management, creating a significant management challenge to address the needs of multiple stakeholders with differing levels of influence and often holding competing views.

The layer of government that is facilitating a study or planning exercise and where it sits in a bureaucracy can influence the way use decisions for cultural assets are made, especially in developing economies. Countries where central governments take the lead in CHM can impose an overall consistent management strategy and objectives. In places like China, however, management of WHS is devolved to local government officials who mostly have no background in heritage management but who often have aspirations to be promoted. Cai (2004 as cited in Li et al. 2008) noted that promotion is often based on reaching economic goals rather than the effectiveness of achievements. As such, few officials make a long-term commitment to the area under their jurisdiction and, instead, are more likely to support opportunistic initiatives that provide the greatest short-term reward. Li et al. (2008) note that policies in the tourist development master plans and WHS are likely to favour exploitation rather than conservation.

Revenue generation and allocation are issues that receive less attention. Heritage assets rarely receive much of the revenue generated from tourism. If the asset is run by government agencies, income goes into 'consolidated revenues' in much the same way as income or sales tax. It is then redistributed at the government's will for whatever purposes it sees fit. Income from tourism sites is seen as a profit generator, where the income generated exceeds the expenses incurred. If it is a public asset that is managed by a private firm under a management contract, then the firm normally agrees to pay a flat fee or a percentage of sales back to the lead agency and retain excess income. In some cases, sites are licenced to private firms, as happens in some developing economies.

Finally, the issue of corruption must be addressed, for it is a big part of the hidden politics of heritage management. Corrupt practices or allegations of corrupt practices in both the awarding of management of commercial contracts and the setting of terms and conditions can also siphon needed monies away from conservation activities. Media reports, for example, have raised questions about 'the irregular' nature of the management contract for Angkor Wat which was awarded to a company with strong connections to a senior Cambodian politician (Sokchea and Di Certo 2012). The company has agreed to pay a nominal fee back to the site, but can keep excess income. An Australian television reporter illustrates that less than $7 of the $20 entry fee paid for a one day pass will go towards managing the site, with the rest of the money being split between the management company, the government and, rumour has it, politicians (Campbell 2008).

World Heritage

World Heritage represents a unique form of cultural heritage. WHS are recognized as having outstanding universal value to humanity. Designation is prized, for it represents an 'International Top Tourism Brand' that places destinations among the pantheon of other world-class destinations. It is for this reason that designation can act as a focal point for national marketing campaigns (Li et al. 2008). While tourism is often the motive behind the pursuit of World Heritage status, tourism potential is not one of the criteria used to identify prospective sites. This duality creates a range of challenges.

UNESCO World Heritage Convention

The 'Convention Concerning the Protection of the World's Cultural and Cultural Heritage,' more commonly referred to as the 'World Heritage Convention' was approved by UNESCO in 1972 and adopted formally in 1976. The objectives of the Convention are to encourage the identification, protection and preservation of cultural heritage properties which "because of their exceptional qualities, can be considered to be of 'Outstanding Universal Value' and as such worthy of special protection against the dangers which increasingly threaten them" (UNESCO WHC 2013: 2). It achieves this goal by encouraging countries to sign the Convention, nominate sites for inclusion, establish management plans and set up reporting systems for sites, assist countries to safeguard WHSs by providing technical assistance and professional training, provide emergency assistance for WHSs in immediate danger, support public awareness-building activities, encourage participation of the local population in the preservation of their cultural and natural heritage, and promote international cooperation in the conservation of our world's cultural and natural heritage (UNESCO 2008). Over the years, the Convention has stayed close to its original promise, although it has been modified from time to time. For example, new heritage categories such as cultural landscapes have been added, revisions have been made to national and international guidelines, changes to the implementation guidelines were introduced, and more emphasis was placed on partnerships with a broader range of stakeholders.

Some authorities have hailed the World Heritage Convention as one of UNESCO's success stories (Stovel 1998; Leask 2006) with over 190 countries or State Parties as signatories and about 1,000 sites placed on the list by mid-2014 (UNESCO WHC 2014a). It was also considered to be innovative for the time by combining cultural and natural heritage. Some even argue it foreshadowed the notion of sustainable development (Cameron and Rössler 2013).

It is one of a set of six UNESCO conventions, (for example UNESCO conventions on diversity of cultural expressions, ICH, illegal transfers of cultural property, underwater cultural heritage, and the protection of cultural property in the advent of armed conflict), which combined contribute to the formation of a core of substantive and procedural obligations that have a common denominator: the principle of "preservation of the great diversity of cultural heritage is part of the general interest of humanity" (Francioni et al. 2014). Recently Director-General of UNESCO, Irina Bokova, noted,

> The UNESCO Culture Conventions are the interface between culture and development – the meeting points between the systems of meaning through which women and men understand the world and the tools with which they shape it. Each Convention is unique – but together, they embody a singular approach to understanding heritage and building on its importance.
>
> (UNESCO WHC News 2014)

The nomination process

The World Heritage Committee (WHC) is the body in charge of the implementation of the Convention. Candidate places must satisfy at least one of ten criteria to be considered for inclusion on the list. Six apply specifically to cultural sites, as follows:

(i)   Represent a masterpiece of human creative genius;

(ii) Exhibit an important interchange of human values, over a span of time or within a cultural area of the world, on developments in architecture or technology, monumental arts, town planning or landscape design;

(iii) Bear a unique or at least exceptional testimony to a cultural tradition or to a civilization, which is living or which has disappeared;

(iv) Be an outstanding example of a type of building, architectural or technological ensemble or landscape, which illustrates (a) significant stage(s) in human history;

(v)   Be an outstanding example of a traditional human settlement, land-use, or sea-use, which is representative of a culture (or cultures), or human interaction with the environment especially when it has become vulnerable under the impact of irreversible change;

(vi) Be directly or tangibly associated with events or living traditions, with ideas, or with beliefs, with artistic and literary works of outstanding universal significance. (The Committee considers that this criterion should preferably be used in conjunction with other criteria.)

(UNESCO 2008: 14)

Only signatory governments can nominate places, with the nomination process following a clearly defined process (UNESCO 2008;DEA 2014). Initially states make an inventory of important natural and cultural heritage sites (the 'Tentative List'), and then they identify specific sites for consideration ('Nomination File'). Nominated properties are then evaluated independently by two non-governmental organizations (NGOs) to ensure they meet the criteria. In the case of cultural properties, ICOMOS and ICCROM evaluate applications and make recommendations with some input from IUCN if properties have mixed cultural and natural values. The WHC meets once a year after this step has been taken to make the final decision on inscription.

The process does not end there, though, for two other factors must also be considered before sites can be inscribed on the World Heritage List. An additional criterion was introduced in 1994 with the introduction of the 'Global Strategy for a Representative, Balanced and Credible World Heritage List' (UNESCO WHC 2014a) to try to get a better balance of sites and locations. Concern grew during the late 1980s and early 1990s that the geographic representation of the List was skewed in favour of European sites, while those from the Asia-Pacific and African economies were under-represented. Likewise, it was observed that historic towns and religious monuments, Christianity, historical periods and 'elitist' architecture (in relation to vernacular) were all over-represented, while other cultural sites and natural heritage sites were under-represented (UNESCO 2008). The causes of this imbalance are either structural (nomination process, managing and protecting cultural properties) or qualitative (how properties are identified, assessed, and evaluated) in nature. In response, some State Parties in Asia have committed extensive funding and loans to local authorities to ensure greater success (Li et al. 2008), while others sought international aid (Galla 2012).

The second factor relates to the introduction of the 'World Heritage Sustainable Tourism Programme' in 2001. The need for this programme grew out of the dual recognition that: 1) inscription could lead to greater visitation of sites which, therefore, demanded stronger management activities; and, 2) the potential for tourism development opportunities may lead some State Parties to misuse the World Heritage brand and trivialize the concept of Outstanding Universal Values for tourism. Ferrucci (2012: 62) has commented that many of the State Parties tend to focus on the economic incentive aspects of the programme, due to their competitive spirit "as each country attempts to gain the most out of the system for self-interested motives". He also notes UNESCO frowns on World Heritage being used as "fodder for 'things to see before you die' coffee-table books" (Ferrucci 2012: 61).

The World Heritage Sustainable Tourism Programme has undergone a number of iterations since it was first launched, with the latest version requiring parties to conduct what is in effect an environmental impact study with the aim of integrating sustainable tourism principles into the mechanisms of the World Heritage Convention. The current programme's objectives are to:

- Integrate sustainable tourism principles into the mechanisms of the World Heritage Convention;
- Strengthen the enabling environment by advocating policies, strategies, frameworks and tools that support sustainable tourism as an important vehicle for protecting and managing cultural and natural heritage of Outstanding Universal Value;
- Promote broad stakeholder engagement in the planning, development and management of sustainable tourism that follows a destination approach to heritage conservation and focuses on empowering local communities;
- Provide World Heritage stakeholders with the capacity and the tools to manage tourism efficiently, responsibly and sustainably based on the local context and needs;
- Promote quality tourism products and services that encourage responsible behaviour among all stakeholders and foster understanding and appreciation of the concept of Outstanding Universal Value and protection of World Heritage.

(UNESCO WHC 2014d)

Does tourism benefit from World Heritage inscription?

Do the benefits of inscription outweigh the costs? Many communities yearn for World Heritage status, in part for civic pride (Harrison and Hitchcock 2005) and because of its brand power (Hall and Piggin 2001). However, World Heritage designation may not yield the tourism benefits desired, and may induce a number of adverse costs. Much research has been published identifying the benefits World Heritage status brings to communities, but its quality is highly variable. As Jansen-Verbeke and McKercher (2013) illustrate, benefits tend to be stated in generic terms relating primarily to revenue generation, job creation, and the power of tourism to displace other more damaging industries, but with little evidence offered to support these claims. Impacts are documented more precisely, but this body of research tends to be fragmented and site specific.

Some sites may witness increased visitor numbers, but many others will see few or no benefits. In many cases, increased visitation is a function of a number of factors that have little to do with designation. Rátz and Puczkó (2003) show WHSs near large source markets attract visitors, while remote sites often receive no benefits from designation. Likewise research from America (Hazen 2008) and New Zealand (Hall and Piggin 2001) suggests designation produces variable impacts on visitation, while a UK study concluded only about one in four sites recorded large increases in visitors after designation, with the majority showing no change (Landorf 2009). Proximity to major tourist nodes (Rátz and Puczkó 2003, DCMS 2008), fame and image prior to designation play critical roles (Evans 2003; Buckley et al. 2004; Dewar et al. 2012). Dewar et al. (2012), for example, illustrate the World Heritage brand is not as strong for heritage assets that are already icons or have some kind of national significance. In addition, such issues as concentration of cultural heritage assets or other attractions nearby can play a role (Caffyn and Lutz 1999; Li et al. 2008), especially if they define a destination (Tufts and Milne 1999). In short, places that are already popular will likely benefit even more, while remote or contested sites may generate few new visitors. Likewise, Yan and Morrison (2007) have argued inscription may play some role in the decision to visit, but that depends on the ability of destinations to place emphasis on the underlying cultural values of sites and to make these elements accessible and interpretable.

Conclusion

A basic understanding of the principles and practices of CHM outlined in this chapter can be used as a guide to the underlying workings of this sector. A summary of the main themes in this respect is presented in Table 4.2. Overall, this discussion also provides a useful counterpoint to the description of how tourism works, presented in Chapter 7. The challenge for cultural tourism is how to integrate the commercial need of tourism with the substantially different social objectives of CHM when these two sectors come together at the meeting table.

Three broad themes identified in Table 4.2 are of particular importance to cultural heritage principles and practices, which also are of relevance to sustainable tourism.

Key learning outcomes

- The main goal of CHM is to conserve a representative sample of our tangible and intangible heritage for future generations.
- Achieving that goal usually involves a five stage learning process.
- CHM traditions differ around the world in terms of focus and development.
- The 'how to' do CHM is inscribed in a series of international charters and codes, which influence both legislation and subsequent management actions.
- Heritage professionals and asset managers are often members of state chapters of international organizations of heritage professionals which allows for a degree of peer review and agreed sets of principles or ethics to guide practice.
- Heritage professionals and asset managers have differing amounts of power and influence in tourism planning both within a country and in different countries and management frameworks.
- Attempts at integrating heritage management into such frameworks vary in success.
- There are good and bad models for involving stakeholders in developing cultural assets for tourism.

Table 4.2 *Cultural heritage management principles and practices*

Cultural heritage management	Sustainability	Stakeholders (including tourism)
Conserve a representative sample of our heritage for future generations	The identification, documentation and conservation of heritage assets are essential parts of sustainability	Most heritage assets have multiple stakeholders. Tourism is one of many possible stakeholders
Conservation of intrinsic values	Each cultural heritage asset has its own meaning and assessable cultural significance or values	Consultation with stakeholders is important to define their needs in the conservation process
Caring for both intangible and tangible heritage is part of CHM	Some cultures differ in their view about how much intervention or change can occur before an asset ceases to be authentic	A stakeholder other than the cultural asset manager may have greater control over the asset
Assets differ in scale, complexity and management challenges	Assets should only be used in culturally appropriate ways	External stakeholders can have a major influence on how the presentation of cultural heritage is planned
The CHM framework is ever evolving	Some assets are too fragile or sacred to be fully accessible to the public	Tourism requirements may sometimes clash with those regarding conservation of an asset
Conservation and CHM are ongoing structured activities		
Most assets are managed to be accessible to the public physically and intellectually		

⬤5 Tangible cultural heritage

Introduction

Tangible cultural heritage includes all assets that have some physical embodiment of cultural values such as heritage cities, historic towns, buildings, archaeological sites, cultural landscapes, cultural objects, collections, and museums (UNESCO WHC et al. 2013; ICOM 2014b). These assets are thought to be easier to manage than intangible heritage assets, for their condition and integrity can be more easily assessed. Even so, tangible heritage is still vulnerable to a wide range of processes that can damage or destroy the asset and its associated cultural values, with tourism recognized as one such stressor agent (Wang 1999; UNESCO and Nordic World Heritage Office 1999; Winter 2002; Staiff and Bushell 2013).

This chapter introduces the reader to a number of issues relating to the management of tangible heritage. The fundamental stages in the conservation planning process are outlined, followed by a discussion of how conservation priorities are set for different types of assets with some examples of best practice in relation to management for tourism. The importance of evaluating cultural significance and its meaning for setting conservation and commodification goals is also dealt with and this leads into a discussion of authenticity and use. Finally, the issues of access to fragile assets and the role of stakeholders in the conservation process are investigated.

Conventions, codes, charters, and declarations

The tangible heritage evaluation and conservation processes are usually guided by a series of international protocols housed in codes, charters, or guidelines. Many of these codes build on the ICOMOS *The Venice Charter* (1994) or its regional variations such as *The Burra Charter* (ICOMOS 2014), while the museum community has developed its own set of the codes for managing collections and exhibitions (ICOM 2014b). Table 5.1 can be used as a handy reference resource as it lists key documents and their respective URLs. Since these articles are revised or amended frequently, the reader is advised to consult the relevant websites for the most up-to-date information. Certain documents listed here will be of key interest to tourism professionals (e.g. UNESCO's World Heritage Convention, the *ICOMOS Cultural Tourism Charter* and the ICOMOS *Ename Charter*), while the others are provided for a general understanding of how protection and professional practice is guided from the regional and international level for specific categories of tangible heritage.

Table 5.1 Key codes, charters, conventions, declarations, and recommendations (with website links) for tangible cultural heritage

Title	Website	Key feature
UNESCO Convention Concerning the Protection of the World Cultural and Natural Heritage	http://whc.unesco.org/en/convention	Defines criteria for inclusion on WHS list for cultural and natural heritage; associated operational guidelines set out obligations of State Parties signatories to Convention responsible for their management.
UNESCO Convention on the Means of Prohibiting and Preventing the Illicit Import, Export and Transfer of Ownership of Cultural Property	http://portal.unesco.org/en/ev.php-URL_ID=13039&URL_DO=DO_TOPIC&URL_SECTION=201.html#STATE_PARTIES	State Parties are obliged to protect the cultural property existing within their territory against the dangers of theft, clandestine excavation and illicit export and guard against illicit import of cultural properties from elsewhere.
UNESCO Recommendation for the Protection of Movable Cultural Property	http://portal.unesco.org/en/ev.php-URL_ID=13137&URL_DO=DO_TOPIC&URL_SECTION=201.html	Adopted eight years after the above it is a more detailed document outlining the responsibility of museums within the borders of UNESCO member State Party countries.
UNESCO Recommendation on the HUL (*HUL Approach*)	http://portal.unesco.org/en/ev.php-URL_ID=48857&URL_DO=DO_TOPIC&URL_SECTION=201.html	This instrument aims to promote greater integration of conservation, planning and land use (including tourism) concerns for HULs.
UNESCO Convention on the Protection of the Underwater Cultural Heritage	http://portal.unesco.org/en/ev.php-URL_ID=13520&URL_DO=DO_TOPIC&URL_SECTION=201.html	Key aims are to protect shipwrecks and other underwater remains *in situ* for research and recreation. Chiefly in place to control destructive commercial exploitation, such as salvage.
UNESCO Memory of the World Programme (and recommendation)	http://www.unesco.org/new/en/communication-and-information/flagship-project-activities/memory-of-the-world/homepage	The List associated with the programme tries to be the equivalent of the WHS List for documentary heritage. An International Advisory Committee, or IAC, administers the programme whose members are appointed by the UNESCO Director-General.
ICOMOS International Charter for the Conservation and Restoration of Monuments and Sites (*The Venice Charter*)	http://www.international.icomos.org/charters/venice_e.pdf	The first set of principles devised to underlie professional practice of restoration and other architectural conservation actions and to guide the professionalization of archaeological practice internationally.

Continued

Table 5.1 Key codes, charters, conventions, declarations and recommendations (with website links) for tangible cultural heritage, continued

Title	Website	Key feature
ICOMOS Historic Gardens (*Florence Charter*)	http://www.international.icomos.org/charters/gardens_e.pdf	One of the first charters to complement *The Venice Charter* and provide guidance for the conservation of heritage with mixed natural and cultural values.
ICOMOS Charter for the Conservation of Historic Towns and Urban Areas (*Washington Charter*)	http://www.international.icomos.org/charters/towns_e.pdf	The first document to deal specifically with urban landscapes. Also, one of the first to advocate multidisciplinary teams for studies.
ICOMOS Charter for the Protection and Management of the Archaeological Heritage	http://www.international.icomos.org/charters/arch_e.pdf	The charter builds on *The Venice Charter's* articles about professionalization of practice to include more detail on conservation, management and, for the first time, presentation and interpretation of archaeological heritage.
ICOMOS Charter on the Protection and Management of the Underwater Cultural Heritage	http://www.international.icomos.org/charters/underwater_e.pdf	Precedes the UNESCO Convention and includes more details on professional conservation principles and practices specific to underwater items than the archaeological heritage charter.
ICOMOS Charter on Cultural Routes	http://www.international.icomos.org/charters/culturalroutes_e.pdf	A newer charter that provides professional guidance for understanding the cultural significance and management issues for this often trans-border, large-scale heritage asset.
ICOMOS Charter on the Built Vernacular Heritage	http://www.international.icomos.org/charters/vernacular_e.pdf	Another charter that complements *The Venice Charter* in that it provides greater clarification on professional practices. It also can be used in advocacy as vernacular heritage is increasingly considered a vulnerable heritage category.
ICOMOS Charter on the Interpretation and Presentation of Cultural Heritage Sites (*Ename Charter*)	http://www.international.icomos.org/charters/interpretation_e.pdf	This charter builds on previous ones that mention this area briefly, because there was a need to broaden and underline how important this aspect is becoming. It is a key charter for tourism professionals to acknowledge.

Title	Website	Key feature
ICOMOS Cultural Tourism Charter – Managing Tourism at Places of Heritage Significance	http://www.international.icomos.org/charters/tourism_e.htm	This charter has been revised several times and has become more positive about tourism collaboration. It also offers guidance on stakeholder collaboration and the nature of the planning process.
The Nara Document on Authenticity (*Nara Declaration*)	http://www.icomos.org/charters/nara-e.pdf	First instrument to recognize differences in cultural traditions of conservation practice. At the time of writing, a conference was being organized to debate and possibly update some sections of it.
Xi'an Declaration on the Conservation of the Setting of Heritage Structures, Sites and Areas	http://www.international.icomos.org/charters/xian-declaration.pdf	Aims similar to the Built Vernacular Heritage Charter, in terms of highlighting the care of 'settings' as an important part of heritage management and the need for specific principles to guide conservation practice.
The Australia ICOMOS Charter for the Conservation of Places of Cultural Significance (*The Burra Charter*)	http://australia.icomos.org/wp-content/uploads/The-Burra-Charter-2013-Adopted-31.10.2013.pdf	First charter developed to deal with regional issues not covered by *The Venice Charter*. *The Burra Charter* was the first document to outline a detailed concept of values-based assessment that should guide the planning and management of a heritage asset.
The Hoi An Declaration on Conservation of Historic Districts of Asia	http://www.international.icomos.org/xian2005/hoi-an-declaration.pdf	A recent example of a regional document, similar to *The Burra Charter*, but with more attention to providing professional guidance on specific issues for Asian historic districts and stakeholder engagement.
Joint ICOMOS – TICCIH Principles for the Conservation of Industrial Heritage Sites, Structures, Areas and Landscapes	http://www.international.icomos.org/Paris2011/GA2011_ICOMOS_TICCIH_joint_principles_EN_FR_final_20120110.pdf	A recent example of a collaboration between ICOMOS and another professional organization, The International Committee for the Conservation of Industrial Heritage, to create a more specialized document.
International Centre for the Study of the Conservation and Restoration of Cultural Property (ICCROM) Statutes	http://www.iccrom.org/about/statutes/	As close to a code or charter as possible for the guidance of professional materials conservation practice (specialist care/ restoration of artefacts, structural elements, artworks and so on).
International Council of Museums (ICOM) Code of Ethics	http://icom.museum/professional-standards/code-of-ethics/	A similar document to the ICOMOS charters, which guides professional museum management principles and practices.

A four stage planning process

Heritage planning generally follows a four stage process of:

1   identification, classification and documentation of the heritage asset and its components;
2   assessment of the cultural values evoked by the physicality of the asset;
3   analysis of the opportunities and constraints which will have a bearing on the production of a conservation and management policy;
4   the implementation of decisions and recommendations, including that of ongoing monitoring or detailed recording prior to removal or conservation work.

(based on Pearson and Sullivan 1995: 8–9; ICCROM 2014)

Documentation is critical. Finding out as much as possible in advance in a systematic way about the asset and its setting, as well as making sure that this information is available to all parties that are involved in the process will help identify intrinsic and extrinsic values associated with assets. Individuals carrying out documentation and research should disclose why the information is needed and include these stakeholders, if interested, in further consultation. In addition, identification of the state of the existing fabric of a tangible heritage asset has been a long-standing part of any conservation planning process, so facilitators of a project should expect that this stage may take some time commensurate with the scale of the asset.

In some countries, non-professionals are encouraged to undertake this work, but refer closely to manuals and resources provided by heritage agencies and regulatory bodies (e.g. Heritage Victoria 2009 *Protecting Local Places* advisory booklet; Canada's *Cultural and Heritage Tourism Handbook*, Whyte et al. 2012; Heritage Preservation 2014 Conservation Assessment Programme). Also, as an aid to capacity building, some cultural tourism and heritage professionals have been known to offer pro-bono advice to local authorities and professionals, as have international designers to community arts organizations trying to develop plans for sensitively commodifying local arts and handicrafts as quality tourism souvenirs (du Cros 2013).

Further, social impact assessments are becoming more common in relation to large-scale projects or World Heritage nomination. They are also appropriate when considering whether or how to develop cultural heritage assets that include social practices, religious rituals, or some potentially sensitive area of a community's daily life. The management or safeguarding of cultural heritage in general and ICH in particular in relation to tourism planning is a relatively new field (UNWTO 2012) so there are rarely any formal requirements for studies. However, most authorities advise that some kind of impact assessment is useful for maintaining a balance in the development process and, moreover, provides a start for any longitudinal studies concerned with discerning thresholds of cultural change in the future.

Identification: differing categories of tangible heritage

Essentially, tangible heritage can be grouped into three broad categories: buildings and archaeological sites; heritage cities, cultural routes and cultural landscapes; and movable cultural property and museum collections.

Buildings and archaeological sites

Buildings and archaeological sites are the most common types of tangible heritage documented. The initial motivation to document them is often to fight to save these structures and sites from destruction, while in the latter stages, the focus tends to shift to finding suitable uses for the conserved assets. Even when tourism is not cited as a conservation rationale, developing appropriate visitor programmes should be an integral part of conservation planning (Pearson and Sullivan 1995, Shackley 1998).

Archaeological sites have special issues for site interpreters and with this in mind the Ename Centre for Public Archaeological and Heritage Presentation worked closely with the ICOMOS International Scientific Committee on Interpretation and Presentation of Cultural Heritage Sites to produce the *Charter on the Interpretation and Presentation of Cultural Heritage Sites* 2008; 2014). (See Plate 5.1).

Plate 5.1 Towers of Silence, Yazd, Iran

The Zoastrian funerary area called Dakhmeh-ye Zartoshtiyun (Towers of Silence), Yazd, Iran, is an archaeological site that requires special sensitivity to its presentation and interpretation. Because archaeological heritage can be culturally sensitive, partly visible, damaged, or incomplete, great care must be taken in presentation and interpretation. A multidisciplinary approach is required to collate background information resources (history, artifact analysis, landscape analysis, and so on). These resources provide context and are the basis of any on-site interpretation for tourists.

Heritage cities, cultural routes and cultural landscapes

Cultural heritage assets can cover entire neighbourhoods, historic cities, routes and broader cultural landscapes. After the initial concentration on individual items, heritage management started to consider more closely how to conserve items in groups at a more collective level. Typically, historic cities and towns are managed through town planning guidelines, by-laws, zoning structures and policies that often include special regulations for heritage precincts or conservation areas (English Heritage 2011). Urban planners, therefore, ultimately set priorities for historic precincts or conservation areas. Their decisions have been made with varying amounts of cooperation from and participation by heritage professionals, individual property owners and the general public.

The identification of special precincts and the subsequent development of a precinct-wide management plan has proven to be quite successful, providing they are discrete areas with clearly defined boundaries and also providing property developers buy into the concept of conserving cultural values. In many cases, however, valuable cultural assets often lie outside specially designated areas. Here, the HUL Approach supported by the UNESCO recommendation represents a major step forward for the care of these kinds of assets. It has as its basis a greater awareness of the "challenges facing urban heritage in the new century" (Bandarin and van Oers 2012: 65).

The HUL Approach is essentially an elaborate toolkit for citywide conservation which also allows for new resources to be added. The approach tries to link issues concerned with sustainability, resilience, adaptation to climate change, and globalization to those of standard urban heritage planning and conservation. Creative industries and tourism are also given a higher status than previously in trying to reach a balance that will satisfy a wide array of stakeholders. The toolkit comprises four areas that need to be addressed simultaneously, due to their interdependence:

- Regulatory systems comprising statutory frameworks, policies and traditional caretaker practices where these exist.
- Community engagement tools to identify key values in their urban areas. For example, cultural mapping exercises which rely on feedback from community focus groups about their histories and traditions. More than that, such tools should also facilitate intercultural dialogue by listening to the needs and aspirations of communities and be able to mediate between conflicting interests and groups.
- Technical tools to protect the integrity and authenticity of the architectural, visual, spatial, and material attributes of urban heritage. For example, studies that acknowledge cultural significance and diversity, and provide measures for monitoring/management of change to improve the quality of life of the community. Also, inventories of natural and cultural features should be undertaken or updated regularly. Cultural heritage and social impacts should be considered a higher priority in development planning that requires environmental impact assessments (EIAs) with the results integrated regularly into urban planning and design.
- Financial tools (mechanisms, incentives, policies and so on) should aim to improve urban areas while safeguarding their tangible and intangible values. Flexible mechanisms are recommended such as micro-credit financing and public–private partnerships facilitated by public sector or not-for-profit organizations.

Overall, the definition of a HUL is one where "the urban settlement is understood as a historic layering of cultural and natural values, extending beyond the notion of 'historic centre' or 'ensemble' to include the broader urban context and its geographical setting" (Bandarin and van Oers 2012: 200). Accordingly, this approach recognizes that this category of heritage asset needs not just a few but all of the above tools for an integrated approach to planning and management to be holistic, inclusive, and participatory.

Even before HUL started to gain popularity, other approaches to linking tangible and intangible heritage in historic cities were being tried to mitigate the pressure of globalization. These measures also try to work to provide a better experience of unique local culture and sense of place for tourists, while mitigating the impacts of tourism in return. Over the last ten years or so, various international bodies have showcased the best examples of integrated urban planning and heritage management these to use as exemplars to other places facing similar problems.

One example from the Best in Heritage organization of an integrated heritage planning project of the kind advocated by the HUL approach and one that links tangible and intangible heritage is the Belgian Heart for People's Cafes project. In 2007 the media in Flanders and Brussels regularly reported on the disappearance of local people's cafes and it soon became clear to the research organization Lebialem Cultural Association (LECA) Belgium that these press reports were only the tip of the iceberg. After doing some preliminary research, LECA noted that people's cafes were closing their doors everywhere and the community was losing public spaces for not only social encounters, but also unique elements of Belgian cultural heritage, which combine architectural, tangible, and intangible elements.

The project was innovative in the way it combined research, policy recommendations, crowdsourcing, and a nationwide communication campaign to achieve its goals. 'Heart for people's cafes' was kicked off with the launch of a website and a widespread call to register extant cafes. In less than 24 hours after the launch, volunteers had entered over 200 people's cafes on the online database.

LECA also published a cycling route 'Visiting people's cafes by bike' brochure for locals and tourists and a coffee table style picture book called 'Volkscafés'. The book showed a contemporary image of the people's cafes and emphasized their social function in Belgian society. Finally, a heritage study and a list of policy recommendations on how to safeguard the remaining people's cafes in Flanders and Brussels in September 2009 was submitted to the secretaries of the relevant government agencies (Best in Heritage 2011).

However, it became evident to many authorities that there were categories of heritage that were beyond these measures and also deserved recognition in some way (Rössler 2006). Cultural routes or sometimes itineraries usually include other categories of heritage, for example, industrial, archaeological, and historic cities, under an umbrella of a shared history and a spatial pattern of activity such as trade, cultural exchange, pilgrimage, or exploration (see Plates 5.2 and 5.3). They have presented some conceptual problems for heritage managers by being often transnational and inclusive of many stakeholders. In 2008, ICOMOS redefined them as representing,

> interactive, dynamic, and evolving processes of human intercultural links that reflect the rich diversity of the contributions of different peoples to cultural heritage.
>
> Though Cultural Routes have resulted historically from both peaceful and hostile encounters, they present a number of shared dimensions, which transcend their original functions …

(ICOMOS 2008: 1)

Plate 5.2 Religious tourists and pilgrims wait in the cathedral forecourt, Santiago de Compostela, Spain

The Way of Saint James is really a network of pilgrimage routes leading to an endpoint in Santiago de Compostela in Spain. The cathedral city is often where pilgrims meet up and celebrate the completion of the journey, and an attraction in itself for them and other touristsas is where they can view the statue of St James, visit his tomb, go to mass, and so on.

Plate 5.3 Sign for the Way of St James

Pilgrims and religious tourists follow the signs and maps for the route. At the end they can request a certificate, issued by the Catholic Church as a souvenir. The Way was the first European Cultural Route declared by the Council of Europe. The key stakeholder, the Catholic Church, with assistance from pilgrimage societies and other organizations, manages it. The provincial governments, either side of the French/Spanish border, undertake tourism promotion and the *Observatorio do Camino* monitors tourism impacts (UNWTO 2012).

Cultural routes in particular are potentially a very marketable type of asset for tourism given the interest in following in the footsteps of ancient travellers or pilgrims (Rosenbaum 1995a, 1995b; Moulin and Boniface 2001). Indeed, they are so popular that tourism marketing organizations and rural communities are working closely to create artificially designed networks between heritage places to encourage tourist use, some with the support of international funding. Examples include the Silk Road and the Tea and Horse Trade Route, site conservation projects for which have received resources from overseas partners and international organizations to commodify them for tourism and build management capacity (Rössler 2006; du Cros 2007b; Whitfield 2009).

Cultural landscapes are another heritage category. They comprise a cultural asset where natural and cultural values are highly integrated and one that embodies how humans influence change in the environment over time by undertaking particular activities. The term also recognizes that tangible and intangible heritage should be protected together, as has been long acknowledged by certain indigenous societies (see Plate 5.4). So it is no surprise that UNESCO included cultural landscapes as a way to broaden the World Heritage List and included them in the operational guidelines when updating the World Heritage Convention (UNESCO WHC 2013). As a consequence of these shifts in focus, a more holistic approach is needed to identify and manage a heritage asset that comprises a broad array of values and elements. It should be seen as a sum of the whole rather than focusing on individual parts (Bandarin and van Oers 2012).

Plate 5.4 Cliffs of Bandiagara (Land of the Dogons) WHS, Mali, West Africa and associated tangible heritage

The cliffs are still managed by local villagers with some assistance from NGOs. Communities have been nestled beside the cliffs for centuries. UNESCO considers it an outstanding example of a cultural landscape of striking cliffs, a sandy plateau, and local traditional architecture (houses, granaries, altars, sanctuaries, and *togu na*, or communal meeting places). Age-old social practices are evident in the area (mask production and performances, feasts, rituals, and ceremonies involving ancestor worship). The geological, archaeological, and ethnological values, together with the scenic nature of the landscape, make the Bandiagara Plateau one of West Africa's WHSs of outstanding universal value.

Movable cultural property, collections and museums

Movable cultural property includes any type of portable heritage object, artwork or arti-fact, such as ancient scrolls, wine bottles from shipwrecks, painted African masks, Hindu sculptures of a deity, or Babylonian pottery sherds. It is an extremely vulnerable type of asset as it can be damaged, sold on the black market, or its intangible values destroyed when it is removed from its original context. Movable archaeological cultural property is also extremely vulnerable to souveniring practices by visitors. Even something as small as a pretty blue bead or broken piece of pottery is easy to pick up and walk away with, which reduces the authenticity of the experience for others and the site's value scientifically.

Management priorities for movable cultural property that has been removed from or has lost its original home differ from those for other heritage assets, because such assets need to be placed in a suitable setting such as a museum, gallery or library (and hopefully can be displayed rather than just stored). When it is an artifact or object that has lost some sense of where it has come from, it cannot be used in displays or research unless a specialist can identify or authenticate it. This is also why documentation is important for verifying art-works and as part of excavation or archaeological rescue work, as there are so many objects that have been removed illegally and have lost all clues to their exact origin and there are not the resources to relocate and recontextualize them all. Although the international conven-tions and documents on movable property have raised the awareness of this problem, there is still a way to go in order to ensure that not only tourists, but art collectors and museums, do not get talked into acquiring illegally sourced objects and artwork.

Sometimes objects may be housed in their original setting, such as agricultural tools in a historic barn. In most cases, though, they have been removed from their setting. In order for them to be exhibited many objects go through commodification by being 'conserved' (work that is carried out by a professional materials conservator to improve or stabilize their physical condition), displayed and interpreted. Many museums place a high priority on appropriate display of their collections to engage visitors in new ways to absorb educational messages about their cultural values (Hein 1998; Falk and Dierking 2000; Hooper-Greenhill 2007). The increasingly constructivist approaches of these institutions allows more room for visitors to experience the collection informally and in their own way. That is, visitors are given opportunities and resources to 'construct' their own meanings (in terms of their own frame of reference) for such objects as a way of learning about them.

Assessing cultural significance: the intrinsic values of tangible heritage

While precise definitions of cultural significance are place-specific to reflect local conser-vation priorities (du Cros and Lee 2007), at their core they espouse a similar philosophy. The concept of assessing cultural significance has been important to heritage manage-ment from the beginning, yet it is only relatively recently that more professionals have accepted that the role of value in decision-making should be made explicit (Clark 2009). The Australia ICOMOS *Burra Charter* was the first set of conservation principles to make this link. It has been influential in the region (du Cros and Lee 2007). Hence, it is described as ICOMOS's first regional charter of conservation principles.

The Burra Charter (of 1979 – revised 1983, 1988, 1999 and 2013) defines cultural sig-nificance as meaning the "aesthetic, historic, scientific, social or spiritual value for past, present or future generations" (Australia ICOMOS 2013: 2). Basic criteria for assessment of significance include rarity, research or teaching potential, representativeness (is it a good example of its kind?), visual appeal, evidence of technical or innovative processes and associations with special individuals, cultural practices or spiritual beliefs. In determining representativeness, the asset must be compared to others of a similar kind locally, regionally or nationally on such aspects as integrity (how complete or intact it is), design or style (if architectural), physical condition and significance to the local or indigenous community. The resultant statement of significance outlining its cultural values (AHC 1998: 36) should be succinct, clear, comprehensive and assist in setting management priorities (ICOMOS 2013). The Charter is clear that the cultural significance should be retained and not adversely affected by any conservation or other activities. It suggests that every professional decision should be based on an understanding of the significance and even a choice of approach should take this into consideration. Hence it is known as a values-based assessment document, a process which influences how proposals for adaptive re-use or commodification for tourism should be handled.

Authenticity

Authenticity is perhaps the one area in CHM and conservation planning where there has been lively debate that has resulted in a noticeable broadening of opinions. The usage of the terms 'authenticity' or 'authentic' has changed markedly over the past 200 years both inside and outside CHM circles (Larsen 1994; Lowenthal 1994). Hence, the concept of 'authenticity' is and deserves to remain in state of flux (Jokilehto 1994; Lowenthal 1994). The word is of Classical Greco-Roman etymological origin and was used initially to indicate a sense of a true, sincere, or original element in a historical context. By 1849, it was defined as meaning "that is authentic, which is sufficient to itself, which commends, sustains, proves itself, and hath credit and authority from itself" (Fitzgerald in Jokilehto 1994: 19).

As the concept of heritage gained currency, the idea of being able to guarantee authenticity became vital when evaluating assets. Artworks, rare books, and other examples of material culture were subjected to scrutiny in various ways, so that they could be affirmed as genuine. During the eighteenth and nineteenth centuries in Europe, authenticity became part of an emerging approach to the conservation of artworks and historical monuments (Jokilehto 1994). Maintaining historical authenticity in building restoration works was promoted strongly by Englishmen John Ruskin and William Morris.

With the advent of increased mass production and a greater homogeneity of material culture in the twentieth century, the focus of much conservation work shifted to the preservation of mostly pre-industrial heritage. The resulting treatment for western-style heritage places tends to emphasize the importance of maintaining the original fabric of the heritage asset (or one phase of development) with as little intervention as possible as certain kinds of built heritage became rare (Jokilehto 1994). Later additions to buildings were torn down, so that they could be returned to their 'authentic' state.

More recently, though, conservation practice has emphasized the importance of acknowledging something from all phases of historical development of many types of heritage assets (e.g. that a youth hostel sits on the site of early cottages) and efforts are now being made to conserve and interpret the entire fabric of a place and not only its original structure. Alternatively, Chinese temples have had a longstanding practice of renewing the fabric completely and then commemorating each renewal with a stone tablet explaining briefly what was done and by whom including, of course, the sponsors. Although, the approach to renewal may be more extreme than what is comfortable for those with the stewardship of other Asian temples that are not in China, it nevertheless falls under the terms of the The Nara Declaration Documentation outlined earlier.

But authenticity is a word that does not always have a counterpart in non-European languages, particularly Japanese. The two closest words are genuineness and reliability. As a result, different approaches to authenticity have evolved to encapsulate a non-European view that is encapsulated in the *Nara Document on Authenticity* (ICOMOS 1994b). The main features of the document are the revised principles on understanding and managing authenticity in a way that takes into account eastern as well as western viewpoints. It also makes some important points about heritage and cultural diversity, which had not been made in previous charters (ICOMOS 1994).

In many parts of Asia, the intangible heritage associated with the fabric is a stronger indicator of authenticity than the fabric of the structure itself, for a couple of reasons. To begin with, many structures were built of wood, and over time, the wood would deteriorate and need replacement. In addition, the religious views held by some cultures (such as animism – sacredness of the surrounding environment) meant that shrines were thought of as having mortal life spans. It was important to renew these structures at regular intervals, so as not to become unclean by death. One 'ancient' temple in Nara, Japan has been on the same site for more than 1,000 years, but the temple itself is completely rebuilt every 20 years in accordance with strict attention to traditional methods. Thus, this shrine has had 61 reconstructions since it was first founded (Ito 1994).

Two other factors have caused cultural heritage managers to pause for thought when considering authenticity. One factor is community opinion, as greater access to the conservation process by local or indigenous community members has caused both sides to appreciate issues, especially religious ones, that are beyond that of the conservation of the fabric. Another factor is the need to set conservation objectives against the backdrop of sustaining cultural identity and diversity. The latter deals with issues of scale, not just of site types (building, town, and heritage route), but also of management policies, which have to accommodate assets with a range of cultural values (Domicelj 1994). Hence, authenticity has been linked to cultural mapping, which recognizes the cultural heritage perceptions of diverse communities and ensures an inclusive study of all elements. Again, these need to be flexible enough to receive input from community cultural heritage mechanisms or consultation processes (Galla 1994, 2012).

Analysis of opportunities: use should not clash with intrinsic cultural values and sustainable levels of use

Contemporary society uses the past in many different ways. It can be a commodity to be bought, sold and consumed. It can be used to control, confirm or confront present beliefs, especially as it relates to national identity. It can provide a venue for leisure and education. And it can articulate national pride or group identity. Who decides the use and management of heritage assets ultimately defines them. This issue affects the cultural tourism community as much as its counterparts in CHM. According to a number of heritage analysts (Spearritt 1991; Tunbridge and Ashworth 1996; Hall and McArthur 1998; du Cros 2002; Clark 2009), such a debate is very important for understanding cultural identity and also a crucial part of any conservation plan for key heritage attractions such as WHSs (UNESCO WHC et al. 2013).

Thus, identifying compatible uses or reuses of tangible heritage is a significant issue for the sustainability of their cultural values (ICOMOS 1993: English Heritage 2011). This consideration extends beyond the immediate curtilage of the asset and also encompasses its surroundings, for a heritage asset can be badly affected by uncontrolled, insensitive development around it (ICOMOS 1993: 15; ICOMOS 2005). Tourism involves a certain amount of unstructured activities. Unsympathetic alteration to the vernacular in historic areas around icon attractions can reduce enjoyment (du Cros et al. 2005). Development that abuts structures can ruin their aesthetic appeal, while developers who want to ensure good views of icon attractions by demolishing structures that interfere with the view can also affect the sense of the place. Where possible, such incursions should be discouraged. If they cannot be ruled out completely, building owners should be encouraged to commission renovations with some measure of sensitivity of design in the architectural style of the construction, as was the case with the Mills Bakery, Royal William Yard, Plymouth, UK (Urban Splash 2014) or the Queen Victoria Building, Sydney (QVB 2014).

Inappropriate activities or even unnecessary repetition of themes and motifs can also lead to an area or structure, and the culture that is associated with it, being trivialized (Cuattingguis 1993; ICOM 2004). It is unfortunately the case that such trivialization can occur as part of tourism development, and the historic character of heritage attractions can become seriously compromised by it. Attention must also be given to the nature and use of the environment and space adjacent to or part of the setting of such an asset in order to sustain its cultural values. Over the last ten years, a number of ICOMOS General Assemblies of heritage professionals have had a number of sessions on this topic. In 2005, the Xi'an Declaration on the Conservation of the Setting of Heritage Structures, Sites and Areas was approved and was supposed to be used to raise awareness of this issue in developing nations. However, the destruction of much of the vernacular heritage and its setting in such places continues apace as do incursions into buffer zones for WHSs, so measures other than charters and other documents are needed in the twenty-first century for these more extreme situations.

Management: visitor accessibility and use

Not all assets should be made accessible to all visitors. Instead, the level of access and types of approved activities need to be defined by the robustness of the asset and its traditional uses. Setting use management priorities lies somewhere along a use/conservation continuum shown in Figure 5.1. For instance, heritage places guided by a conservation only ethos will need to adopt measures to reduce visitation and minimize or mitigate impacts. Alternatively, places with high use potential can be managed in such a way as to encourage visitation. Usually a balance of use and conservation considerations will drive management decisions (du Cros 2000).

However, there are some exceptions. Remote assets that can cope with heavy visitation will likely not be visited often. As such, a conservation-oriented management approach may be desired. Assets that are fragile but potentially popular might require the development of associated, highly commodified, museum-type attractions where visitors are directed to a reconstruction as an alternative (Brooks 1993). This situation has occurred in Lascaux, France where the Paleolithic rock art found in the caves is at risk from too many tourists. A purpose-built museum and visitor centre has been developed to shift visitors away from the original caves. Some heritage assets cannot be viewed or talked about outside certain circles in order to retain aspects of sacredness that are part of the

Figure 5.1 Management option continuum

conservation of their intangible heritage values (Deacon 2004). Information on sensitive assets may be presented instead in a range of other ways including DVDs, education resource kits, documentaries, or publications and, more recently, in virtual reconstructions and the immersive experiences discussed earlier.

Issues about maintaining authenticity in terms of what kind of intervention is required to conserve the physical fabric and its cultural values need to be discussed. In setting commodification priorities that can affect both fabric and cultural values, tourism can be a much more powerful stakeholder than the host community or the heritage manager. How a partnership or an arrangement can be reached between all these stakeholders on this important issue is the subject of the next chapter.

Key learning outcomes

- A vast array of charters, principles and practices guide CHM of tangible heritage worldwide.
- Each cultural heritage asset is unique, due to its complexity, scale, location, and setting.
- Illegal practices can complicate matters, especially artefact provenance.
- Different views on managing authenticity in architectural conservation have led to a recognition that a plurality of approaches to heritage management is possible.
- A values-based assessment approach can work well with an integrated planning process for cultural tourism.

6 Intangible cultural heritage and creative arts

Introduction

If tangible heritage represents a community's hardware, ICH represents its software. This chapter explains some of the core concepts behind ICH and also some of its unique management challenges, especially for tourism. The definitions used in the *UNESCO Convention for the Safeguarding of the Intangible Cultural Heritage,* 2003 state that ICH

> means the practices, representations, expressions, knowledge, skills – as well as the instruments, objects, artifacts and cultural spaces associated therewith – that communities, groups and, in some cases, individuals recognize as part of their cultural heritage. This intangible cultural heritage, transmitted from generation to generation, is constantly recreated by communities and groups in response to their environment, their interaction with nature and their history, and provides them with a sense of identity and continuity, thus promoting respect for cultural diversity and human creativity.
>
> (UNESCO 2014)

ICOM has had more to do with this Convention than ICOMOS, so far. ICOM has set the following actions as important in relation to implementing the 2003 Convention, that its members:

- value human creativity and its contribution to understanding the past, shaping the present and mapping the future;
- believe heritage has a humanistic value;
- value global dialogue based on intellectual, cultural and social diversity;
- value transparent dialogue including cross-cultural understanding of human rights;
- recognize their museums' responsibility to society through their engagement with public issues of social change.

(ICOM Australia 2008)

Conventions, codes, charters, and declarations

As with tangible cultural heritage, a variety of international codes, charters, and conventions have been developed to help identify and manage ICH. (Table 6.1 identifies the key conventions and their web links.) But, unlike tangible cultural heritage where the mandate is to conserve, here, the mandate changes to 'safeguarding' intangible heritage, in recognition

Table 6.1 *Key international conventions, charters, and recommendations for safeguarding intangible cultural heritage (with website links)*

Title	Website link	Key feature
UNESCO Convention for the Safeguarding of the Intangible Cultural Heritage	http://portal.unesco.org/en/ev.php-URL_ID=17716&URL_DO=DO_TOPIC&URL_SECTION=201.html	Defines main categories of ICH and outlines a process to safeguard cultural values and promote knowledge transfer with some official recognition of outstanding examples
UNESCO Proclamation of Masterpieces of Oral and Intangible Heritage of Humanity	http://www.unesco.org/culture/intangible-heritage/	A precursor to the UNESCO ICH Convention in terms of providing recognition of outstanding examples
UNESCO Convention on the Diversity of Cultural Expressions	http://portal.unesco.org/en/ev.php-URL_ID=31038&URL_DO=DO_TOPIC&URL_SECTION=201.html	Links human rights and freedom of expression to management of what is mostly ICH to promote cultural diversity
ICOM Declaration of Seoul on the Intangible Heritage	http://icom.museum/the-governance/general-assembly/resolutions-adopted-by-icoms-general-assemblies-1946-to-date/seoul-2004/	Outlines the nature of ICOM's support for the UNESCO ICH Convention and some responses to operationalizing it
ICOM Shanghai Charter: Museums, Intangible Heritage and Globalization	http://icom.museum/programmes/intangible-heritage/	A set of principles to guide how museum professionals should safeguard ICH values
UNWTO Ninh Binh Declaration on Spiritual Tourism for Sustainable Development	http://media.unwto.org/news/2013-11-29/viet-nam-hosts-1st-international-conference-spiritual-tourism	A set of principles for both heritage and tourism community to use to develop cultural sensitive spiritual tourism products
UNESCO Declaration on Cultural Diversity	http://portal.unesco.org/en/ev.php-URL_ID=13179&URL_DO=DO_TOPIC&URL_SECTION=201.html	A precursor to the Convention on Cultural Diversity with the key principles in a simplified form for easy use

of its dynamic nature. Conservation may lead to fossilization and museumification of traditions, while safeguarding seeks to keep them alive and vibrant.

Consequently, a different set of issues is raised. Intangible heritage is by definition people-orientated rather than object-centred. At its core, implementation of the UNESCO Convention could transform the relationships between museums and their audiences and stakeholders (Boylan 2006). Knowledge transfer and education programmes that use tradition bearers, living treasures, artists, and performers play an important role in promoting the continuity of ICH. But education programmes require close coordination with the community, as these people may not want to spend their entire time as performers or demonstrators to masses of museum visitors. Many of these people belong to indigenous groups and many are community leaders. They often welcome the opportunity to perform or demonstrate their arts and knowledge to students of all ages as an opportunity for cultural exchange and celebration of their survival.

As of mid-2014, 158 states have signed the Convention and 156 NGOs have been accredited as part of the capacity building programme (UNESCO 2014). Japan and the Republic of South Korea have been instrumental in the early promotion of the Convention by holding international conferences. These countries were also the first to have legal recognition of intangible heritage, and were also the key drivers of the push to recognize living cultural treasures.

A three stage approach to safeguarding intangible cultural heritage

Museums, cultural community centres and institutes, among others from the public and not-for-profit sectors, have been involved at the local level in the increasingly systematic approach to safeguarding ICH. Although the development of widely adopted management approaches is still in its early stages, overall it appears that most countries seem to have adopted a three stage approach, comprising:

1   involvement of communities;
2   documentation and developing an inventory;
3   building capacity within communities to continue transmission of ICH.

Again, as with tangible heritage, any type of management system should not try to conserve heritage as an end in itself. The management philosophy is more about identifying particular values that a community wants to continue to transmit to future generations, through various manifestations of its intangible heritage, than about maintaining these expressions in an unchanging, stagnant state.

Museums have an important role to play in intangible heritage management and knowledge transfer through investigation, documentation, and assisting communities to build capacity in the transmission of these techniques and skills (Boylan 2006). Museums can provide space and facilitate programmes to match visitors with tradition bearers, practitioners, and artists, especially in cases where knowledge and skills are under threat of disappearing as occurred in a hand-knitting frame project in Leicester, England, and Cantonese opera in Hong Kong (see Plate 6.1) (Liu and du Cros 2012). In recognizing this role, ICOM has also assisted at the international and national level in capacity building for documentation and public awareness programmes about the need to safeguard ICH (ICOM 2014a).

Key producers, performers and bearers of intangible cultural heritage

Part of the difference between tangible and intangible heritage is that the latter requires the presence of people to give it life. Consequently the cooperation and participation of

Plate 6.1 Cantonese Opera being performed by Hong Kong schoolchildren

New measures to integrate learning about this local performing art are being trialled in schools with assistance from the Chinese Artists Association of Hong Kong, Hong Kong Institute of Education, and the Hong Kong Museum of Heritage. Ideally, it is important for all students in Hong Kong, whether ethnic Chinese or not, to understand the culture behind such ICH items. Better understanding of the role that locally derived ICH assets, such as Cantonese Opera, play in society is important for building civic pride and creating a sense of shared cultural identity. This sense of pride and place can be also relayed to visitors, whether they experience the asset personally or not.

'folk', 'tradition bearers', 'living treasures', '*sifus* or masters/mistresses' and others is essential, otherwise, it becomes little more than shallow performance. Likewise, the setting is important, for intangible heritage is intrinsically linked to place. From a tourism perspective, as well, seeing an 'authentic' individual demonstrating ICH in a 'real' place enhances the experience.

Performers and artisans using traditional methods or modes of cultural expression play a key role in the maintenance of traditions and the presentation of these traditions to tourists. Consequently, tradition bearers, custodians, and religious figures with special knowledge are becoming involved in the delivery of tourism products. They may be secular, sacred, or a mixture of both. These individuals see themselves primarily as custodians of knowledge, and their role as presenters of knowledge for tourists as secondary. Increasingly, indigenous custodians are being asked to co-manage places that hold important spiritual significance to traditional owners (Uluru-Kata Tjuta National Park 2010). Growing interest in learning something about indigenous culture also places greater pressure on tradition bearers, custodians and religious figures to share their knowledge with tourists. (See Plates 6.2, 6.3 and 6.4).

Plate 6.2 Sovereign Hill, Australia

The role of performers and artisans varies depending on the nature of the cultural attraction. Sometimes actors may be hired to perform specific roles at cultural theme parks, as shown in the photo of Sovereign Hill in Australia, billed as an open air museum and family tourist attraction. In some cases, staff are assigned to play the role of historic figures, while in extreme cases, scripted performances are offered at regular intervals.

Plate 6.3 Tjabukai Aboriginal Cultural Park, Australia.

In other cases, local indigenous people are hired as performers as shown in the photo taken at Tjabukai Aboriginal Cultural Park in Australia. These types of performance for smaller groups are less commodified than that provided at Sovereign Hill.

Plate 6.4 Aboriginal cultural tour in Uluru, Central Australia.

Alternately, local residents may also become involved as performers, as shown in the case of a locally owned Aboriginal cultural tour in Uluru, Central Australia. Here local tradition bearers are employed to share their culture, stories and traditions with tourists.

Plate 6.5 Living treasure: weaver, Vigan, Philippines

Living human treasures represent another special group of custodians that are rarely encountered by tourists. UNESCO (2014) recognizes that the declining numbers of practitioners of traditional craftsmanship, music, dance, or theatre pose the greatest threat to the viability of much ICH. In order to help conserve this knowledge, UNESCO is encouraging states to develop national systems of 'Living Human Treasures' (see Plate 6.5). They are defined as 'persons who possess to a high degree the knowledge and skills required for performing or re-creating specific elements of the intangible cultural heritage'. Japan was the first country to recognize the value of ICH with its Living Human Treasures Programme, which began in 1950. This programme allows 'living national treasures' or 'holders of important intangible cultural properties' to be identified individually or collectively. Although the legislation does not necessarily bring with it greater protection or invigoration of intangible heritage, it does provide a basis for a more general recognition of the role of special individuals "as transmitters of traditions" (Larsen in Nishimura 1994: 179; Wantanabe 2006). The Korean *Cultural Properties Protection Act* of 1962 allows for a similar category of heritage protection. It was enacted in response to the realization that rapid modernization following the Korean Conflict was producing a reduction in interest in traditional skills and crafts. (See Plate 6.5)

Categories of intangible cultural heritage and their commodification for tourism

Sometimes it is not clear what and how to commodify ICH for tourism in a sustainable way. This issue is not covered well in any of the charters or codes listed, which are more about recognizing and safeguarding it in the face of cultural change and globalization. The closest any of them come to explicitly dealing with the issue is the most recent – the UNWTO Ninh Binh Declaration on Spiritual Tourism for Sustainable Development, 2013 (see Table 6.1 and Plate 6.6).

Plate 6.6 Christian church, Vietnam

A Christian congregation worshipping in a Vietnamese church, unaware that they may soon be part of a tourism product. UNWTO has just developed a new declaration on spiritual tourism to encourage more cultural sensitivity in developing and managing these assets for tourism. It has called for the support of governments, destinations, tourism businesses, and religious leaders to facilitate networking and to exchange best practices and case studies at the global level and support the Ninh Binh Declaration on Spiritual Tourism (see Table 6.1).

Using the UNESCO Convention as a basis to explore this issue further in relation to ICH as a whole, five main domains of intangible heritage that also have potential for tourism commodification are:

1   traditional craftsmanship;
2   social practices, rituals and festive events;
3   performing arts;
4   oral traditions and expressions, including language as a vehicle of the ICH;
5   knowledge and practices concerning nature and the universe.

Traditional craftsmanship

Handicrafts have been the mainstay of the material culture offered to tourists as souvenirs. Like any product, purchasing handicrafts satisfies a range of personal needs, wants and desires. They include household products, traditional beauty products, cosmetics and medicines, clothing, art, paintings, sculptures, pottery, traditional ceremonial artifacts, and even industrial goods including farm implements, tools, and industrial artifacts (Marwick 2001).

Unlike other types of souvenirs, handicrafts play a much more personal role in shaping the tourist experience (Marwick 2001), fostering long-term memories and associations with a place. As such, they are valued more highly than most other souvenirs. They are one of the few items that reflect authentic local culture in a globalized world (see Plate 6.7). It is becoming increasingly hard to find things that are truly unique and authentic. Yet, tourists are looking for original, authentic items and want to buy them at their place of origin (Ventacachellum 2004). Handicrafts have a deep association with a place, its people, their ways of life and/or a certain period of time.

Folk arts and handicrafts can be conceived of as products that reflect a country, region, or local community's cultural heritage and traditions. They may be evocative of past practices but may also reflect current practices. They are associated with a place and have value because they reflect a place and the people who produce them. In fact, any skill, no matter how broadly 'skill' is defined, can become a handicraft. The Canadian government suggests that craftspeople can be divided into trade families by medium, such as wood, ceramics, fibre, leathers and skins, glass, paper, print and binding, metals, and multidisciplinary (Anon 2001).

The touristic commercialization of handicrafts usually requires some type of adaptation of the original product. Gigantism where goods are enlarged to make them more appealing, or miniaturization where they are reduced in size, is common. Original materials, such as fur, sometimes have to be changed to avoid conflict with the law or public opinion (Muller and Petterrson 2001), while substitute materials like plastics or wood can be used to make a product that is more durable or lighter. The platform where indigenous motifs are presented may also need to be changed to facilitate tourist consumption. Aboriginal drawings are printed on T-shirts, even though they were not traditionally found on them. The same situation applies in performance, where a dedicated venue and a short performance showing highlights of traditional dances leads to the production of an appealing product. (See Plate 6.8).

Many pro-poor tourism projects focus on handicraft production as an attractive and economically viable way for communities to become involved in tourism indirectly. Their low barriers to entry enable people to enter this sector with minimal capital and debt load (Jamieson 2000; Marwick 2001). Government programmes to provide seeding loans, training programmes, and assistance with the legal requirements to establish enterprises

Plate 6.7 Miniature painter, Isfahan, Iran

Master Iranian miniature painter doing individual pictures for tourists visiting his shop, whether or not they bought his pictures as souvenirs.

Plate 6.8 Mask performance by Dogon villagers, Mali, West Africa

Mask performances by Dogon villagers, Mali, West Africa are held using masks that are generally not for sale to tourists. Alternative masks are for sale (that are handmade), although a few instances of mass production have been noted in the more popular spots for tourists. Other souvenirs include indigo dyed fabric and carved wooden granary doors.

often yield positive results. Crafts enable members of agricultural communities to supplement their income with off-season employment (Theerapappisit 2009). Importantly, they provide much needed employment and income opportunities for people traditionally excluded from local economies, including women, members of ethnic minorities, young people, unskilled workers, people with disabilities, and the elderly. Crafts may also provide important income streams for museums and historic sites. Handicraft tourism can help diversify local economies, especially in rural areas of the less developed world (Ashley et al. 2000).

Social practices, rituals, and festive events

Social practices, rituals, and festive events are defined by UNESCO (2014) as "habitual activities that structure the lives of communities and groups and that are shared by and relevant to many of their members". Many ethnographic, social history, and local history museums and NGOs have been engaged in the documentation and promotion of such practices, in part because they are so vulnerable to changes brought about by globalization. These types of activities are significant because they help affirm individual, group, or society identity and, more importantly, are related to important events. Harvest festivals, birth rituals, religious celebrations, and a wide range of other activities fall into this class. Scale can vary from small family rituals to community or nationwide celebrations. (See Plate 6.9).

Plate 6.9 Dervishes, Turkey

Rumi, aka Mevlana, was a thirteenth century poet and mystic and founder of the Dervishes. His tomb is in Konya at the Mevlana dervish lodge (now a museum on the WHS List). Every week the Dervishes perform the Sema in the grounds of the Mevlana to honour the poet. Tourists can attend providing they are respectful.

Rituals and festive events tend to be more public. They occur either at special times of the year (Thanksgiving, Christmas, Chinese New Year) or in special places (grave sweeping). Some are closed to the public, while in many other cases the public is welcome. Festive events and rituals hold special appeal for tourists who are looking to gain a deeper understanding of the local culture being visited. It is believed that community festivals, in particular, hold much appeal, for they celebrate both group and place identity (de Bres and Davis 2001). Moreover, since each community is unique, its festive events are also unique (Getz 1989). Visiting festivals and participating in rituals, even as an onlooker, enables tourists to experience authentic cultural ambience, meet local residents, and partake in something authentically indigenous (Getz 1989). (See Plate 6.10).

Gastronomic heritage also comes under the umbrella of social practices. Particular aspects of a cuisine are either promoted singly or bundled with other practices to be a strong tourism draw card for many destinations (UNWTO 2012). Mak et al. (2012) when reviewing the literature observed that food consumption can be considered as more than just sustenance and, instead, can be viewed in social, cultural, and political terms. They note further that food consumption bears symbolic significance as a marker of social distinction and as a way to encounter and experience other cultures. Gastronomy, therefore, and especially gastronomic festivals and activities, represent a popular category used by destination marketing organizations to position themselves uniquely. A variety of food festivals, cooking tours, and food souvenirs have been developed to entice tourists by highlighting local cultures and traditions (du Cros 2013). (See Plate 6.11).

Wine tourism could also be considered as part of cultural tourism, when it is heavily based in historic districts or cultural landscapes that provide more context than pure wine tasting and consumption. Portugal has recognized the opportunity this provides for highlighting its role in the production of fortified and table wines over the years, as have many other European countries.

Performing arts and performance

Performing arts, including traditional and contemporary music, dance, and theatre, represent a third category of ICH (UNESCO 2014) that is frequently the subject of tourism commodification because of its often vibrant and dynamic nature. The cultural assets can vary in size from full theatre productions and symphony orchestra performances to a single storyteller or street performer. The geographic scale can be as large as a theatre district in cities like London or New York, or as small as a street corner. Likewise, venues may be purpose-built or spontaneously created. The artificial distinction between high and low culture in performing arts, no longer applies, as so-called low culture is often a reflection of the cultural behaviour of the masses. Indeed, Xie et al. (2007) discuss the emergence of 'hip hop' tourism as a form of intangible cultural tourism and the potential to commodify it for large-scale touristic consumption.

Temporary exhibitions also have a role to play in this area just as they do with objects. One example is that of the 2011 Airarang Exhibition at the National Folk Museum of Korea. *Airarang* is a Korean folk song, which is considered to be the country's unofficial national anthem in the same way as 'Waltzing Matilda' is for Australia. As well as artifacts associated with the song's creation and performance over the years, there was an area set aside for spontaneous amateur performances. Promoting this activity allowed an inclusive and multi-sensory appreciation of the subject of the exhibition for visitors, which they enjoyed immensely (Cheon 2012).

Plate 6.10 Floating children parade, Cheung Chau Festival

Local festivals often provide a fascinating glimpse of customs, traditions and lifestyles. However, few of them function as successful tourism products (McKercher et al. 2006) for several reasons. First, and foremost, most tourists are unaware of local festivals prior to arriving at their destination and, therefore, do not consider them as part of their product choice set when visiting. Second, participation in these festivals often requires a significant amount of time, especially if they are located outside of traditional tourism nodes. The combination of lack of awareness and significant time commitment make attending these events risky especially in light of other better-known higher priority activities that could be pursued. Local festivals tend to attract long stay tourists who have sufficient time budgets to engage in more discretionary activities. To increase the chance of spontaneous visitation, festivals need to be located in or near a tourism node.

Plate 6.11 'Food Street', Kaohsiung, Taiwan

Participating in the same types of activities as local residents provides an opportunity for tourists to engage in local intangible cultural experiences. Food is one such activity. 'Food Street' in Kaohsiung is an open air night market that occupies a number of blocks in the centre of the city. Local residents and tourists alike wander along the street and sample the local delicacies.

Oral traditions and expressions, including language as a vehicle of the intangible cultural heritage

Oral traditions encompass a wide variety of spoken activities that can include proverbs, riddles, tales, nursery rhymes, legends, myths, epic songs and poems, charms, prayers, chants, songs, dramatic performances, and more (UNESCO 2014). Historically, they were used to pass knowledge, social values, and collective memories across generations. As such, they are felt to play a key role in keeping cultures alive. However, UNESCO (2014) points out that like other forms of ICH, oral traditions are threatened by globalization, urbanization, migration, industrialization and, in particular, the spread of mass media that tends to present a homogeneous westernized view of the world.

Tourism can be both a saviour and threat to oral traditions. On the one hand, storytelling cultural exchange with tourists is beneficial, especially if it helps them understand indigenous cultural practices. It can also provide employment for traditional storytellers, and in doing so, keep these traditions alive. However, tourists want products and experiences that are easy to consume, and given their limited time budgets, quick to consume. As such, epic poems that once took several days to recite now have to be presented in 10 or 15 minutes, while Australian Aboriginal corroborees that used to take many days are now presented as evening theatre.

The tourismification of oral traditions can be challenging, especially in traditional collectivist societies. Cheer et al. (2013) note tensions can surround the juxtaposition of tourism and traditional culture when the economic utility of that culture becomes integral to contemporary local livelihoods. In particular, their study of Vanuatu pointed out that traditional peoples were communal, and as such, their intellectual and material property was viewed as a collective asset presided over by a hierarchy of leaders. This social structure conflicted with the needs of commercial tourism enterprises which function best in an individualistic context. Schmiechen et al. (2010) identified a further ethical issue in their study of Aboriginal cultural tourism in Australia. Again, they note that indigenous arts, crafts, designs, symbols and oral stories are communally, not individually, owned, but the development of successful tourism products may involve recording, photographing or videotaping people, stories, songs, dances, and ecological knowledge, with the resulting question of who owns the subsequent intellectual property rights.

Knowledge and practices concerning nature and the universe

This category includes knowledge, knowhow, skills, practices, and representations developed by communities by interacting with the natural environment (UNESCO 2014). This domain emerged out of the recognition that different communities think about the universe in different ways and have developed a series of oral traditions, place attachments, and memories of place that reflect that memory. How different groups think about nature and the universe also underlies many social practices and cultural traditions. Traditionally, life for most agricultural and nomadic communities was driven by the seasons. Food was also seasonal, with different foods in abundance or shortage at different times of the year.

Many science museums, community-based museums, as well as ethnographic and historical museums acknowledge the need to conserve such knowledge and practices as a core mandate. It is also where the recent change in mindset on museum curation practices towards the 'éco muse' (eco museum) or 'new' museum approach probably took root. For instance, the !Khwa ttu Education Centre in South Africa showcases San historical agricultural and eco-friendly traditional practices inside and outside the facility on a tour that is set on an existing farm with food cooked by the San (!Khwa ttu 2014).

Tourism, authenticity, and intangible cultural heritage

The greatest challenge facing the tourist provision of ICH is how to convert something that is essentially private and personal into something to be consumed by tourists, for the very commodification of ICH must lead to some compromises in presenting cultural values, especially when trying to present traditions, family practices, and private events (weddings, funerals, initiations, family meals and so on) for tourists. Either there is the potential for a massive invasion of privacy or some kind of trivialization of the asset. Either community amenity or authenticity suffers. (See Plate 6.12).

One solution has been to turn these events into performances. Doing so separates them from the local community, reducing the potential for adverse impacts, and can also create an authentic tourist experience. But, performance by its very nature, especially touristic performance where events have to be shrunk into a very short time frame, means that much of the meaning and value of the experience will be lost.

This issue is not particularly relevant when intangible heritage is performed with the community's whole-hearted support in the public domain, as in the case of many performances of festive occasions and events. The challenge then becomes how to provide an easily accessible experience that tourists can enjoy any time they visit as against only

Plate 6.12 Church, Dalian, China

The removal of ICH from its physical and social setting can result in its trivialization, sometimes to the extent that it becomes little more than a hollow parody of itself. This replication of the church from Pennsylvania, USA, was built in a cultural theme park outside Dalian, China, primarily to act as a wedding venue. The physical structure of the church is an exact replica of the original, but the interior is devoid of any reference to Christianity. Wedding packages are sold by showing pictures of a wedding in the original church and duplicate photos of a copy wedding here, down to the last detail. Celebrants can, therefore, enjoy all the physical trappings of a western wedding, including the ritualistic limousine ride, white gowns, bridesmaids and church-like service. However, the celebration is completely lacking any of the associated intangible cultural significance and meaning associated with Christian weddings.

when the traditional event or practice is held. Although communities may be positive about this change it can mean some subtle changes that may steamroll over the years and need careful monitoring to see if they are affecting the core cultural values of the community. This is where collaboration with professional anthropologists can be useful for communities in terms of setting up and managing longitudinal studies of such impacts. An anthropological study of *eisā*, a Japanese art form held in traditional temples and for festivals, is now accessible in transformed settings (e.g. theme parks). Previously little known outside Okinawa, the tourism development of this asset has shown how a performing art can also transform the local and national imagination. The movement of *eisā* from sacred to secular contexts also illustrates how the art form has significance today as a marker of cultural identity for Okinawans and other Japanese alike. Okinawa is considered by mainstream Japanese society to be one of Japan's 'others' (almost like the Ainu), which is why it is so popular as a tourist attraction (the unfamiliar within the familiar).

The dance form of *eisā* involves both music and dance, whether for religious, entertainment, or economic reasons. In each context, it is believed by researchers that when Okinawans are performing, they are 'performing Okinawa'. This is done largely in cultural theme parks themed to showcase local Okinawan culture and in a recently created summer arts festivals themed to *eisā*. Also, several of the larger Okinawan theme parks are designed specifically to relive an Okinawan historical past. For example, Oceanic Culture Hall (Kaiyō Bunkakan) has a native Okinawan village (Okinawa Kyōdo Mura) within it. At another location near a popular natural heritage site, Gyokusendō, a traditional village theme park has been constructed to feature *eisā* and other local arts and crafts. Local custodians have close control over the latter and the way the art forms are presented.

Meanwhile, recently created festivals have become media spectacles in Japan promoted by city authorities. Examples of these events include: Zenkoku Eisā Fesutibaru (Island-Wide Eisā Festival), Zen-Okinawa Kodomo Eisā, Matsuri (Okinawa Island-Wide Children's Eisā Festival) and Ichiman Eisā (10,000 Eisā Dance Parade). Ichiman Eisā, for example, is a vibrant and colourful parade along the main commercial street of the capital Naha and is part of a week-long event celebrating *eisā*. It showcases many *eisā* styles, old and new, and the performers are of all ages and both genders.

Authenticity, in terms of the timing of traditional events and their duration, does not work in favour of tourism, hence much of the commodification into theme parks and specially timed island-wide festivals. For visitors without access to theme parks, it might be difficult during a short stay on the island to visit a *sanshin* (musical instrument) maker or see an *eisā* performance, especially since the religious and secular events are held at certain times of the year. Anthropologists have argued that seeing both of these symbols of Okinawan identity at a theme park allows the visitor to enter a liminal (fantasy) world where the experience of Okinawa can be consumed the whole year round. Meanwhile, away from the theme parks local custodians can continue the training for and practice of *eisā* without too much touristic attention (Johnson 2008; Cooper et al. 2008). In summary, although the community seems happy with the attention, the tourist commodification has added a strong secular element to a cultural asset that was previously considered to be more in the sacred realm, so there has been a change to the core cultural values.

However, what happens if there are problems with the local community or with domestic tourists witnessing a version of their culture that they are uncomfortable with? This is an interesting issue and a pertinent one, as the advent of budget airlines and the rising incomes in developing countries mean that the old 'staged authenticity' cultural shows may be threatened in order to appeal to these new markets. In particular, new strategies and techniques will be needed that are still entertaining, but also inclusive of domestic tourists. Especially in that they avoid the most common cultural stereotyping and include more authentic representations of local living culture.

For example, a study of cultural performances for tourists at the Victoria Falls, Zimbabwe employed a combined traditional and online ethnography (netnography) to explore western and African tourist perspectives of their cultural experiences of such performances in Victoria Falls' restaurants. It emerged that in the case of (indigenous) Zimbabwean tourists, who formed the majority of African tourists, there is no vernacular (in the *Shona* and *Ndebele* languages) equivalent term for authenticity. If 'cultural authenticity' is a foreign concept for these tourists, it may be also for the local providers of such cultural experiences.

Mkono (2013) concluded that the African tourists would rather just enjoy themselves for the most part without reading too deeply into what they encountered as 'staged culture'. If they thought too much about these cultural performances being representations of themselves, then, focusing only on the 'fun' dimension offered an escape from contemplating what might be uncomfortable or stereotypical caricatures of their African identity. However, some African tourists sought to distance themselves from the show when interviewed, arguing that it clashed with their personal/religious belief systems. In some cases, they expressed resentment at what they saw as a stereotypical portrayal of 'Africanness' in the show and worried what the international tourists thought of them and other Africans after seeing the show.

Contemporary culture and the advent of creative tourism

Much of the focus of cultural tourism is placed on historic sites and ancient traditions. Yet, the range of cultural tourism products extends to include the contemporary, from the tangible (iconic buildings and other structures) to the intangible (performing and visual arts, events, festivals, etc.). AM authority Derik Chong (2009) notes that discussion of contemporary arts is often placed within a context of CM where much overlap is noted between CM and CHM in the organization, management and delivery of experiences. Cultural policy and AM authorities are increasingly trying to encourage the co-creation of contemporary arts activities events, with many activities of interest to tourists.

Producers of contemporary culture are increasingly describing themselves as more than just artists, writers, inventors, communications or IT types. Instead, they prefer the broader term 'creatives', partially in response to Florida's (2002) identification of a 'creative class' and also because much of the work transcends traditional labels. In a similar manner, they prefer to use the term 'art ecologies' (Chong 2009; Hager and Sung 2012) to describe the intricate linkages and interdependent relationships that exist between and among stakeholders, the community, and the general public. Understanding the nature and health of arts ecologies is important for the establishment of a place-based sustainable advantage that makes the most of available creative capital (creativity, creatives, creative processes and arts ecologies) (du Cros and Jolliffe 2014).

Collectively, the identification of creatives and art ecologies has led to the emergence of 'creative tourism' as an increasingly popular offering. It has been defined as "travel directed toward an engaged and authentic experience, with participative learning in the arts, heritage, or special character of a place, and it provides a connection with those who reside in this place and create this living culture" (UNESCO Creative Cities Network 2006: 3). This definition follows from the original one offered by Richards and Raymond (2000: 18), who defined it as a form of "tourism, which offers visitors the opportunity to develop their creative potential through active participation in courses and learning experiences which are characteristic of the holiday destination where they are undertaken."

Creative tourism first gained prominence in Europe, South Korea, Australia and New Zealand, when both the tourism industry and creatives recognized the role each can play in providing more interactive, mindful and diverse cultural tourism products. However, its potential was recognized at the 2009 Asia-Pacific Creativity Forum in South Korea; former Secretary of the UNWTO Francesco Frangialli observed, "the cultural personality specific to a country or to a destination … must assert itself in the global market (Frangialli 2009: 10). He also advised that new products were needed that reflect and "unleash the forces of cultural creation" for the benefit of tourists to a destination. (See Plates 6.13 and 6.14).

An example of one such product is Edventures in Fredericton (New Brunswick, Canada). It provides enriching experiences to tourists in a range of arts and crafts as well as some other activities. This event promotes itself as providing 'vacation learning in craft and culture' within the areas of: Visual Art, Mixed Media and Design; Fashion and Sewing; Jewellery and Metalwork; Photography and Digital Media; Pottery and Glass; Textiles; Heritage Offerings (such as Canadian Aboriginal Paddle Making), and Writing. The event is held over the summer months of July and August and has the capacity to attract more than 900 participants, who are mainly adults. Edventures' vision reflects a creative tourism ethos:

> to provide an exceptional learning experience from top-quality, experienced instructors in a refreshing, easy-going atmosphere. We'll weave that first-rate learning opportunity in a rich tapestry of exciting cultural offerings and connections to our friendly people.
>
> (Edventures 2013)

Plate 6.13 Fotanian Festival workshop, Hong Kong

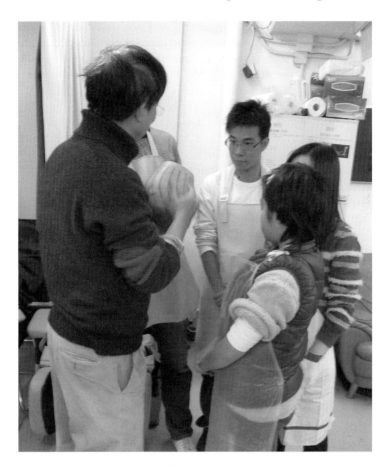

Plate 6.14 Fotanian Festival artist and participants, Hong Kong

Participatory activities are becoming a more frequent part of the Fotanian Festival, where artist studios are open to the public for several weekends over January each year. Artists from the Fotanian Artist Collective that runs the festival estimate that between 26,000 and 30,000 attend the unticketed event. The studio hop is an example of a bundled urban arts experience that attracts both tourists and locals (du Cros and Jolliffe 2011). Artists interviewed by the author at the 2014 event observed that many of the tourists they spoke to were also artists themselves.

Audience participation is necessary for creative tourism. Gordin and Matetskaya's (2012) study of arts festivals identified the following factors that could make them participatory:

- inclusion of interactive events in the festival programme;
- competitive events (preferably ones where entry requirements favour tourists and locals equally);
- educational events (master classes, public lectures, workshops, and so on);
- sub-events oriented towards promoting professional communication (seminars, conferences, panel debates);
- sub-events oriented towards non-professional communication (meeting actors, visiting backstage spaces, artist studios, and participating in activities there).

Meanwhile, other European examples of creative tourism activities provided by creative networks in Barcelona, Paris, and Austria offer a range of creative experiences for visitors including visual, performing and culinary arts, fashion and design, writing and philosophy, and gardening. In Austria, leisure pursuits are being brought together with a range of creative experiences at various 'creative hotspots' around the country. Creative Tourism Austria has also devised a model to manage this collaboration by developing close relationships with commercial partners, including hotels and spas, drawing these new partners into the arts/cultural ecology responsible for the activities. The model works to ensure a more holistic arts/education/leisure experience for tourists and more benefits for the creatives involved (Richards and Marques 2012). There is also more that public sector authorities can do in relation to creative tourism. One example known to the authors is where the Ministry of Culture and Tourism of the Republic of South Korea runs regular arts and crafts workshops for tourists in transit at its souvenir shops within Incheon International Airport, Seoul. Many of the activities are suitable for children as well as adults, giving parents a break from the stress of family travel while their children are both entertained and educated by the activity.

By their very nature, contemporary arts can take more risks than more traditional intangible cultural tourism activities. But, risk taking is also somewhat dangerous for it can either enhance or detract from the long-term management and success of the activities. A lack of creativity or too much creativity may alienate stakeholders and visitors alike. Taking too many risks may result in censorship or running foul of current political sentiments, especially in more repressive societies where free speech is seen as a threat. Bad initial conceptualization may represent a fatal flaw, while changing circumstances may result in a loss of funding.

Conversely, some events may prove to be too popular, which also creates problems. The Glastonbury Festival of the Contemporary Performing Arts (colloquially known as Glastonbury) was closed for a year after 2000 because of overcrowding due to gatecrashers, putting it in breach of licenced attendance numbers. Much tighter security and ticket management measures were introduced to limit attendance to around 130,000, when estimates for the year 2000 suggested as many 250,000 people attended, even though only 100,000 tickets had been sold (BBC News 2013, Glastonbury Festival 2014).

Conclusion

ICH raises a number of interesting issues for the tourism sector. At a simplistic level, it provides a means for tourists to gain a deeper understanding of the local culture. Moreover, the public nature of much intangible heritage, manifested through performance, festivals, handicrafts, listening to storytellers, food-tasting, local markets, and so on, creates appealing products that encourage deeper engagement. But their delivery ultimately also leads to the need to commodify, modify, and standardize experiences. Thus, one could also ask whether tourists are consuming ICH or simply seeing performance. What are they really learning about another culture, if anything? Tourism's commodification needs may mean that little of the 'culture' tourists consume is indeed representative of authentic intangible heritage, for it is divorced from the host community and its place. That is fine if the community is happy for that to occur, and many are, otherwise problems will arise for the supplier of these experiences.

Key learning outcomes

- An awareness of what sets of principles and practices guide CHM of ICH worldwide.
- An appreciation of the differences between tangible and intangible heritage as cultural assets and who the main stakeholders are for the latter.
- Comprehension of the basic issues and current approaches for commodifying different categories of ICH sensitively for cultural tourism.
- A recognition of how creative arts and creative tourism are providing new opportunities for cultural tourism.

Part C

Tourism, the tourist, and stakeholders

7 How tourism works

Introduction

People sometimes lose sight of the fact that cultural tourism is first and foremost a form of tourism. They forget that the word 'cultural' is an adjective that modifies the noun 'tourism'. Thus, while cultural tourism uses the cultural assets of a destination, its performance is guided by the same principles that drive any other form of tourism. Understanding cultural tourism, therefore, is predicated on developing an understanding of what tourism is, how it works, and what drives tourism decisions. Yet, while many are keen to express an opinion about how tourism *should* work, relatively few really understand the underlying factors that determine how tourism *does* work. This chapter seeks to address that knowledge gap, at least partially, through the identification of 19 underlying principles or structural realities that drive tourism. They are summarized in Table 7.1. Some relate to tourism in general, while others relate to how cultural assets are used for tourism purposes. You may not agree with them all, but at least consider them before commenting on tourism in the future.

The nature of tourism

It is important to understand what tourism is, how it works, why people travel, and what they expect when travelling. One must also appreciate that the benefits and costs of tourism are uneven; not everyone will benefit and not everyone who benefits will benefit equally.

Tourism is a commercial activity

Tourism is, essentially, a commercial activity. This axiomatic principle seems to be overlooked in much of the literature examining tourism from different academic or intellectual perspectives. While tourism may be an interesting intellectual phenomenon, in practice it is a business: a big business. Businesses enter the tourism sector in the hope of profiting by providing goods and services for the billions of people who travel domestically and internationally every year. Destinations pursue tourism because of the economic benefits it provides and for the ensuing social benefits that accrue from its wealth generation. States and provinces pursue tourism because it generates new money for their jurisdictions. Nations pursue tourism because it is such a valuable source of foreign exchange. While we may travel to satisfy inner needs such as escape, rest, recreation, status, or learning, destinations pursue tourism for the economic benefits it provides.

But tourism is unique in that facilitators of experiences rather than experience providers generate the majority of revenue. The 'tourism industry' enables tourists to consume

Table 7.1 *Underlying principles of cultural tourism*

The Nature of Tourism	Tourism is a commercial activity
	Tourism involves the consumption of experiences
	Tourism is entertainment
	Tourism is a demand driven activity that is difficult to control
Attractions Drive Tourism	Not all tourism attractions are equal
	Cultural heritage attractions are part of tourism
	Not all cultural assets are cultural tourist attractions
	World Heritage (or other) designation does not mean an automatic influx of tourists
Factors Influencing Visitation Levels	Access and proximity dictate the potential number of visitors
	Time availability influences the quality and depth of experience sought
Tourist Behaviour	There is no difference between a tourist and a traveller
	The tourist experience must be controlled, which in turn controls the actions of the tourist
	Tourists want controlled experiences
	The more mainstream (or mass) the market being targeted, the more quickly and easily the tourism product must be able to be consumed
	The mass market has not fractured
	Tourists seeking deep experiences exist but represent only a small share of the market
Cultural Tourism	Not all cultural tourists are alike
	Cultural tourism products may be presented in a challenging and confronting manner but cannot be presented in an intimidating or accusatory manner
	Tourists want 'authenticity' but not necessarily reality

experiences, but does not necessarily provide the experiences. Businesses that generate income from tourism, such as airlines, travel agents, hotels, or tour operators, facilitate consumption of the product but are not the product themselves. Few people fly because they like flying. They do so to get to a destination. Few people stay in hotels because they like hotels. Instead, hotels provide a base from which the destination can be explored. Indeed, only a small fraction of the cost of a tour is spent at what can be called attractions; the rest is spent on transport, accommodation, food, drink, tips, sightseeing, and commissions to the travel trade. Yet, it is these attractions that draw the tourist to a region in the first place, enabling the rest of the benefits to accrue. One of the great challenges of cultural tourism is that the products tourists seek are often in the public domain and are available free of charge or at minimal cost. As such, while these attractions provide the product, they often generate little economic benefits, but have to address the costs associated with overcrowding, over-use and/or misuse.

Tourism involves the consumption of experiences

Tourists satisfy their personal needs by consuming enjoyable experiences (Urry 2002; Sharpley 2000). Some commentators decry tourism consumption as being nothing more than a search for photo opportunities (Allcock 1995; Richards 1996; Human 1999). Meanwhile, others argue that consumption of experiences is a worthy goal in itself (Pine and Gilmore 1999; Sharpley 2000). Cultural tourism is no different than any other form of tourism in that cultural tourists are interested in consuming experiences. But tourism represents an insidious form of consumption (McKercher 1993) for its attractions are intrinsically linked to the social fabric of the host community, and therefore subject to competition and over-use.

Tourism activities can be invasive, especially when tourism has been imposed on host communities, and local residents have been turned into tourist attractions against their will. Tourists who consume heritage places for their extrinsic tourism values and local residents who use the same places for their intrinsic cultural values have radically differing needs. How to address these differences poses the greatest challenge for the cultural tourism sector, for the 'tourismification' of cultural assets necessarily involves some change in their use (Cheung 1999, Chhabra 2008; du Cros and Jolliffe 2011).

Tourism is entertainment

Most tourism experiences have their basis in entertainment. To be successful, and therefore commercially viable, the tourism product must be manipulated and packaged in a way that allows it to be consumed easily by the public (Cohen 1972; McKercher 2003). Tight tour schedules, limited time budgets, and the need to process large numbers of visitors mean that the product must often be modified to provide regular show times and a guaranteed experience. As one ex-president of the Hawaiian Visitors Bureau said many years ago, "since real events do not always occur on schedule, we invent pseudo events for tour operators who must have a dance of the vestal virgins precisely at 10 am every Wednesday" (Stalker 1984: 8). While dated, this observation still applies. We have seen tour guides pour soap down a geyser in New Zealand to ensure it erupts promptly at 10.30 every morning to illustrate the story of how it was discovered by accident over 100 years ago by a sleeping sheep herder.

Clearly learning opportunities can be created from the experiences, but their primary role is to entertain. Even museums and art galleries that are developed to provide educational and cultural enlightenment have recognized that they are also in the entertainment business and have arranged their displays accordingly (Prideaux and Kinnimont 1999; McKercher et al. 2005). Often edutainment is the desired outcome rather than education, for only a small number of tourists really want a deep learning experience when they travel. The rest are travelling for pleasure or escapist reasons and wish to participate in activities that will provide a sense of enjoyment. (See Plate 7.1).

Art museums, particularly the larger and sometimes specialist ones, are shaping their experiences in more leisure-focused ways to broaden their market appeal. For instance, the Asian Art Museum in San Francisco has run activities with attention grabbing promotions on YouTube and out in public places, to attract more than the usual art gallery goers. Other examples used by the same museum are tattoo demonstrations and 'the wandering samurai' (see Asian Art Museum 2009a and b; Dante 2013). In much the same way,

Plate 7.1 Dubai Cultural Centre, UAE

Cultural experiences can be both fun and educational. In Dubai, the Sheikh Mohammed Centre for Cultural Understanding organizes tours of the Jumeriah Mosque to help raise awareness of and demystify the local culture, customs, and religion of the United Arab Emirates. The Centre also runs a range of other activities, including heritage tours, walking tours, Arabic lessons, and introductions to local cuisine. The Centre is located in a traditional wind tower house and directs tours to the Jumeriah Mosque.

blockbuster exhibitions can draw record-breaking audiences, while bringing art to the public has been the subject of many smaller exhibitions held at shopping malls and other public spaces (Dicks 2003).

Tourism is a demand driven activity that is difficult to control

One of the great myths of tourism promoted by public sector tourism agencies and NGOs is that it can be controlled. History suggests otherwise. Visitor numbers may be able to be controlled at an enterprise level, but are almost impossible to control at a destination level unless via a top down management approach, as noted in Bhutan. The best governments can do is hope to influence the direction tourism will take.

Ultimately tourism is a demand driven activity that is influenced more by market forces (the tourist and the industry that seeks to satisfy the tourists' needs) than by governments that try to control or manage it. The ability to control tourism must be predicated on the assumption of being able to control tourists. But proponents of a complexity theory (Faulkner and Russell 1997; Russell and Faulkner 1999) illustrate that tourism markets are dynamic, erratic, and non-linear and are noted for their great volatility. If the driving force behind tourism functions in a chaotic manner, then the entire system will be driven by the principles of chaos and complexity. Tourism, tourists, and the tourism industry behave in a manner similar to a bottom up, self-organizing, living ecosystem that can rarely be controlled using traditional top down management approaches.

Further, it has been our experience that many advocates of the belief that supply can control tourism are elitist in their attitudes. They assert that encouraging the 'right' type of development will attract the 'right' type of provider, which will appeal to the 'right' travel distributor that will reach the 'right' type of tourist. This person is usually an affluent experienced traveller who is aware of and sensitive to local cultures, will want to stay in local accommodation, eat locally produced food, and who will be satisfied with basic facilities, at the same time paying high tariffs. The problem is that this type of person represents a tiny portion of the travelling public. How do you satisfy the needs of the vast majority of people who will travel anyway, even if they do not fit this ideal? They are not going to stop travelling and will continue to demand services and facilities.

Attractions drive tourism

Not all tourism attractions are equal

Tourism is driven by attractions or, in marketing terms, demand generators. However, not all tourism attractions have equal demand generation potential. That is, not all attractions have an equal amount of market appeal. A clear hierarchy of tourist attractions exists that can be defined according to the degree of compulsion felt by tourists to visit them: the more dominant the attraction, the greater the sense of obligation to visit it. However, the purchase decision becomes increasingly discretionary for lower order attractions, where visits to the lowest order ones are typified by low involvement decisions. It is also important to appreciate where any attraction sits in this hierarchy, for its position will dictate how much visitation it will receive and how it will be used. People who intend to visit

Plate 7.2 Zadar Castle, Croatia

Understanding where the destination fits in the overall hierarchy of destinations within a country is arguably more important than understanding where an attraction fits within a local destination's attractions hierarchy. Many second and third tier cities have outstanding cultural heritage assets, but are visited rarely because the destination itself is not seen as being a high enough priority to warrant visitation. This situation exists in Zadar, Croatia, located on the north coast of the Adriatic Sea. It has been settled continuously since at least 400 BC and contains significant Roman and early Christian ruins. Yet relatively few international tourists visit compared to the more well-known Croatian destinations of Zagreb, Split, and Dubrovnik.

primary attractions are likely to do so. But if the attraction is perceived to be more discretionary (second or third choice to visit), the likelihood of visiting declines, even if tourists intended to visit prior to arrival at the destination (see Plate 7.2). Instead, the lower the activity is in the priority list, the more likely it is to be substitutable for almost anything else. People may substitute a chance to visit a museum for the opportunity to go shopping, do some sightseeing, have a drink, or participate in some other activity if the museum was not high on their list of priorities (McKercher and Lau 2007).

Cultural heritage attractions are part of tourism

Cultural tourism attractions form an important element of the tourism mix of any destination. Some heritage managers, though, seem to resist accepting that the assets they manage have touristic appeal. As a result they resist introducing management structures that will both optimize the quality of the experience provided, while at the same time minimize the impacts that tourism may have. Plus, it also means that cultural attractions must not only compete with other attractions in the same product class, but they must also compete with other attractions in completely different product classes, especially if they are regarded as lower order attractions.

The first step in successful management of any cultural heritage tourism attraction is to accept that it is indeed a tourism attraction and, as such, must be managed, at least in part, for tourism use. The same situation applies at many cultural events, where a local authority has decided to either revive or create a cultural festival as a tourist attraction. Visitation will occur, regardless of whether or not it is wanted by the local heritage agency or community, and regardless of what management structures are imposed. Accepting this reality means that proactive managers need to develop management plans that will ensure the needs, wants, and desires of tourists visiting the assets are satisfied, while at the same time ensuring that the cultural value and integrity of the asset is maintained.

Not all cultural assets are cultural tourist attractions

Cultural assets are considered significant and worth keeping by communities for reasons other than their tourism potential (Jamieson 1994; du Cros 2006b). But, by the same token, it does not mean they automatically have tourism potential. They may be locally significant assets or may be locally unusual. But just because an asset is listed or culturally mapped does not mean that it will be attractive to tourists. Many honest, yet costly mistakes are made by well meaning people who have over-inflated the perceived tourism value of an asset, when it has limited appeal. Valuable resources have been wasted developing infrastructure and services to cater for anticipated tourist use that never eventuates. (See Plate 7.3 and 7.4).

World Heritage (or other) designation does not mean an automatic influx of tourists

Many destinations chase World Heritage status or some other international designation in the belief that the granting of such status will give the asset top brand recognition and generate significant visitation (Buckley et al. 2004). But the relationship between World Heritage designation and increased visitation is not absolute (Patuelli et al. 2013). (See Plate 7.5). As discussed in some detail in Chapter 4, inscription on World Heritage Lists

Plate 7.3 Hong Kong heritage trail (above left)

There is a significant difference between a cultural heritage asset and a cultural tourism product. An evaluation of the cultural significance in question represents the first stage of successful product development. Being locally significant may not warrant tourismification, especially if the asset in question is a remnant asset that has meaning only to a small number of users. A number of self-guided heritage walking trails have been developed for Hong Kong that take people through a series of small villages, ancestral halls and ancient temples. The Tang Chung Ling Ancestral Hall (left photograph) is popular. This building houses soul tablets of the village's ancestors, including one of a Song Dynasty princess who migrated here during a period of political upheaval in China in the twelfth century. The connection to royalty makes the place unique and gives this asset significance beyond the local community.

Plate 7.4 Wall remnant in village setting, Hong Kong (above right)

By contrast, no one stops at the remnant wall of another village a few hundred metres away because it is not seen to have any significance worth noting.

Plate 7.5 Rideau Canal, Canada

Many national, state, and local governments pursue World Heritage designation as a form of top brand, in the hope that it will stimulate increased visitation. The effect of such designation on visitation is mixed, though. In general, designation does increase visitor numbers, but the impact is highly variable. Popularity prior to designation, proximity to large source markets, and an existing tourism reputation of the broader destination region seem to have a greater impact on visitor arrivals than designation itself. World Heritage designation has little incremental impact on already popular places, such as the Rideau Canal in Canada (Donohoe 2010). Likewise, extremely remote places will not see much increased visitation unless access is improved significantly. Visitation is likely to increase the most and management challenges are likely to arise at newly designated sites in close proximity to large urban centres that did not have a prior history of involvement in tourism. In these situations the World Heritage brand signifies these sites as places to visit for the day trip and short break markets.

may or may not result in greater visitation. Its impact depends on a number of other factors, including proximity to markets, prior fame, clustering of attractions, and the like.

Factors influencing visitation levels

Access and proximity dictate the potential number of visitors

Demand for tourism products is influenced by a range of factors, including distance (McKercher et al. 2008), market access (Pearce 1989, McKercher 1998), and time availability (McKean et al. 1995). Distance decay theory shows how demand declines exponentially as distance increases, whether it is between the person's home and possible destinations or from the person's hotel and possible attractions. Similarly, market access states that demand is influenced by the number of similar and competing products/destinations available between the tourist's home and the prospective product/destination. Time availability has been shown to accentuate or minimize the effect of market access and distance decay (Johannson and Montagari 1996; Sjorgren and Brannas 1996).

The proximity of an attraction to a large population base, a major tourism destination, or a gateway (e.g. airport or other transport hub) will influence visitation and consequently how the asset is used. Demand, in turn, influences the revenue generation potential for the asset, which should, therefore, influence the size, level of development, and level of investment. The basic rule of thumb is that attractions that are located close to large population or tourist centres will attract significantly larger numbers of visitors than more distant attractions. The same maxim holds true on a micro or destination specific scale. Readily accessible attractions will enjoy greater visitation levels than out of the way assets, unless the compulsion to visit them is so great that remoteness becomes a non-issue. Museums located in downtown areas or in tourist precincts, for example, will enjoy greater visitation than isolated museums located in outer suburbs. Therefore, the physical location of the asset vis à vis its major markets must be taken into consideration when assessing its tourism potential. Only truly superlative assets are capable of overcoming the realities of distance and market access. Their drawing power must be so strong that people are motivated to see them, regardless of the time, effort, cost, or distance involved.

Time availability influences the quality and depth of experience sought

Most tourists have limited time budgets, with many having their time strictly controlled by tour operators, the needs of children, and other travel companions or flight schedules. They only have a limited amount of time available at any one destination and, being rational consumers, will choose to spend that time in the most cost-effective manner (Shoval and Raveh 2004). As such, many tourists will seek to consume as many experiences as possible during their stay and will show a predilection for those activities that can be consumed quickly and easily and where they feel certain they will get a guaranteed experience. Especially when culture represents an incidental aspect of the trip, the amount of time a tourist is willing to allocate to experiences will depend on the amount of discretionary time available and the number of possible competing uses for that time. Those experiences that consume large blocks of time will tend to be avoided if an attractive alternative exists. Bear in mind that in tourism terms, large blocks of time can be counted in hours, and not days.

Unfortunately, the very nature of cultural tourism often demands that substantial amounts of time or emotional effort be expended to fully appreciate the experience. This creates two challenges for providers. On the one hand, providing experiences that require greater effort to consume may result in lower visitation, which could affect the commercial viability of a product. On the other hand, making the product simple to consume may result in higher visitation, but at cost to the quality of the message being sent.

Tourist behaviour

There is no difference between a tourist and a traveller

Often, comments about the benefits or risk of tourism are biased and highly value laden. A case in point is the artificial distinction made between tourists and travellers. Travellers are felt to be the superior type of person who is seeking a deeper experience, while the term tourist is often used in a derogatory fashion to connote someone who is less sophisticated, does not care about the destination, and behaves inappropriately (Leiper 2004). We all want to see ourselves as being special and want to look at our own tourism experience as being unique and so try to disassociate ourselves from the masses. In reality, there is no difference between a tourist and a traveller, other than the observation that 'I am a traveller, while everyone else is a tourist.'

The tourist experience must be controlled, which in turn controls the actions of the tourist

The best way to control tourists and, therefore, to limit the adverse impacts of tourism on cultural heritage is to control the tourism experience. The best way to control the tourist experience is to standardize, modify, and commodify that experience. For many, this is heresy, especially given the significant volume of literature that condemns tourism for the commodification and trivialization of culture. Yet, the standardization, modification, and commodification of the experience represent a pragmatic means of controlling the movement of people, while ensuring the visitor gains as much as possible from the experience. It is for this reason that purpose-built heritage products often function better as tourism attractions than extant assets, especially if significant asset modification is required to cater for the needs of the tourist.

The problem has been and continues to be that the experience is being standardized and commodified by the tourism industry for the benefit of tourist operators and not by asset managers or asset owners as the best interpretation and protection of the asset's fabric. The challenge for the asset manager or museum board is to control the experience on site and to wrest control from the tour operator or their employees.

Tourists want controlled experiences

It may be difficult for many to appreciate but most tourists actually want to have their experience controlled and are amenable to having the asset presented in a manner that facilitates easy consumption. The reason is that most domestic tourists and the vast majority of international tourists may only visit an asset once in their lifetime, and consequently wish to get the most out of the experience. Standardizing the presentation ensures consistency in experience delivery. Controlling the experience also ensures that people on limited time budgets can experience the essence of the attraction while not wasting their time consuming elements that they feel are not essential to the core experience. Further, standardization, modification, and commodification that add value justify charging an admission fee. (See Plates 7.6 and 7.7).

Plate 7.6 Pompeii with crowds

One of the ironies of tourism is that people want to explore a destination or attraction on their own terms and, yet, also seek to have their experience controlled. Tourists who make one-off, short duration visits to attractions want to ensure that they do not miss the highlights or key features of that attraction. The provision of a guide map directs people where to go and also, by inference, identifies parts of the attraction that they can avoid without missing out on any part of the experience. The result is that independent tourists will behave in a collective manner that, in many ways, is similar to that of package tourists. Following a guide map produces a standardized experience that can also lead to crowding at popular sites. In Pompeii, Italy, for example, most tourists will follow the suggested route, making it difficult to avoid crowds and to experience the ruins at a more personal level.

Plate 7.7 Pompeii without crowds

Yet, by moving only one street away, the visitor has a completely different experience. Crowds vanish, noise vanishes and the ruins come alive. As a result, overcrowding can be spatially and temporarily uneven, with crowding at peak moments and site deterioration in specific areas, while other areas may register small numbers of visitors (Russo 2002).

The more mainstream (or mass) the market being targeted, the more quickly and easily the tourism product must be able to be consumed

The more mainstream or mass the market being drawn to the attraction is, the easier the product must be to consume. Two factors are at play here. Mainstream tourists are usually motivated by pleasure or escape reasons. They are seeking enjoyable experiences that do not tax them mentally or ideologically. They cannot be confused with anthropologists or archaeologists (de Kadt 1979). D'Sa (1999: 65) adds to this idea when he reports on the opinions of some in the travel trade: "the major motive of tourism is recreation…we are in no position to educate our clients".

Furthermore, many of these people will be fundamentally ignorant of the assets they are visiting because they have not visited them before or do not come from the destination. The more culturally distant the asset is from the individual's own frame of reference, the greater the likelihood of ignorance about it (Sizer 1999), while ironically the greater the interest in experiencing cultural tourism (McKercher and Chow 2001). At best, many tourists have not studied history, music, or art formally beyond the level of elementary or lower level high school. At worst, they have not studied it at all in relation to the asset. As such, they often have the same real knowledge as a 12 to 14 year-old. Whatever additional knowledge they will have acquired would have likely come from the mass media, documentary and lifestyle television shows, and the cinema. This information often presents a distorted vision. This, of course, raises the ethical question of whether and how to present assets, and further drives home the need to control the experience and the actions of the tourist.

The mass market has not fractured

There is a long-standing belief that the mass market has fractured and that we are now in the age of mass individualism. It originated from the convergence of a number of events. However, evidence of the fracturing of the mass market is difficult to come by. The idea was promoted initially by the marketing consultant Auliana Poon (1988, 1994) who promoted the idea of 'new tourism' whereby mass tourism was being replaced by a new form of tourism driven by advances in technology, greater sensitivity in consumer tastes, and a new type of tourist who is looking for a more sustainable, authentic experience. Her work also coincided with the emergence of alternative tourism, anti-tourism, and other forms of non-mass tourism in the popular lexicon, as affluent baby boomers did not want to be associated with the standard sun, sand and beach holiday they took as children. The myth was further enhanced by the popularization of eco-tourism and its promotion by global tourism stakeholders as being reflective of a new form of ethically appropriate activity that attracted a new type of ethically superior tourist. The maturation of destination marketing was the second piece of the equation. Traditionally, destination marketers pushed products, but as marketing matured they realized they needed to promote experiences that could satisfy their consumers' needs. What better way to do this than to identify market niches that seemed to evoke experiential responses? Finally, the emergence of easy to use statistical analysis packages permitted researchers to conduct market segmentation studies, often by comparing the profile of people who participated in certain activities with those who did not.

The end result was the identification and pursuit of a range of niche markets. We have seen the rise and eventual fall of any number of specialist products/markets that were hailed as the next big thing but never materialized. They follow the same evolutionary path from hope, to hype, to unrealized expectations, to a final recognition that it is niche activity that appeals to a small number of people who want to pursue it in a limited number of destinations. It has taken the World Tourism Organization (WTO), for example, close to 20 years to recognize that ecotourism is a "small niche market in constant growth" (UNWTO 2002: 111) and not a mass market.

One reason is that while the range of activities that can satisfy tourists' varied needs has increased exponentially, the core reasons for travel have not really changed much. Pearce and Lee (2005) suggest that needs such as novelty, escape/relaxation, relationship-building, and self-development represent the backbone or skeleton of all travel motivation patterns. Other motives may complement these core elements, but rarely supersede them, except for the true niche, specialist tourist. However, tourists now have a far greater selection of both destinations and activities within destinations to satisfy their needs. So, if one only looks at activities, it appears that the market has fractured. But remember, many activities are pursued as complementary actions that may only relate peripherally to the core motives.

Tourists seeking deep experiences exist but represent only a small share of the market

A market does exist for the person who is seeking a deeper experience, but it tends to be rather small. Specialist educational products, voluntourism, history-themed tours, cooking and handicraft workshops appeal to this type of consumer. But, the deep tourist represents only a tiny portion of any specialist market, sometimes 2 percent or less.

Cultural tourism

Not all cultural tourists are alike

The UNWTO estimates that 40 percent of international tourists are cultural tourists (Richards 2011). This figure is derived from applying an operational definition of a cultural tourist as someone who visits a cultural or heritage attraction, goes to a museum or attends a performance sometime during their trip. It is a mistake to assume all tourists are equal in that they all want a quintessentially deep experience. Instead, many shades of cultural tourist exist that can be defined by the centrality of purpose and the depth of experience sought. Five types of cultural tourist exist (serendipitous, purposeful, incidental, casual, and sightseeing) with each group seeking a qualitatively different experience and preferring different attractions.

Cultural tourism products may be presented in a challenging and confronting manner but cannot be presented in an intimidating or accusatory manner

Some cultural attractions have a dark side and one that may relate to past or present activities of the country or cultural group to which a tourist may belong. Remember, most tourists are on holiday and are looking for a break from their normal stressful, hectic lives. Most do not want to be challenged and, if confronted, most are not receptive to accept such a message. Cultural heritage products can be presented in an emotionally demanding manner but cannot be presented in an intimidating or accusatory manner.

Even here, the degree of challenge will depend on the type of tourist being attracted, with the incidental and casual segments less willing to be challenged than the purposeful segment.

This statement does not mean that cultural heritage products cannot and should not be presented in a challenging manner. Indeed, it can be a useful strategy to differentiate the product from the array of other cultural tourism products available in the marketplace. It may also be regarded as necessary if the asset is a heritage place that is associated with a particularly gruesome or reprehensible experience in the past. But, few assets work as cultural tourism products if they are presented in an intimidating or accusatory manner that blames the visitor as being the cause of the problem. The exception is when societal attitudes change, enabling individuals to share collective guilt.

Many tourists visiting heritage attractions seem to be seeking affirmation of how modern they are and how much modern society has evolved from the past. As Craik (1997: 115) states so eloquently "tourism is a process of seeing and experiencing the other, but it is not about otherness, except as a means of coming to terms with one's own culture". Cultural tourism product designers think that tourists do not want to be reminded that many social ills (oppression, racism, and so on) outlined in site interpretation remain unresolved today. It is for this reason that many attractions present the past as being a vestige of a bygone era, unless it is part of a national myth (e.g. the Great War battlefield of Gallipoli, Turkey, is closely associated with travel for honouring departed war heroes annually on ANZAAC Day, see Cooper 2014), or part of a public policy that uses such attractions to support calls for social unity (Nyiri 2006).

People want 'authenticity' but not necessarily reality

Tourists want authentic experience, but do not necessarily want to experience reality. This point is driven home in Salazar's (2005) observation about the glocalization of tourism, discussed earlier. Authenticity is a social construct that is determined in part by the individual's own knowledge and frame of reference. Many tourists are interested in cultural heritage, but most have minimal knowledge about the past. As such, they may be travelling to have their stereotypical or romantic images of a destination reinforced or possible challenged, depending on their political leaning.

People going to cultural heritage attractions, be they historic parks, forts, prisons, or purpose-built historic theme parks, may be seeking a clichéd image of the past (Sizer 1999). It has been observed that travel is about reaffirmation and not change and that resources that make up tourism are transformed into elements of a symbolic system (Craik 1999). The past is seen as very distant, and as such, many historic assets are presented in an idyllic manner, with pristine gardens, clean streets, paved roads and neat buildings (Lowenthal 1985). The reality of pollution, oppression, poor sewerage, and indifferent maintenance of some landscapes (particularly penal, industrial, and urban) is not an experience tourists can easily put in context without extensive historical and archaeological knowledge of the asset's era. Much of this information would be considered 'overkill' by tourists. Many tourists wish, therefore, to experience what they are happy to believe to be authenticity at an attraction, but not necessarily reality.

Identifying what is meant by 'authenticity' is difficult, for there is no consensus as to what it means within a tourism context, unlike in CHM. Scholars talk about three main types of authenticity: objective, constructive, and existential. Objective authenticity focuses on the actual toured object, such as works of art or historical artifacts, where tourism can serve as a catalyst for the destruction of authenticity of cultural assets (Kim and Jamal 2007). Cohen (1988), however, adopts a constructivist view and argues that authenticity is not a given, but rather 'negotiable' and is socially constructed by the visitor, who actively imputes meaning to the cultural tourism experience. While objective and constructive authenticities both concern toured objects, existential authenticity disregards the object completely. Instead, this approach focuses more on recurring themes in philosophy and psychology studies of "self-identity, individuality, meaning-making, and anxiety" (Steiner and Reisinger 2006: 300). While these interpretations make for fascinating scholarly research, most tourists do not care about exact details. Instead, they want what they feel is a genuine, real, or original experience. As a result, authentic cultural experiences can be enjoyed just as easily in purpose-built theme parks, and at cultural shows, as they can by wandering through neighbourhoods and talking to local residents.

Most often, people experiencing a heritage attraction for the first time are assailed by its 'feeling value' or apparent authenticity. Even when little is known or understood about the monument, object, or site it will convey a sense of history, an aura, or the trace of something almost nostalgic (Walle 1993; Petzet 1994; Sharples et al. 1999; Wang 1999). This sentiment has led some people to argue that assets can undergo near total transformation and still retain their authenticity as far as many tourists are concerned. The architectural compromise of preserving the façade of historic buildings designated for redevelopment has its roots in this belief. Again, the view that authenticity is relative makes us view this strategy as only a compromise, given that saving the whole building would increase its feeling value. However, when its cultural significance is fully considered it would embody "the place itself, its fabric, setting, use, associations, meanings, records, related places and related objects" (Australia ICOMOS 2013: 2). In an ideal situation, most cultural heritage managers interested in the latest best practices advocated by ICOMOS in the Asia Pacific region would be aiming for the latter in line with *The Burra Charter*, which is the ICOMOS charter most recently updated at the time of writing.

Authenticity must also include a cultural element. The patina of age and the subliminal feeling that many tangible heritage assets provide is difficult to fake at a theme park. Many visitors from Europe would consider these places to be less than authentic. However, visitors with an eastern background to heritage would see most heritage attractions' level of authenticity as acceptable even if some theme park elements were included in larger ones. How far a heritage attraction goes in trying to satisfy both markets (one wanting authentic fabric and one not so bothered as long as it is authenticish) is a dilemma that should be solved in the early stages of its planning as it could be difficult and expensive to change direction later on.

Conclusion

Successful tourism development does not occur by chance. Many people have the misconception that if they put up a sign saying 'tourists welcome' or 'George Washington slept here' hordes of tourists will flood to their attraction. The reality is quite different. Developing successful tourism attractions involves first and foremost understanding what tourism is and how it works. The preceding discussion has identified what we feel are 19 key principles of tourism. Others no doubt exist. These principles explain the rationale behind entering this sector; what attracts people to destinations, the factors that encourage or inhibit visitation, and why tourists behave the way they do.

Key learning outcomes

- Tourism is a commercial activity pursued by destinations for economic benefits and associated social benefits.
- Attractions drive tourism, and if a destination does not have a sufficient breadth and depth of attractions it will struggle.
- Cultural assets as tourism attractions must compete against non-cultural attractions.
- Time limits the depth of experience most people can have.
- Tourists want to believe they are independent but at the same time want to have their experiences controlled.
- The mass market has not fractured.
- Tourists want authenticity but not necessarily reality.

8 The cultural tourism market

A cultural tourism typology

Introduction

Our knowledge of the cultural tourism market has changed dramatically in the last ten years. Whereas once it was assumed to be homogenous, now it is recognized as being heterogeneous, consisting of a number of clearly defined segments differentiated by the importance of culture as a travel motive and the depth of experience sought. Different segments, in turn, seek different products and different experiences, and respond to different marketing messages. This chapter discusses the cultural tourism market. It begins with an overview of the definitional challenge that has confused attempts to define the size of the market. A five segment cultural tourism is then discussed. Finally, the chapter concludes with a cautionary note about research findings that appear too good to be true.

Cultural tourists

Who are cultural tourists? This simply question has proven to be difficult to answer because two different philosophical approaches have been used to define the market and its behaviour. Each approach produces dramatically different conclusions about its size and importance (Vong 2013a). One approach defines the market on the basis of activities pursued in the destination, while another assesses the importance of cultural tourism as a trip motive. Marketing consultant Bob Dauner (nd) unintentionally captured the confusion when he used both measures to define the cultural tourism segment as being "comprised of a select group of travelers who either plan a trip to attend a cultural activity or who actively participate in cultural activities while on a trip, even if they are traveling for other reasons".

But, there is a significant difference between someone who visits a cultural attraction regardless of the reasons they chose the destination and someone who was attracted to the destination because of its cultural attributes. Part of the problem lies in an efficient but sloppy use of the English language that conflates the two ideas. It is clearly more efficient to use a simple descriptor of 'cultural tourist' when using an activities-based approach, rather than using the more accurate term of a 'tourist who visits an attraction that may or may not reflect the cultural heritage of the destination for reasons that may or may not have anything to do with learning about that attraction's cultural significance'. But this term infers trip purpose, in much the same way that labelling someone as a business or transit tourist does, when no such inference can be made.

A second issue is operational. Most studies that attempt to quantify the size of the market rely on secondary analysis of data gathered by national and state tourism organizations in their departing visitor surveys. These surveys consist of a number of sections, including specific questions about trip purpose and activities pursued. Trip purpose questions usually offer a limited number of choices (typically pleasure, business, visiting friends, and maybe one or two other options) and require respondents to select one item only. Activity questions include a much larger array of possible answers (up to 120 in some cases) and allow respondents to select all that they or members of their travel party participated in during the visit. Historically 'cultural tourism' is listed rarely, if ever, as a trip purpose option and so researchers had to rely on analysing activity questions to gain a better understanding of what people did in the destination. The volume of visitors who participate in activities can be determined by counting participation rates in the set of activities that are thought to be evocative of the specialist interest under examination.

This method is appealing for a number of reasons. First, anyone with access to the data set and a statistical software package can analyse the data and determine the market 'size' by tabulating raw participation rates as a share of all visitors. Second, it is possible to compare participants and non-participants and to look for similarities and differences between markets. Most importantly, though, this method produces 'good' numbers. By 'good' numbers we mean large numbers, which in turn have been used by stakeholders to argue that the activity and institutions supporting the activity are wanted and needed by the constituency that ultimately pays for them (Cameron 1997). The UNWTO has estimated that cultural tourism accounts for 40 percent of all tourist trips (Richards 2011). US-based studies indicate that more than three-quarters of domestic tourists are cultural/heritage travellers (Mandala 2013; McCormack 2010). Studies in Australia suggest 85 percent of the Australian population aged 15 and over had attended at least one cultural venue or participated in at least one cultural activity (TQ nd) and that 58 percent of all overnight international visitors are cultural tourists (TV 2013). Canadian research reported that more than 40 percent of Canadian domestic and US inbound tourists visit historic sites, museums, and art galleries while almost one-third participate in fairs and festivals (Whyte et al. 2012). Antolovic (1999) indicates that 70 percent of all Americans travelling to Europe seek a cultural heritage experience and that about two-thirds of all of visitors to the UK are seeking a cultural heritage tourism experience as part of their trip but not necessarily as the main reason to visit the UK. This method has also been used to 'prove' cultural tourists spend more, stay longer, travel more frequently and participate in more activities and are older, better educated, and more affluent than the travelling public as a whole.

There is only one problem. This method is so flawed conceptually that the results are meaningless, and worse, dangerous (McKercher and Chan 2005). The reasons why will be explained more at the end of the chapter, but, basically the method uses activities undertaken to infer trip purpose, when no such association can be made. Conceptually, as well, this approach assumes the market is homogeneous, when in fact many shades of cultural tourist exist. Croes and Semrad (2013), for example, remind us that tourists often travel for a mixture of cultural and recreational reasons, but that most statistics generated by an activities-based method cannot track the role of different motives separately. In addition an implied assumption is that all cultural tourists reflect the prototypical deep cultural tourist who travels primarily for the pursuit of culture and who is looking for a meaningful experience in accordance with the definition of special interest tourism as "the hub around which the total travel experience is planned and developed" (Read 1980 as cited in Hall and Weiler 1992). Using this definition, special interest tourists are likely to visit attractions that reflect their specialist interest. However, while the belief that 'motivation influences activities' has merit, the opposite assumption that 'activities reflect motives' does not exist, for people may visit attractions to have a variety of other needs met (McKercher and Chan 2005; Croes and Semrad 2013). Hughes and Allen

(2005), for example, note that visitors to cultural attractions are often labelled as cultural tourists, regardless of their motives.

Fortunately, a trip purpose-based approach is gaining favour, as the limitations of the activities-based model are becoming recognized. This approach recognizes interest in this activity exists along a continuum. For some, the pursuit of culture represents a dominant trip purpose, while for others it can be considered as part of the basket of motives that influence destination choice, and for others still it may play little or no role in the trip decision process. Yet, they will still visit cultural attractions in the destination. Indeed, the prototypical, deep experience seeking, 'purposeful' cultural tourist is now recognized as representing only a small portion of the total market (VW 2009; Le and Pearce 2011; Mandala 2013).

Segmenting the cultural tourism market

Segmentation research recognizes that any market consists of a number of groups, each with a slightly different reason for visiting a destination, each having different goals, and each looking for different activities to satisfy these goals (Dolnicar 2007). Within these differences, though, some commonalities can also be found, where some groups of tourists are more similar than others. Segmentation, then, tries to divide a heterogeneous market into homogeneous groups of customers who experience a similar problem and react to market stimuli in the same way (Sollner and Rese 2001). It must be remembered, though, that segments are not discrete units. Rather, the boundaries between groups may be fuzzy, especially if the segments can be aligned along a continuum. Thus, while members of each segment have clearly identifiable features, the differences between individuals at the edge of segments may be smaller than the differences within each segment (McKercher et al. 2002). Segmenting the market permits the destination or product supplier to shape experiences for different groups, optimize promotional efforts and maximize tourist enjoyment (Dolnicar 2007). Ideally, segments should satisfy the following criteria:

- share common values and interests that are sufficiently different and distinct from other segments;
- be sufficiently large to give the organization a return for its effort;
- be easy to reach through promotional media and other marketing activities at an affordable cost;
- have their needs satisfied by the products being offered.

A cultural tourist typology: centrality of motive and depth of experience

The cultural tourism market consists of five segments based on the role that culture plays as a trip motivator and the depth of experience. These segments are shown in Figure 8.1. This framework was developed by the authors (McKercher 2002; McKercher and du Cros 2003) and has been verified by a number of other studies. It has now been adopted widely by governmental and quasi-governmental agencies (Beesley 2005; ETC 2005; AL 2010; Failte Ireland (2012); Latvia 2006; VB 2010; Williams 2010; CTC 2013; CBI 2014; COE nd).

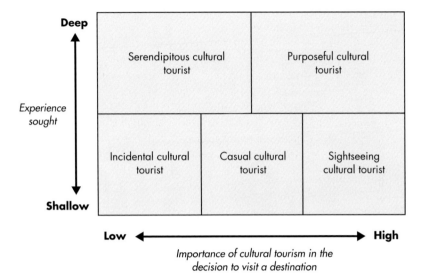

Figure 8.1 A cultural tourist typology

The horizontal axis reflects the centrality of a cultural tourism in the overall trip decision-making process. It recognizes the role of culture can vary in importance from being the main or only reason to visit to playing no role at all in the decision-making process, even though the tourist may still participate in some cultural activities. The vertical axis represents depth of experience. This axis recognizes that not all tourists want or can have a deep experience. Instead, a range of experiences can exist. (See Plates 8.1 and 8.2). The five types of cultural tourist that emerge from the matrix are the:

• purposeful cultural tourist: cultural tourism is the primary motive for visiting a destination and the individual has a deep cultural experience;
• sightseeing cultural tourist: cultural tourism is a primary or major reason for visiting a destination but the experience is more shallow;
• serendipitous cultural tourist: a tourist who does not travel for cultural tourism reasons but who, after participating, ends up having a deep cultural tourism experience;
• casual cultural tourist: cultural tourism is a weak motive for visiting a destination and the resultant experience is shallow;
• incidental cultural tourist: who does not travel for cultural tourism reasons but who nonetheless participates in some activities and has a shallow experience.

The centrality dimension

A number of studies have shown that the importance of culture in the trip decision process lies along a continuum from those who see it as a critical driving force in their travel decisions to those for whom it plays little or no role in the decision. Moreover, as shown in Table 8.1, the findings of these studies map well onto the typology used in this book. The only exception is the case of the 'serendipitous cultural tourist' whose primary point of differentiation is depth of experience. Early studies adopted a binary importance/unimportance segmentation approach (Richards 1996; Stebbins 1996; Santana 2003) that

Plate 8.1 Tourists visiting built heritage

Different types of tourists look for and are capable of having completely different experiences. Sightseeing cultural tourists (as shown above) may have an interest in learning about the destination's cultural heritage but are often limited in their ability to have deep experience due to time constraints, different interests of members of the travel party, and their own level of interest and knowledge of the subject matter.

Plate 8.2 Tourists visiting rock art

By comparison, a group of archaeologists visiting rock art sites in South Africa are typical of the extremely purposeful cultural tourist who is very knowledgeable about the area being visited and who is also looking for a deep learning experience.

sought to identify whether culture was the primary motive for visitation. However, as with any emerging field, latter research sought to identify more subtle divisions within the market, identifying three or four segments along a continuum.

In most cases, the market is dominated by incidental and casual cultural tourism segments with the purposeful segment being the smallest. The initial Hong Kong study found that about 50 percent of all people who visited cultural attractions fell into the casual or incidental segments, indicating that culture played little or no role in their decision to visit. A further 30 percent were classified as sightseeing cultural tourists, who felt culture did play a strong role in their decision to visit, but who also had a fairly shallow experience. Only 6 percent were classified as purposeful cultural tourists. Vong (2013a) came to similar conclusions in her study of Macau. Casual cultural tourists represented 53.5 percent of her sample, while purposeful (5.6 percent) and sightseeing (4 percent) constituted a small share of visitors. Visit Wales (VW 2009) describes the pure cultural tourist as representing a small minority of the population, while the casual cultural tourist represents the majority of respondents in their study. Liu (2013) found the 'Arts and Museum with high motive' segment representing about one-third of his sample in a study conducted in Taiwan, while Le and Pearce (2011) determined that 'Passive' battlefield tourists, scoring lowest in all motivational factors, represented more than half of the visitors to Vietnam War era sites. Lord (2002) indicates the 'Greatly Motivated' segment is the smallest of the four segments identified by his company at 15 percent of visitors. Table 8.1 compares our classification of the five main types of cultural tourists (see Figure 8.1) earlier with that of other authorities with those who have the most types closest to ours at the top of the table.

Depth of experience

Depth of experience or level of engagement is the other dimension to be considered, for not everyone is interested in or capable of having a qualitatively similar experience. Experience has received much more attention in tourism recently, as a link between satisfaction and deeper engagement has been shown (Beesley 2005). This idea has grown out of the broader literature on the experience economy, where consumer attention has shifted away from pushing products to the delivery of experiences that offer consumers added value (Mehmetoglu and Engen 2011). Experiences are not absolute, though. Instead the degree to which a tourist can and will engage in a cultural experience is influenced in part by motivation but also by connectivity with the experience and level of participation (Beesley 2005). An individual's capacity to have a deep experience at cultural attractions is also affected by a number of factors, including time availability, prior knowledge, cultural affinity with the asset, education level, and other issues.

Stebbins (1996: 948) uses the concept of 'serious leisure' to explain this phenomenon. He defines serious leisure as a "systematic pursuit of an amateur, hobbyist, or volunteer activity sufficiently substantial and interesting in nature for the participant to find a career there acquiring and expressing a combination of its special skills, knowledge, and experience." To him, the cultural tourist is akin to a hobbyist whom he defines as someone who has a profound interest in a topic and who exhibits a certain level of skill, knowledge, conditioning or experience in pursuit of the hobby. While cultural tourism may be a major motivation for travel, Stebbins identifies two quite different types of hobbyist cultural tourists. The generalized cultural tourist makes a hobby of visiting a variety of different assets and regions. Over time, this cultural tourist acquires a broad general knowledge of different cultures. The specialized cultural tourist, on the other hand, focuses his or her efforts on one or a small number of geographic sites or cultural entities. This tourist repeatedly visits a particular city or country in search of a deeper cultural understanding

Table 8.1 *Motivation-based segmentation studies*

Author	Year	Segmentation variable	Cultural tourism types				
			Purposeful	Sightseeing	Casual	Incidental	Serendipitous
Academic							
McKercher and du Cros	2003	Centrality of cultural motive & depth of experience	Purposeful	Sightseeing	Casual	Incidental	Serendipitous
Silberberg	1995	Motivation	Greatly motivated	In part	Adjunct	Accidental	
Richards	1996	Motivation	Specific	General		General	
Stebbins	1996	Interest and motive		Specialized		General	
Hughes	2002	Interest	Primary	Multi-primary	Incidental	Accidental	
Santana	2003	Motive	Real			Free time consumers of cultural heritage	
Le and Pearce	2011	Motive and personal connection	Battlefield tourist		Opportunist	Passive	
Möller and Deckert	2009	Motive, visit history and duration	Heavy User	Multiple user	Newcomer	Excursionist	
Barbieri and Mahoney	2010	Behaviour and preference	Omnivore	Univore	Sporadic		
Lade	2010	Motive, visit history and duration	Highly motivated people	People motivated in part	People with other primary interests	Accidental visitors	
Özel and Kozak	2012	Overall travel motives	Achievement and autonomy	Escape	Family togetherness	Sports and socialization	Rest and relaxation

Author	Year	Segmentation variable	Cultural tourism types				
Liu	2013	Image attributes and motive		Living culture with low motive	Living culture with medium motive	Heritage with medium motive	Arts and museum with high motive
van der Ark and Richards	2006	Participation and enjoyment	Class 1 – low participation and high attractiveness		Class 3 – high participation and low attractiveness	Class 2 – high participation and high attractiveness	Class 2 – high participation and high attractiveness
Petroman et al.	2013	Motive		Incidental/Accidental	Occasional	Tour-amateur	Purposeful
Sintas and Alvarez	2005	Performing arts consumption patterns + high and low culture		Sporadic	Popular	Omnivorous	Snob
Industry/Government							
DKS	1999	Motive			Low	Moderate	Core
Lord	2002	Motive		Accidental	Adjunct	Motivated in part	Greatly motivated
MTC (Ontario, Canada)	2009	Motive			Partake in cultural activities	Partially motivated	Wholly motivated
EU	2009	Motive		Casual	Interested		Committed
Failte Ireland	2012	Motive & depth of interest in culture		Incidental		Inspired	Motivated
Mandala	2013	Intensity and motive		Self guided/accidental	Aspirational	Well rounded/active	Passionate

of that place or goes to different cities, regions, or countries in search of exemplars of a specific kind of art, history, festival, or museum.

Timothy (1997) addresses the issue of depth of experience from the perspective of the individual's connectivity to an asset. He identifies four levels of heritage tourism attractions: world, national, local, and personal and suggests that tourists have different levels of connectivity to each type of asset and therefore, by implication, have different depths of experience depending on which type of asset is visited. MacIntosh and Prentice (1999) in particular explored the relationship between perceived authenticity gained by tourists and their emotive processes with attractions' settings. They found that the depth or the quality of the depth of the experience visitors had to British socio-industrial cultural heritage attractions depended both on the individual thought processes when visiting these attractions and the resultant perceived levels of commodification. (See Plate 8.3).

The typology in practice

All five types of cultural tourists can be found simultaneously in a destination. The mix of tourist types, though, will vary from destination to destination depending on the destination itself, the asset being visited within the destination and the origin of the tourist. Purposeful and sightseeing cultural tourists see their trip as a chance to grow personally,

Plate 8.3 Sovereign Hill, Australia

Sovereign Hill is a cultural theme park, which is a historically speculative reconstruction of the Ballarat Goldfields of the mid to late nineteenth century, in Victoria, Australia. Casual and incidental cultural tourists travel primarily for reasons related to recreation, escape, fun, relaxation, and the chance to spend time with family and friends. They are not looking for an intellectually or emotionally challenging experience. These groups of tourists represent the largest share of cultural tourists, especially in multiproduct destinations. They are looking for enjoyable, easy to consume edutainment experiences. Kantanen and Tikkanen (2006) indicate they are looking for a delightful experience when they travel, and respond well to 'do-learn-feel' advertising materials. Highly commodified, interactive products, such as theme parks are very appealing to them. They may learn while being entertained.

and are motivated to travel more for cultural and educational reasons or to learn about the destination's cultural heritage. By contrast, casual, incidental, and serendipitous cultural tourists travel primarily for recreation, and fun, relaxation, and to spend time with family and friends.

In addition, a relationship has been noted between type and physical distance travelled or cultural distance encountered. Long haul tourists are far more likely to be represented in the purposeful and sightseeing cultural segments, while short haul international tourists tend to be clustered in the incidental and casual segments. Likewise, the greater the cultural distance between the host culture and the traveller's own culture, the greater the likelihood that the destination will attract purposeful cultural tourists, while visitors from culturally similar markets are over-represented in the incidental and casual segments (McKercher and Chow 2001, Croes and Semrad 2013). A somewhat different scenario exists with domestic tourists. Here the closer the cultural or heritage attraction is to the core values of the domestic market, the more they reflect durable national ideals or the collective core values of the nation and the greater the likelihood of drawing purposeful or sightseeing cultural tourists.

The underlying factors translate into and explain different preferred activities, as shown in Table 8.2. Sightseeing and purposeful cultural tourists are motivated to visit to learn about a destination's cultural heritage but are seeking qualitatively different experiences to satisfy that motive. The purposeful cultural tourist is the greatest consumer of museum experiences, in general, and of fine arts museums, art galleries, pottery museums, and high culture in particular (Niemcyzk 2013). He or she also chooses to visit lesser-known temples and heritage assets and seeks to immerse him or herself in the local culture by going to local food markets. He or she also tends to spend a long time at each place, learning about its features (Nyaupune et al. 2006; Vong 2013a). The sightseeing cultural tourist, on the other hand, is more interested in collecting a wide array of experiences rather than pursuing any one activity in any depth. The quantity of experiences consumed matters more than the depth of any one experience. This tourist is mostly likely to visit icon attractions and is also most likely to travel widely throughout the destination. Sightseeing and absorbing the streetscape are popular activities reported. They are the most active and prefer sightseeing to shopping. They will also be the ones with the most photos in their blogs and social media sites of the key cultural tourism attractions and experiences.

Casual and incidental markets prefer low engagement and low involvement cultural experiences that highlight fun, enjoyment, and the opportunity to spend time with family and friends. They want highly commodified experiences such as theme parks, festivals, large public art galleries, and museums. Their preferences tend towards popular culture, arts, and performance. Physically or architecturally impressive built heritage appeals to them, while shopping is as important as visiting cultural sites. The casual cultural tourist also appears more willing to sightsee and take photos than the incidental cultural tourist, but less intensely than the purposeful cultural tourist.

Incidental cultural tourists visit convenience-based attractions located in tourist nodes that are easy to consume and not particularly emotionally or intellectually challenging. Space and science museums are appealing, as are theme park experiences but only if they are positioned as one of the destination's icon attractions. Here, as well, the experience will be superficial.

The behaviour of serendipitous cultural tourists is the hardest to describe in general terms. Their experiences seem to involve an element of exploration whereby the individual comes upon a site, attraction, or performance and is enthralled by it. Vong (2013a) concludes they are the most inquisitive of all tourists and tend to spend the longest time

Table 8.2 Preferred activities by type of cultural tourist

Author Location	Serendipitous	Incidental	Casual	Sightseeing	Purposeful
Liu (2013) Taiwan	Living culture	Living culture Popular culture	Living culture	Heritage High culture	Arts/heritage
Kantanen and Tikkanen (2006) Finland	Contemporary art museums	Fortresses	Fortresses	Opera/museums	Opera/museums
Vong (2013b) Macau	Longest time visiting heritage attractions Sightseeing/local street food Visited less prominent sites Explore	Street food Sightseeing Visited fewest sites		Heritage attractions/ least time shopping	Longest time visiting heritage attractions Sightseeing Local street food
Le and Pearce (2011) Vietnam			Bus tour		Private tour
Croes and Semrad (2013) Aruba	Beaches Shopping Some cultural or historic sites	Little interest in cultural attractions	Natural landscape/ national park Visit historic building	Island touring Heritage sites Gastronomy plus beaches, shopping	Visit cultural site/ participate in events Eat local food Visit museums, galleries Beaches, shopping and sightseeing were less appealing
Niemcyzk (2013) Poland		Religious/monuments		Monuments	Events

Author Location	Serendipitous	Incidental	Casual	Sightseeing	Purposeful
Sintas and Alvarez (2005) Spain		Spends very little of their leisure time attending or going to any performance	Consistent pattern of attending popular performances but almost no attendance at highbrow performances	Insatiable demand for a variety of cultural genres	Attendance at the highbrow performances, particularly classical music concerts, light opera and ballet/dance Searches for specific local cultural jewels, alongside most famous and visited sites
McKercher (2002) Hong Kong	Highly personal	Convenience-based attractions	Temples, mainstream cultural attractions	Sightseeing/collecting experiences/travel widely	Museums/art galleries/lesser known sites
McKercher and du Cros (2003) Hong Kong		Theme park IMAX theatre Brand name stores Icon attractions	British colonial attractions in downtown core	General sightseeing/ travel widely	British colonial Chinese heritage Prefer museums to shopping Out of the way places Local markets

at individual places once they visit. Discovering something new or unusual about the destination or visiting an attraction with a new or different twist provides a pleasurable and unexpectedly deep experience.

Interestingly, as well, a similar pattern was found with attendance at contemporary cultural attractions, as noted by Sintas and Alvarez (2005) in their study of consumption patterns of performing arts in Spain. It is perhaps why Carpenter (2008a) argues that cultural and arts programming needs to learn from the leisure studies sector (and by extension tourism) in order to attract more visitors. He notes leisure behaviour is often typified as pleasurable and necessary to human development and a sense of social civility but that participation is influenced by a range of socio-psychological factors such as family and peer preferences, time constraints, previous experiences, and how actively individuals wish to participate.

Implications for cultural tourism

Cultural tourism participation may be a mass market activity but the core or purposeful cultural tourism market is still a small, niche market. Most people who engage in cultural tourism activities see them as lower order complementary activities that enhance the total visitor experience. Different approaches and different marketing messages, therefore, are required to appeal to each segment. Kantanen and Tikannen (2006) conducted a study on advertising effectiveness in attractions that appealed to different segments, while others have commented on their search strategies (Le and Pearce 2011; Kastenholz et al. 2013; Vong 2013a). Purposeful cultural tourists need to understand the meaning of the wider cultural connections of the attraction before they experience it. They often conduct extensive research through a wide range of media. Advertising works best when it has a persuasive element that encourages learning (Kantanen and Tikkanen 2006). Descriptive, accurate, and factual promotional materials are most effective.

Promotional messages targeted at sightseeing cultural tourists are similar to those aimed at the purposeful cultural tourist. They are sensitive to information and want to learn about the attraction. They respond to learn-feel-do calls to action, as they are motivated by learning new things, sightseeing, and experiencing different cultures (Kastenholz et al. 2013). However, their level of interest and willingness to engage is much less than the purposeful cultural tourist and, this being the case, materials must focus on the provision of an enjoyable experience rather than a deep learning one.

Incidental and casual cultural tourists, on the other hand, do not invest heavily in the experience and do not want to be deeply engaged in it. As Kantanen and Tikkanen (2006) suggest, a cultural attraction is just one means of filling time in a destination for them. They are motivated by activities that entertain or inspire awe, and appear willing to engage in cultural activities if they reflect positively on the destination's core image (Kastenholz et al. 2013). Novelty seeking is important but they base their cultural experiences on well-known attractions. Convenience is critical as they will not travel to out of the way places if other activities more easily accessible at the destination have higher importance. Promotional messages that encourage people to 'come and enjoy' and marketing tactics that emphasize do-learn-feel or partake in 'delightful experiences' have proven to be effective. Advertising also works that emphasizes the age, uniqueness or otherwise, or exceptional characteristics of a place.

A few words of caution about numbers that appear too good to be true

Be careful about research that comes up with fantastic estimates of the size of the market or identified differences between cultural and other tourists that seem too impressive. The likelihood is that the method used to derive these figures is highly flawed. If the numbers seem too good to be true, chances are they are. A degree of scepticism always helps. Ask what method was used and make sure researchers discuss it clearly.

McKercher and Chan (2005) conducted a detailed study on the validity of the activity-based method used to define special interest markets. This study revealed the basic assumptions underlying its use are so flawed that it renders it completely invalid. To recap, activity-based studies rely on secondary analysis of visitor data. Secondary analysis is a valid method providing that the survey instrument and resultant data satisfy fitness, validity reliability and sensitivity, criteria for the desired purpose (McKercher and Chan 2005). Reliability and sensitivity criteria relate to the extent to which data can provide consistent results and fine enough detail for the purpose of the research. Logically, data collected for one purpose may not be relevant, timely, or suitable for another purpose. Validity refers to the degree to which the instrument can predict a criterion. Reliability and sensitivity are normally not an issue in the survey data gathered by state or national tourism organizations. Usually, the data are gathered in a rigorous method, the sampling technique is valid and the questionnaire is well thought through.

However, fitness and validity do become issues. In the case of activity-based segmentation, an assumption is made that participation is a valid proxy for trip purpose. This assumption is false as people may visit attractions for a wide variety of reasons that may have little to do with its ostensible purpose. Thus, analysing activities to infer purpose fails the fitness test. The data also fail the validity test. Studies comparing cultural tourists with others to draw conclusions about expenditure, length of stay, activities pursued and the like infer a causal relationship exists. For example, many of the studies suggest that visiting a museum causes a person to stay longer, spend more, or do more things in the destination. But is this assumption valid? Activity questions record what people did in the destination and not why they are visited. In other words, they record an effect of visitation. Activities pursued are then compared to other effects of visitation (how long they stayed, how much they spent, how many other activities they pursued) or who exhibited this behaviour (older, higher income earners, etc.) in an effort to show causality. In reality, what is being tested is an effect-effect relationship and not a cause-and-effect relationship. Relationships may be found but they will be casual and most likely incidental.

One cannot draw any inferences about cultural tourism 'causing' something to happen just by looking at behaviour. Making such a claim is the equivalent of suggesting that wearing pyjamas causes people to eat more breakfast cereal. If you were a marketing person and saw this relationship, the logical conclusion would be to run a campaign encouraging people to put on pyjamas at lunchtime with the result that breakfast cereal consumption would increase exponentially. Of course, such a statement is ludicrous. Yet some researchers, consultants, and government workers who are not familiar with the rules of secondary data analysis persist in arguing that data show conclusively that encouraging people to visit a museum will induce them to extend their stay in a destination.

In reality, the relationship between breakfast cereal and pyjamas is coincidental. Both are a function of a more profound underlying cause, in this case time of day. Likewise, the relationship between visitation, extended stay, higher participation rates, and extra expenditure is also coincidental and can be attributed to a number of other causal agents. First-time visitors tend to do much more in the destination than repeat visitors. People who identify a place as their main destination are also more active, in part because they tend to stay longer and in part because they have a greater emotional investment. Finally, people who participate in package tours also tend to be seen to do a lot more when surveyed. In fact, in most instances, cultural tourism participation is an opportunistic beneficiary of these underlying factors. Cultural tourism rarely causes people to stay longer, but the longer staying guest is more likely to engage in cultural activities.

So, how to explain the apparent significant differences between people who participate in cultural tourism and those who don't? The simple solution is that the tourism market is diverse, and that regardless of how it is segmented, statistically significant differences will emerge. Again, McKercher and Chan (2005) compared 24 different types of activities on 33 motivation, demographic, and trip profile variables to determine the meaningfulness of identifying significant differences. On average, 19.2 statistically significant differences were identified between participants and non-participants per activity. Valid conclusions can be drawn about differences between cultural and other tourists and the impact of cultural tourism on behaviour if, and only if, specific questions are asked about the role of cultural tourism plays as a trip motive. No valid conclusions can be reached by analysing activities.

Key learning outcomes

- Five types of cultural tourist can be identified based on trip purpose and depth of experience. Each type seeks different types of products and responds to different promotional messages.
- Most cultural tourists at a multi-product destination can be classified as casual or incidental.
- The share of purposeful cultural tourists at most places is quite small, meaning products must be geared for a tourist seeking a shallower experience.
- Caution must be used when considering the size of the market. An activities-based approach will likely overstate the size and importance of this sector.

9 Tourist attractions system, markers, and gatekeepers

Introduction

Having a significant cultural asset means little if nobody knows about it. Neil Leiper (1990) wrote about this very issue when he conceptualized tourist attractions as a system that includes the attraction itself, the tourist, and markers that connect the tourist to the attraction. His model explains that if no tourists visit, or if visitation is infrequent, then a site cannot be considered to be a tourist attraction. More importantly, he identifies the role of markers and information gatekeepers in stimulating visits, shaping expectations, and ultimately shaping experiences. This chapter begins with a review of the tourist attraction system, explores the idea of markers, and concludes by discussing the role of information gatekeepers.

Tourist attraction systems

Building on the work of the sociologist Dean MacCannell, Leiper (1990: 370) defined a tourist attraction as a system comprising three elements: a tourist, a nucleus or attraction, and a marker. Each plays a fundamental role in explaining how places attract tourists and how tourists consume sites. The tourist is the central part of the system, for without tourists places would not be thought of as attractions. He explains that the essence of touristic behaviour involves searching for satisfying experiences away from home, which can be achieved through consuming suitable attractions. This issue is critical for it reminds us that successful attractions must be meaningful to tourists. Many cultural attractions fail as tourism products because tourists do not understand their significance, consider them common and easily substitutable, or cannot relate to them.

The nucleus itself represents the second element of the attractions system. A nucleus is defined as any feature or characteristic of a place that a traveller contemplates visiting or actually visits. The use of the word 'nucleus' rather than 'attraction' is intentional, for it deviates significantly from accepted definitions of attractions as specific, named places that are managed for tourists. Instead, a nucleus is a broader term which captures the touristic experience more fully. Enjoying streetscapes, wandering through historic neighbourhoods, eating different foods, or participating in activities that are developed primarily for the benefit of local residents (such as local festivals) are legitimate and highly sought after tourism activities that do not fit the standard definition of an attraction. It is also important to appreciate that tourists rarely travel for the exclusive purpose of seeking a singular experience that can be satisfied by one nucleus. Instead, most people seek a combination of nuclei to satisfy their multiple needs and wants. Thus, the idea of the 'nuclear mix' emerges to reflect the role that different attractions, activities, and experiences play.

Some nuclei are so significant that they can function as stand-alone products. But such instances are rare. Instead, powerful nuclei tend to stimulate the development of many lower order nuclei where visitation occurs opportunistically around them. Few cultural assets have the ability to function as powerful stand-alone nuclei, for many archaeological sites, historic buildings, and other cultural assets are located far from recognized tourism nodes, are relatively small in scale, and are physically isolated from other potential nuclei. As such, they neither have the drawing power on their own to warrant visitation, nor can they piggyback on the other immediate nuclei to create an appealing touristic node in themselves.

Markers

Markers are items of information about the site or nucleus that are communicated to tourists formally or informally and serve as the catalyst for visiting (Culler 1988; Leiper 1990; Olsson 2010). Culler (1988: 5) defines them as "any kind of information or representation that constitutes a sight as a sight: by giving information about it, representing it, making it recognizable." MacCannell (2001) adds further, they signal the place as being something worth seeing. Moreover, as Clark (2009: 111) notes "because markers function to trigger motivation, they often contain information or present an image about what might be experienced at the sites concerned".

They can include, but are not limited to, formal promotional information, advertising and other collateral materials generated by the tourism sector. Their intent clearly is to create awareness, stimulate interest, motivate desire, and ultimately induce action. But markers include far more than commercial promotional materials. Wong and McKercher (2013), reviewing the literature, indicate that markers can include other forms of information, including common knowledge that is not attributable to any single source, movies, novels, and magazines, ICH associated with destinations, information provided by key informants, including staff at tourist information centres, souvenirs that remind the individual and others of the site or experience, word-of-mouth information from other tourists, lifestyle television programmes, asking other tourists, tour guide narratives, inscriptions of sites and monuments and, increasingly, social networking sites. Souvenirs function as markers that act as effigies of a site visited and in doing so create a direct link to a personal past tourist experience and also play an important role in stimulating visits by potential tourists, for their ubiquity signifies those nuclei as must see places. (See Plate 9.1).

In some cases, the marker itself can become an attraction. Roura (2009), for example, writes about the airship mooring mast at Ny-Ålesund, Svalbard. He indicates the mast itself is a plain utilitarian structure, and in the absence of markers could be regarded as a rusting metal structure standing outside an arctic village. The presence of markers converts this mast into an attraction. In doing so, the attraction becomes a marker that symbolizes the much broader examination of polar exploration and the quest for the North Pole.

Markers can be found either in the tourist-generating region or in the destination area. In a similar manner, online markers can be targeted at tourists in their home country when planning their trip or in the destination region. Generating markers focuses on imparting information and creating awareness of the destination, with the idea of stimulating visitation (Wong and McKercher 2013). They tend to be generic, factual, and focused on sightseeing-oriented experiences. Relatively few sites are identified, especially on the front pages of websites. One has to dig deeply to find markers that signify lower order

Plate 9.1 Tourism markers

Markers convey information about sites that signifies their importance. Markers form the catalytic link between the tourist and the nucleus or attraction in the tourist attraction's system. In doing so they also announce the nucleus as places worth visiting, give an indication of the type of experience to be had, and the type of behaviour that is expected. Markers include tourism promotional literature, directional signage, souvenirs, word-of–mouth information, other symbols that suggest an unusual experience and, especially, the presence of other tourists.

attractions. This is perhaps not surprising given that generating markers are likely to be associated with icon sites (Litvin and Mouri, 2009), since these places define the destination. The number, sophistication and specificity of markers increase in the destination. Here the intent is to stimulate action. More specific details are provided, more action-orientated verbs are used, and textual references imply a deeper experiential encounter. However, in-destination markers are much less effective in generating visitation, especially if someone has a limited time budget, for these people often pre-plan their activities before departure and rarely deviate from them (Shoval and Raveh 2004).

Why are markers so important? Clearly, without markers signifying the importance of a place, people will not visit. Roura (2009) adds they help us understand historic sites and, in doing so, can play a key role in helping protect them by underscoring the significance of the material remains that would otherwise be seen as rubbish. Clark (2009) discusses how markers enable tourists to form images about the type of experience to be had and also to create positive or negative connotations that may stimulate visits. He uses the examples of famous destinations such as the Costa del Sol (Coast of the Sun) in Spain or Surfers Paradise in Australia as place name markers that connote the expectations of a certain type of experience. By contrast, he suggests that if the site names are dysfunctional, or if either the name or the type of information conveyed by markers does not work, then a range of management problems may result, including graffiti, vandalism and destruction of the site. It is for this reason that the marker must convey a clear and unambiguous image of both the significance of the site and appropriate behaviour within it.

We have talked about how many of the adverse impacts of tourism are the result of failure to manage sites and associated tourism activities. By extension, the failure to manage markers can be a stimulus for inappropriate behaviour. Lovelock (2004) writes about the importance of who controls the marker, as whoever does so essentially controls the image of the site and, therefore, influences expectations of accepted and expected behaviour. Ideally, the cultural asset managers, custodians, and stakeholders should control the markers or at least have some influence over how the trade conveys messages. In practice, though, the asset often has little real control over the type, quality, and veracity of information imparted to the visitor, for it is the last stop on the information chain for most visitors, rather than the first. Instead knowledge dissemination is vested in a large number of intermediaries that act as an information gatekeeper (Seaton and Bennett 1996). Moreover, Lovelock (2004) indicates that in the early phase of development, either tourists or the travel trade are responsible for the initial creation of markers and asset managers become involved only after visitation occurs. By then the image and expected uses of the asset may be well established.

Gatekeepers and knowledge brokers

The terms 'gatekeeper' and 'knowledge broker' are often used interchangeably, for both are involved in gathering information, processing it, and then retransmitting it either to other gatekeepers along the communication chain or directly to the tourist. Collectively gatekeepers may intentionally or unintentionally inform the initial expectations of a holiday, affect activity selection, and influence the quality of experience (Solomon 1997; Palmer 2000). Moreover, the type of information provided may be selectively modified to suit the gatekeeper's own needs, to comply with political objectives, to suit the gatekeeper's perceptions of the tourists' needs, or simply out of ignorance (Dahles 2002; Jennings and Weiler 2006; Wong and McKercher 2010).

Gatekeepers, then, act as mediators that provide or limit access to information, sites and experiences (Jennings and Weiler 2006). Jennings and Weiler (2006) continue to observe that tour guides and others may prescribe itineraries and even scripts that limit where visitors can be taken and what guides can say. Sometime this occurs overtly, as Dahles (2002) noted, for example, where the government of Indonesia sees the tour guide's role as extending well beyond welcoming and informing guests and instead entrusts them with a public relations function aimed at encapsulating the essence of the destination and conveying ideas of national significance. The guide is expected to channel people into the right places at the right times to produce controlled experiences designed to create a positive impression of the country and shield tourists from its politically less palatable aspects. Such actions can undermine the provision of alternative histories or messages by individuals or groups who are not members of the power elite (Palmer 2000). At other times it can be more subtle, whereby the manner in which information is provided or withheld can add an affective dimension that reinforces or overpowers the spoken word. For example, Jennings and Weiler (2006), writing about wildlife viewing, indicate some guides withhold information about how to spot hard to locate wildlife, thereby increasing their own authority over the experience but, at the same time, limiting the tourist's access to it.

Who are these gatekeepers? They comprise all potential intermediaries who advise tourists at all stages of the trip. The list includes the commercial travel trade, local tour guides, destination marketing organizations, producers of travel guidebooks, and even family and friends. The exact number is debatable. Ten layers of information gatekeeper are identified as shown in Figure 9.1. Clearly, not all of them will be relevant to all

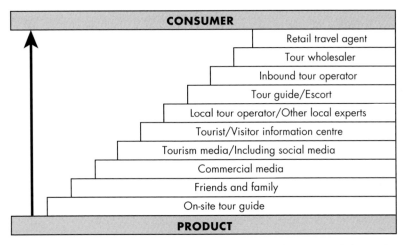

Figure 9.1 Gatekeepers controlling the information flow between the asset and the tourist

tourists in all instances. Many independent travellers will have no need of gatekeepers associated with the commercial travel trade. Likewise, others may use them selectively, seeking advice from a trusted travel agent, accessing a destination website, and talking to friends or family members. Yet, regardless of the number of gatekeepers involved, tourists see them as trusted and knowledgeable key informants.

The role of gatekeepers in conveying messages

The more gatekeepers involved, the greater the likelihood the message will be presented in a simplified, commodified or inaccurate manner. The cultural values for which the attraction is known, for example, may be trivialized or over-simplified to gain the attention of the consumer. Thus, at every gatekeeping stage, some control over the information disseminated is lost, which, in turn, means some loss of control over the asset. The inability to control the information imparted means that the asset loses the ability to ensure that the desired message is sent to prospective visitors in a desired way, which, in turn, means a loss of control over how the asset is portrayed and, therefore, a loss of control over what type of experience can be expected.

Seaton and Bennett (1996) identify two types of gatekeepers: opinion formers and opinion leaders. Opinion formers are generally regarded as being highly credible by virtue of their perceived expertise, while the latter are individuals who are close to the person and who share the same attitudes. Palmer (2000) builds on this idea by classifying them according to their location in the tourism system and the intensity of interaction between the tourist and the gatekeeper. Those who have direct contact with tourists exercise the greatest control over their movements. Retail travel agents, travel representatives, hotel staff, tour guides and friends, family or other close informants fall into this category. Increasingly, as well, social networking sites fall into this category, as people are now looking to such online travel sites as Lonely Planet's Thorn Tree, Trip Advisor, or Expedia as providers of unbiased reliable information. Gatekeepers with less direct contact with the tourist play a lesser but often quite insidious role, as the information they provide to physically distance gatekeepers who have direct contact with the tourist (such as travel agents) will influence what knowledge these individuals have.

Five general features apply to the gatekeeping process. First, the greater the physical distance between the tourist and the destination, the greater the number of intervening gatekeepers likely to be involved. The need to purchase airfares and accommodation from a distance often necessitates the use of a retail travel agent, which opens the prospect of purchasing a fully or partially packaged tour. Second, the less the person knows about the place being visited, the greater the number of gatekeepers used or the wider the information search (Stewart and Vogt 1999). First time visitors, for example, are far more likely to purchase local tours than repeat visitors and are also more likely to seek more travel information. Destination-naive visitors are most likely to use a travel agent (Snepenger et al. 1990). Third, the less knowledgeable the tourist is about the culture or heritage of the destination, the more likely he or she will be to use the services of a gatekeeper to provide that information. Fourth, the more reliant the tourist is on the commercial travel trade, the greater the number of gatekeepers. Fifth and finally, the emergence of social networking sites and Web 2.0 technologies has effectively removed much personal interaction from the gatekeeping process. Whereas once a tourist could rely on a trusted travel agent who he or she knew, today the tourist often has to rely on an anonymous third party.

The asset

The asset forms the starting point of this discussion. Direct communication between the asset, or more accurately its managers, and the tourist enables a desired message to be imparted unimpeded. The message sent is pure. Clearly, this situation is ideal but it occurs only rarely. Most visitors need to be made aware of the asset before they will visit it. This awareness-making process is usually the responsibility of destination marketers, tourism operators, or the travel trade. So unless the tourist stumbles upon the asset by accident, or has access to restricted information gathered by the asset's managers somehow, it is likely that other gatekeepers will have had some influence in the awareness creation process.

The Internet has created more opportunities for direct communication between the tourist and the asset manager. However, the level of use is rather limited. Instead, the asset's message is often conveyed through travel related intermediaries in general and the local DMO in particular. The DMO is likely to offer a superficial overview of the intrinsic cultural significance that indicates its otherness and appeal to the tourist, and rarely produces detailed information about its significance. Many DMOs will add a link to the website of the local heritage or arts organization associated with the attraction, suggesting tourists can visit it if they want more information. But, as Vong (2013b) found in her study of Macau, the purposeful and serendipitous cultural segments were the only ones to engage in such a deep information search. Most others seemed to be satisfied with information produced by intermediaries.

On-site guide/interpreter

The on-site guide represents the first knowledge gatekeeper who may modify the message. Studies have indicated that substantial differences exist in the ability of interpreters/ guides to impart information effectively to visitors (Ryan and Dewar 1995). The visitor is reliant on the guide to make the asset come alive and to tell its story. The ability to do so effectively is related directly to the guide's own knowledge, the effectiveness of training programmes and to specific job descriptions. In some cases, the quality of the interpretation is excellent. Archaeologists and cultural heritage experts, art experts and the like interact with tourists effectively and provide a high quality experience. In other instances though, the guides are little more than costumed performers who assume a persona. Moreover, well meaning but ignorant staff may simplify the message and in doing so may reinforce stereotypical attitudes, rather than foster real learning. We have observed this situation especially at well meaning theme parks in China that have tried to present 'international culture' by having local costumed performers play the role of North American First Nations people, for example. The performance becomes little more than a culturally insensitive agglomerated stereotype of 'Red Indians'. (See Plate 9.2).

The guide's ability to convey certain messages may be inhibited by the need to follow a pre-determined script. On a recent trip to Israel, for example, one of the authors was surprised at the almost complete omission of almost 1,900 years of history that coincided with non-Jewish occupation of the area. Interpretation focused on Israeli history prior to about 100 AD and then leapfrogged to the early 1900s. The same situation is evident in much of the presentation of China's cultural heritage, where ancient history is presented, the recent past is omitted and the dialogue recommences with the onset of the Communist Revolution, and then fast forwards to the late 1970s with Deng Xiaoping's reformist efforts to open up China (du Cros 2006b). Histories of Hong Kong, likewise, tend to focus on its connections to China (since the handover of sovereignty to China in 1997), with scarce mention of the 150 year long British Colonial era (du Cros 2004).

Plate 9.2 Ranger at Alcatraz, USA

The ability of asset managers to convey a desired message will be influenced by the amount of information or misinformation the tourist brings to the experience. If the asset manager can reach an open uncluttered mind, he or she has a chance to educate the tourist. If, on the other hand, the tourist's mind is already cluttered with misinformation, the task of changing attitudes and imparting accurate information becomes challenging – before accurate information can be provided, misinformation must be challenged. This task is done effectively at Alcatraz Island in San Francisco. On arrival, visitors are greeted by a park ranger who asks a series of questions about tourists' knowledge of the island and why it is part of a national park. In a very gentle manner, the guide debunks a number of myths (the Birdman of Alcatraz did all his experiments in Leavenworth Prison and not at Alcatraz; he was a psychopath and not the sympathetic figure portrayed in the movies; prisoners were criminals and not movie stars or folk heroes; the island is not at all like it is portrayed in the movies – there is no lower lighthouse and no series of tunnels) and discreetly reminds the visitor why the island is nationally significant (its military history is the reason it is proclaimed part of the national park, not its history as a prison; the Native American occupation in the early 1970s was a socially and historically significant event). In this manner, the rangers strive to dispel some of the Hollywood myths about the place in the hope that visitors can appreciate it for what it is and not what its image is.

On the other hand, the guide may adjust the message in an attempt to satisfy the perceived interests of tourists from different source markets. Wong (2013) found that tours of Macau targeted at the China mainland market almost totally eschew any reference to its Portuguese colonial history, in contrast to the interpretation presented to non-Chinese visitors. Macau exercises strict control over the quality of the product knowledge of its tour guides, with all guides being required to attend a 180-hour tour guide training programme. She also observed that the majority of the guides in her study complied with the official historical interpretation as taught in the programme which emphasized the dominant hegemonic view that Macau has a history of intercultural exchange between the east and the west. But because the guides feel tourists from different markets have varying degrees of interest, the length, depth and details of interpretation provided vary according to the signals given by tourists. She concludes from interviews with the tour guides indicate that they tend at the outset to take the same view of Macau as the one the government is promoting, but that, when dealing with a non-Chinese group, only a modest degree of encouragement by the tourists will get them to actually present Macau's colonial history, warts and all. In contrast, when guiding Chinese groups, they do not receive such encouragement.

Friends and family

Friends and family potentially exert a great deal of influence in the selection of and expectations for the use of cultural or heritage assets. They are known trusted 'experts' who have visited the place in question and are, therefore, qualified to offer advice. Yet these people are likely to be just as ignorant about the cultural values of a region as the person seeking advice. Indeed, friends are often important but unreliable gatekeepers. If the friends' visit was part of a short holiday, if they themselves are not knowledgeable about the cultural values of the place, and if they have not conducted adequate research, then their advice will be suspect. (See Plate 9.3).

Commercial media

Travel-oriented lifestyle, infotainment and edutainment television shows, radio shows, and magazines are ubiquitous. These gatekeepers justify their existence as information sources for people planning to visit the destinations highlighted. But producers know that only a small percentage of their audience will ever travel to the destinations highlighted and most will consume the product vicariously as armchair travellers. Places featured tend to be presented as having spectacular scenery, idyllic spots, up-market resorts and smiling natives. What cultural features are shown tend to be presented in a 'wow isn't this spectacular' manner or as part of a theme park attraction. As a result, destinations are presented in either a highly idealized or very commodified manner, with their features presented as products to be consumed. This approach is suitable if the product is a recreational escapist experience. But it does create problems if the cultural or heritage asset does not promote itself for such consumption.

Plate 9.3 Haw Par Villa and garden, Confucian Morality Theme Park, Singapore

Some DMOs have noted the important role that residents play in presenting a destination's arts and heritage. For instance, the Singapore Tourism Board recently promoted free tours of Haw Par Villa and its garden to local residents to relive their memories of one of Singapore's oldest cultural tourism attractions and create new ones with visiting friends and family. The asset has been a tourist attraction since 1937 and is basically a cultural theme park that contains over 1,000 statues and 150 giant dioramas established by Burmese–Chinese brothers who made their money selling a popular remedy called Tiger Balm. By taking the tours, local residents can provide some context to the attraction's Confucian morality and folk tales for visitors who may not know about this aspect of Chinese culture. The Singapore Tourism Board also hoped that such 'tourism ambassadors' would promote the attraction to a new audience through posting photos and comments on social media (Chow 2014).

Tourism media including tourism social networking sites

Tourism promotional literature comes in two forms: material presented by destination marketing organizations, and material presented by independent media. Each plays a slightly different role. Information provided by destination marketing organizations is designed to encourage visitation and, further, to stimulate heavy consumption while in the region. The area's assets are presented as products to be consumed. The message is usually simple and single minded.

Independent media, such as the material produced by such publishers as Lonely Planet, Fodor's, or automobile associations, have greater scope to present a more balanced and detailed overview of the destination. Background information on the cultural values of the destination are often included, as are suggestions on appropriate behaviour. But, like all other gatekeepers, these media have limited space to convey the message about the places being described, which means that the message must be condensed into its core features. In doing so, some of the richness of the asset must be lost. A commercial guidebook might devote only a few column inches to a key attraction. For example, a well-known guide book on Washington DC devoted less than one column to the Vietnam Memorial. It contains a brief description of its physical layout and a few sentences about how controversial it is.

Social networking sites are playing an increasingly important role as gatekeepers, for many people see the type of information shared on these sites as being more reliable and unbiased than materials posted by some DMOs (Mack et al. 2008; Zheng and Gretzel 2010). Traditionally, the message was controlled by the DMO with a vested interest in providing information in a controlled and predictable manner. However, the emergence of many social networking sites has shifted that power balance to the extent that citizen reporters can share their own experiences and impressions about places being visited. DMOs and tourist industry must now compete with a wide range of non-commercial materials posted by tourists, to the extent that these information providers are now felt to exert a significant influence on the tourist's decision-making behaviour (Akehurst 2009).

Accordingly, much has been written in the last eight years on the usefulness of tourism forums and online diaries of travellers for tourism (Pan et al. 2007). Other tourism researchers, in turn, have looked to tourism blogs as research materials and spaces for understanding tourist characteristics, motivations, and preferences (Carson 2008; Wenger 2008), tourists' decision-making (Litvin et al. 2007), and the ways in which destination images are framed (Pan and Ryan 2007). Existing research has also considered the role of tourism blogs as tools for facilitating travel planning (Sharda and Ponnada 2008) or as a vehicle for facilitating human interactions (Thevenot 2007). Inevitably, youth tourists, as present and potential cultural tourists, are most likely to be open to the Internet and social media to blog and chat about their travel experiences (UNWTO 2008a) and in one way or another reveal something of the kind and depth of experience of local culture for which they are looking and how they are doing it (du Cros and Liu 2013; du Cros 2014). Interestingly, though, while tourists of all ages are eager to share their opinions, most will still restrict their activities to visits to icon attractions and a destination's better-known cultural assets. As such, markers relating to lesser-known sites are still notable by their absence on the web. (See Plate 9.4).

Tourist information centres

The local tourist information centres are often seen as the first point of contact for visitors. Their function has not changed over the years, although the media they use have.

Plate 9.4 Tonka wedding, Hong Kong

A Chinese independent cultural youth tourist (left) has a serendipitous experience when invited to dress up and take part in a Tonka fisherperson's wedding in Hong Kong. Only a small percentage of youth cultural tourists are looking for deep experiences within their own region, especially for Asia given the overall size of potential travelling public. Accordingly some assets will need to be managed carefully, if the demand for experiences like the above becomes popularized by exposure within travel cyber-communities.

Essentially, their role is to disseminate information to tourists about the destination with the hope of influencing behaviour in a positive manner (Fesenmaier et al. 1993). Deery et al. (2007) note that with their expertise in local knowledge, a visit can help reduce uncertainty for visitors whose information needs cannot be fully met by use of the Internet or from other information sources. But their effectiveness depends on the quality, accuracy, and relevance of the information provided by their staff. Deery et al. (2007) indicate that in most regional centres volunteers constitute a large proportion of the staff. While they enjoy engaging with tourists and are generally helpful, they may have limited knowledge.

A number of other factors may also affect their ability to satisfy tourists' needs. Wong and McKercher (2010) conducted a study specifically seeking to understand how well staff could satisfy the needs of tourists who were looking for a more unusual cultural tourism experience and who wanted to visit lesser-known attractions. The results were not encouraging as most study participants reported an unsatisfying experience. Most encounters lasted between three and seven minutes, with short encounters tending to occur when the centre was busy. Few staff seemed to be able to respond to specific requests. Instead, most made a series of judgements about what type of experience they thought people wanted based on non-verbal cues of travel party size and composition, age of participant, assumed fitness level, ethnic profile, and other factors, rather than on the formal requests made. Staff later confirmed that based on their experience, they could 'pick' what type of experience people wanted almost as soon as they entered the visitor centre. These initial errors of attribution subsequently coloured the entire information exchange process.

Moreover, questions were raised about the breadth and depth of knowledge of information centre staff. Breadth of knowledge related to apparent awareness of the range of activities, options and places to visit, while depth of knowledge related to the specific significance of individual sites. While some staff could identify a progressively deeper range of lower order attractions, many others could not or would not progress beyond the main attractions. Study participants also observed that depth of knowledge relating to the cultural significance of places tended to relate to the extrinsic appeal of such places as tourist attractions rather than to their intrinsic cultural or heritage values. Participants were advised to visit historic sites because they were 'very famous', 'important', 'significant' or 'nice' But, when pressed for more details, few answers were provided. Indeed, the lack of knowledge led to the demarketing of some places because when study participants asked about specific lower order attractions they were encouraged not to go.

Local tour operators

Local tour operators take tourists on short duration tours (half to one day) of the local area. They are normally independent businesses or local franchises of tour companies. The operator provides transport, access to attractions, commentary, and may also include meals and a souvenir. The sector is dominated by bus tour operators which offer generic sightseeing tours. These tours may include cultural or heritage components but only if they are considered to be icon attractions. In recent years, some specialist tour operators have emerged that focus exclusively on cultural, heritage, or ecotourism. They are typically small-scale operations that have limited market appeal. Their role is to offer the visitor a taste of the destination's sights and sounds. Most include a series of brief stops at key attractions or points of interests that preclude the visitor from doing much more than sightseeing, photography, or having a drink and toilet stop.

Described as cultural brokers, tour operators are recognized as playing a key role in both shaping the experience and in presenting material to tourists (Welgemoed 1996). But the most important qualification required in order to become a local tour operator/ guide is a commercial bus licence. It is rare to find a tour operator who possesses formal qualifications in history or CHM. Indeed, most knowledge comes from the completion of a short in-house or external training programme, the guide's own personal initiative, or local knowledge.

However, some alternatives to this arrangement have emerged in places where community-based tourism projects have been linked to training programmes, or specialist training programmes have been initiated or funded by UNESCO, government development aid, or not-for-profit organizations. For instance, UNESCO Bangkok has run a specialist WHS guide training programme in conjunction with the Institute for Tourism Studies (IFT) in Macau for almost 10 years. It includes a more intensive review of CHM, site interpretation and presentation for WHSs than is possible in a regular guide-training course (IFT 2014). Examples of community-based projects that provide guide training to local people and refresher courses to existing guides include ViaVia Village Tours, Yogyakarta, Java, Indonesia and Roi Mata Cultural Tour Community Project for the Chief Roi Mata's Domain WHS, Vanuatu. The latter required a capacity building programme to assist the community to manage its own tours that was funded by WHC International Assistance,

UNESCO Apia Office, an Australian federal government aid programme, and the Non-State Actors Funding (European Union). The project allowed the community to have better control of what information about its intangible and tangible heritage could be shared with tourists, and safeguard any it considered sensitive by applying the Australian participatory tourism planning process 'Stepping Stones for Heritage and Tourism' (UNWTO 2012).

The Economic Planning Group of Canada (EPGC 1995) stresses that effective tours must be experience-based and developed around a cohesive theme that meets the needs of the target audience. Tours are typically built around a destination's primary attractions with additional stops at lower order attractions included to add value and variety to the tour and provide an opportunity for tourists to gain deeper insights into the destination. Tour composition, the amount of time spent at any one location and, therefore, the depth and quality of the message imparted are affected by a number of pragmatic operational considerations. Traffic congestion and on-site crowding, in particular, can disrupt the pacing of the tour and the selection of the itinerary (du Cros 2009). As a result, some otherwise desirable places may be excluded from itineraries if they are located in remote parts of the destination, or if their location is inconvenient. In addition, the amount of time spent at individual attractions may need to be curtailed in order to fit the rest of the itinerary into the tour if many stops are included. Moreover, as noted, politics can play an important role in determining both the itinerary and the subsequent commentary (Cheong and Miller 2000), especially at sites that are framed ideologically within history and national identity (Johnson 1999).

Tour escort

The tour escort accompanies a tour group for the duration of that group's visit. Whereas the tour guide is responsible for the activities at one destination, the tour escort will join the group on arrival and travel with it for the duration of its stay in a country. The escort's primary role is to ensure that the tour runs smoothly and that any problems are resolved. But this person also plays a similar cultural broker's role to the local tour operator, setting the context for the places to be visited and providing continuity between places visited. By virtue of being a resident of the host country, the tour escort also assumes the mantle of 'local expert' How she presents or interprets information influences the overall quality of the cultural experience the group receives.

But, again like the tour operator, the escort is usually employed for reasons other than his or her cultural or heritage background. Unless this person is trained specifically, apart from on-site exposure, the escort may have little real knowledge of places outside their normal home environment. As a result, this expert, on whom the group relies, may not be particularly expert.

Inbound tour operator

The next category of gatekeepers constitutes an insiders group that is commonly referred to as 'the travel trade'. Their role is to link consumers to producers through various commercial arrangements. The inbound tour operator assembles the land content of a visit for overseas wholesalers and travel agents. The role, therefore, is akin to a small manufacturer that assembles components into a product. To succeed, the inbound tour operator must produce an attractive package and position it uniquely in the marketplace. Unless the tour package is themed around culture, an in-depth cultural tourism experience becomes a low order goal.

Tour wholesaler

The tour wholesaler assembles ground content with transportation to provide products for sale through retail outlets. The ground content can be provided by the inbound tour operator or, if the wholesaler is sufficiently large, can be assembled by itself. Although some small speciality tour wholesalers exist, for the most part these types of operations are high volume low margin businesses that supply the mass market. They do this by providing a series of regularized, standardized, and commodified products that can be consumed efficiently, safely, and profitably.

Seeing many places or doing many things in a short period of time is more important than spending long periods of time at any one destination. It is common, for example, for tours of Europe to spend only two nights in Paris, including the arrival night after a full day's bus journey and a mid-afternoon departure after the second night. Thus, the tourist may spend as few as 40 hours in Paris, including two nights' sleep. The result is that the experience provided must, by definition, be superficial, spending only small amounts of time at any one attraction.

Space restrictions on brochures and/or websites limit the amount of information tour wholesalers can impart. An analysis of web markers produced by tour wholesalers (Wong and McKercher 2013) suggests that the branding of the tour assumes greater or equal importance to the component destinations, while the destinations themselves take precedence over specific attractions within any destination. Moreover, tours are promoted as a chance for visitors to explore a region, engage in a long journey, or visit the great sites of a particular destination area. Scarce details are provided about specific attractions and when included tend to focus on icon sites. Likewise, photographs are limited to scenic views and the text tends to be passive, suggesting people can enjoy or see various places, but not really engage the destination. In short, they are marked as appealing to either the sightseeing, casual, or incidental cultural tourist.

Retail travel agents

Retail travel agents provide the direct connection between the tourist and the travel experience. Although the Internet is changing their role, travel agents still represent, arguably, the most important gatekeeper in the travel purchase decision-making process. Their stock and trade is knowledge, and it is that knowledge that they sell to clients. Their recommendations carry a great deal of weight in the final purchase decision. The travel agent represents the most accessible local expert who is a trained professional in satisfying their client's travel needs.

But what many people do not realize is that the recommendations agents make may be influenced as much by agent self-interest as by client needs. Agencies work on very tight margins that are getting tighter all the time. To survive they must sell profitable products. Profitable products are those that offer the highest commission rates or the ones that are the most time-efficient to book. Cost considerations dictate that most retail travel agents will look first at mass tourism products provided by large national or multinational organizations. Few will seek small specialist tour operators who may offer the type of cultural tour people want unless the tour is specifically requested.

Agents acquire information on destinations from the material presented to them by tour wholesalers or, if they are lucky, by participating in familiarization tours offered by the wholesaler or the local DMO. As stated above, while they act as trusted sources of intelligence on destinations, their knowledge base is limited to products they sell and the message imparted to them by their suppliers. By their nature, therefore, they tend to view destinations as products and to view its assets as commodities to consume while at a destination.

Effect of multiple gatekeepers on the message passed to the tourist

Each of the gatekeepers has a different geographic proximity to the asset (proximate to distant), different levels of contact with the asset (frequent to infrequent/never), different levels of awareness of it (may be aware or may never have heard of it before), different knowledge levels (high to none) and different reasons for wanting to impart certain information (to sell a product, to induce visitation, to impart knowledge). Moreover, the individuals involved at each gatekeeper stage will also have different interests, educational backgrounds, jobs, clients they must serve, and professional obligations about how they portray the asset.

As a result, the focus, function, and information needs change significantly at different levels of the communication chain. The closer the gatekeeper is to the asset, the more dominant CHM objectives become. On the other hand, the closer the gatekeeper is to the tourist, the more tourism product focused the gatekeeper becomes. Because of these different professional functions and different levels of knowledge, the type of message transmitted will likely be significantly different. The cultural heritage manager will be interested in imparting a message that promotes the cultural values of the asset. The tourism professional will impart a consumptive message as a means of helping close a sale.

The following features can occur at each stage of the gatekeeping process for heritage assets in particular in that the:

* asset manager loses control over the message that is conveyed and the manner in which it is conveyed;
* desired message gets distorted as it is reinterpreted and represented by an increasing number of gatekeepers;
* message gets simplified as the messenger becomes less aware of cultural values and more aware of tourism products;
* message gets conveyed in the cultural context of the potential visitor and not in the cultural context of the destination area;
* message gets commodified to make it easier to convey it clearly to the consumer and to position the asset in a more appealing manner;
* less important assets are ignored (those assets that gatekeepers deem to be secondary or tertiary attractions), while primary attractions are highlighted;
* expectations about being able to consume the product quickly increase, inhibiting the setting of expectations for a deep experience;
* messenger becomes progressively less familiar with the product and is, therefore, less able to convey information in detail;
* messenger becomes progressively less interested in the arts or heritage message and more interested in the tourism message;
* potential visitor's expectations of the asset will change as a changed meaning is conveyed;
* expectations about appropriate behaviour on site can be modified which may result in inappropriate activities undertaken by the tourist.

The end result is that by the time the visitor arrives on site, he or she may be expecting quite a different experience from the one being offered. That may be a minor annoyance in some instances. But in other cases, problems can arise when large numbers of tourists arrive expecting a certain experience, only to be confronted by a different one. A similar problem can occur at arts events, for these events must be matched to the right market to provide satisfactory experiences.

Key learning outcomes

- The tourist attraction system consists of three components:
  1 the nucleus or attraction;
  2 the tourist;
  3 the marker that connects the two.
- The market is the most important for it signals a place as being worth visiting and also signals the types of activity likely to be acceptable.
- Markers consist of both commercial and non-commercial pieces of information.
- The tourism information system is controlled by a series of gatekeepers, some of whom are close to the asset, while many others are physically and emotionally quite distant.
- Gatekeepers control the information presented and, in doing so, shape expectations and resultant experiences.

Part D

Products

10 Cultural tourism products

Introduction

Two features drive tourism: attractions and access. If neither exists, then tourism does not exist. Attractions are demand generators that give the customer a reason to visit a destination, while access provides a means to reach the destination or the product within the destination. These two must work within a fine balance. Clearly, if demand generators do not exist, people will not visit, regardless of how strong the access is. No destination can succeed without a suitable breadth and depth of attractions, first to draw tourists and secondly to retain them for long periods. Likewise, if access is poor, people will have difficulty visiting even if latent demand is high. As a general rule of thumb, then, the potential appeal of the product must exceed the potential cost associated (in time, money, or effort) to access it. If costs are low, people will participate even if the assumed benefit is modest. But, if access costs are high and anticipated reward low, people will not visit.

The critical feature within a cultural tourism context, therefore, is to create a sufficiently satisfying experience that is unique, exciting, and offers 'one of a kind' encounters that appeal to the target market to warrant the cost associated with reaching the attraction or destination. Failte Ireland (2012) talks about the need to create memorable moments to make customers feel valued, by providing the right products, right quality, right quantity, right time, and right place. Cultural tourists have been described as creative tourists (Lord 2002) where experiences must be provided to allow visitors to exercise their creativity. The Province of Ontario, Canada identifies the need for the establishment of creative destinations that offer unique participatory experiences (MTC 2009), while others are even more succinct, suggesting that experience is the product (Latvia 2006).

Cataloguing an area's cultural or heritage assets is an important first step in evaluating the cultural tourism potential of a destination (CTC 2004; Snowden 2008), just as cataloguing assets is the first step in CHM. Tangible and intangible cultural tourism assets, including local festivals (Felsenstein and Fleischer 2003), are thought to be ideally suited to be developed as tourism demand generators, for they encompass the unique features of a place that reflect its culture, history, or environment and, by their experiential nature, promote the rich tapestry of its cultural traditions, ethnic backgrounds, and landscapes (Copley and Robson 1996, Blackwell 1997). However, a cultural asset is not necessarily a cultural tourist attraction. An old building is an old building – nothing more or nothing less. It must be transformed into something than can be consumed before it can be considered as a product. However, the transformation process is challenging (EU 2009; Lade 2010), especially for smaller regional attractions or where consumers perceive its appeal as being boring or irrelevant.

This part of the book examines cultural tourism products. This chapter looks at the general concept of products, examines the idea of products as tourist attractions, and discusses the need to commodify and standardize product offering. The following chapters examine the processes involved in product evaluation and discuss some success factors.

Before beginning this discussion, let us review some features of tourism. It is important to remember that destinations pursue tourism largely for the economic and flow-on social benefits. They do this by promoting their wide array of community assets as products to be experienced by the visitor. It is also important to remember that, apart from purpose-built attractions, the commercial sector plays a unique role as facilitator of experiences, rather than experience provider. In the past, these two elements (experiences and facilitator) operated in somewhat of a parasitic relationship: the facilitators relied on the experience providers to bring people to the region, exploited them and returned little. Increasingly, though, we are realizing that the convergence of tourism and cultural consumption is not coincidental. Rather, both sectors are involved in the co-creation and co-management of tourism products and, therefore, must function in a symbiotic manner for their mutual benefit. Cultural tourism represents the result of wider social changes where culture provision is becoming commercialized. In many ways, culture is being moulded successfully for tourist consumption through the development of such products and experiences as tourist arts, festivals and purpose-built theme parks targeted at tourists (Craik 1997).

Cultural assets as tourism products

The concept of a tourism product is complex as it involves elements of service, hospitality, free choice, consumer involvement, and consumption of experiences that must be actualized in some way (Hsu et al. 2008). Products can be natural, built, fixed or mobile, ongoing or temporary. At its core, though, a product has been defined as "anything that can be offered to a market for attention, acquisition, use or consumption that might satisfy and need or want' (Kotler and Turner 1989: 435). The key words here are "consumption that might satisfy a need or want". In other words, people do not buy products for the sake of the product itself, they buy them for the benefits they provide or the problems they solve. Accordingly products can be described simply as solution-providers for real or latent problems. These solutions are packaged into something tangible that the person can consume.

Think about why you buy toothpaste? All toothpastes are pretty much the same. So why do people prefer different brands? It is because each brand is positioned to provide different solutions to real or imagined problems. Some people want whiter teeth, some want cavity reduction, some want better breath or a nicer smile, and some want a better sex life. Each product succeeds because its manufacturer knows the benefits it offers to its target markets and has devised the product accordingly.

The same situation exists in cultural tourism. To succeed, a product must be seen to satisfy the core needs of its target audience. Its success, therefore, depends on the ability of the producers to understand the needs of the consumer and to shape the product to suit those needs and then to convey the benefits of consuming that product to the appropriate audience (Failte Ireland 2012). Any discussion of products, therefore, must always occur from the perspective of the consumer (Thorne 2008).

Thinking conceptually of products

A product can be conceived conceptually as having three levels or dimensions: core, tangible, and augmented (see Figure 10.1). The core product is the most important feature

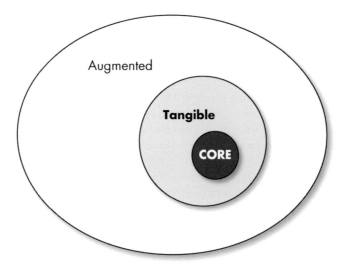

Figure 10.1 The three levels of a product

for it describes the core benefit or solution provided by its use. It answers the questions of 'what personal needs is the product really satisfying' and 'what benefits does it offer ME'? No product can succeed unless these questions are both asked and answered succinctly. As a result, the product development process begins by thinking about who will use the product and what needs it will satisfy. The appeal of adopting a marketing approach is that the core problem being solved can vary widely, even for largely similar products. This variation enables different providers to position their product uniquely according to the benefits being promoted.

Identifying the core product and the core audience is vital in the sustainable development of cultural tourism. Defining the core product facilitates a range of marketing tactics that can communicate an effective message about the key attributes of the attraction, stimulate some to visit and also discourage others from visiting. It sets expectations of the type of experience to be gained, modulates demand by discouraging peak season use, and controls visitor's actions while at the attraction (McKercher and Ho 2003). In addition responsible marketing must take into account the needs of the host population, which may be quite different from those of tourists.

The tangible product represents the second level. It represents the physical manifestation of the core product that facilitates the need satisfaction. In short, it is the physical product or service that is purchased. It is the historic fort that is entered, the battlefield site that is visited, the museum that is seen, the cultural tour that is joined, or the festival that is attended. The tangible product is *not* the core experience provided. It is the means by which the core need can be satisfied. This concept is difficult for many people to appreciate for most people are so attuned to purchasing tangible products that they do not think about the deeper needs being satisfied. Indeed, one of the powerful features of cultural tourism is that its tangible products subliminally signal an expected experience so effectively that people will respond to the product without thinking about why. A fort signals history and struggle, an art gallery signals beauty, ruins signal the deep past, and so on.

The third element of a product is the augmented product. Augmented products provide additional features above and beyond the tangible product that add value and facilitate easier satisfaction of the core need. It could be something such as a free shuttle to and from the hotel, the provision of umbrellas for rainy days, a souvenir at the end of a tour, or a money back guarantee.

Ideally product development begins with the identification of the core product, which then informs the creation of the tangible product, which is then supplemented by adding features of the augmented product that are seen to add value to the consumer, as shown in Figure 10.2a. The marketing message associated with the core product is ideally controlled or influenced largely by the enterprise that produces the product. This situation occurs often, but not exclusively, within cultural tourism. It is certainly evident in purpose-built attractions, including theme parks and museums, as well as festivals, events, and the performing arts.

But a different situation exists when efforts are made to convert extant historic structures or living culture into a tourist product as shown in Figure 10.2b. Here the product development process has to begin with the existing tangible or intangible asset, especially if legislation restricts the ability to modify a structure, or if the community wishes to continue the structure's existing practices. Starting with an existing tangible asset, especially one that is currently used by local residents for non-tourism purposes, may both limit the range of suitable development options and, depending on its size, the ability of the asset to withstand increased visitation. This separation of asset managers and custodians from tourism product developers and promoters also creates an enhanced potential for conflict between the two groups, as one either resists the development of tourism or the other imposes inappropriate types of tourism activities. In such situations, the existing structure or tradition will dictate the type of volume of use. From here, then, an appropriate core product can be defined, which will influence new tangible and augmented products.

Products exist to satisfy consumer needs

Historically products were developed and markets were sought that might be interested in purchasing the product. This push approach adopted the 'if we build it they will come' philosophy and has resulted in some of the great product failures of our time. Now, product development begins by understanding what the market wants and then devising goods and services that satisfy those wants. This lesson is slowly being learned by the tourism industry, and especially by not-for-profit community organizations offering cultural experiences for tourists (Ashley et al. 2005; Snowden 2008). It is understandable, though,

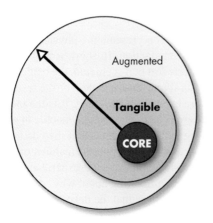
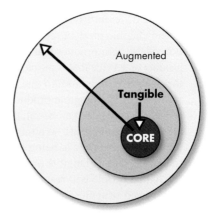

Figure 10.2 Elements of a product

given that few have studied business and that most managers are charged with protecting and conserving tangible assets, rather than providing tourism experiences. But if the decision is made to allow people to visit an asset, consumption of a product will occur.

Thorne (2008) distinguishes between an attractions-based push strategy and a consumer-oriented pull strategy. He illustrates that attractions-based strategies have worked in the past when primary attractions are involved or for marquee events but do not work as well for lower order attractions. Each may be successful but each is supplier driven, being conceived from the standpoint of the individual provider that wants to gain unique benefits from the specialist product or activity being offered. Conversely, a customer-orientation adopts a more holistic approach and views the provision of product development from the perspective of the type of tourist a destination wishes to attract. In doing so, consumer behaviour drives product development, whereby the destination's entire suite of products is evaluated to see where each fits in the hierarchy and the product is then promoted to maximize the destination benefits.

Cultural products should be treated initially no differently than toothpaste when considering how to actualize their potential. Tourism is the quintessential example of a sector that must adopt a marketing approach to products, for it sells dreams. People participate in cultural and heritage tourism to have an inner need satisfied, regardless of whether the person is seeking a deep or shallow experience. People do not go to Civil War battlefield sites to look at an empty field with a monument. Rather they go to gain an appreciation of American history, to visit hallowed ground, to honour the memory of those soldiers who fought and died (Gallagher 1995), to connect to their own cultural roots, to marvel at the incredible waste of war and loss of life, or even to try to imagine how they would react if they were placed in a similar circumstance. Sometimes the motive is more banal, as shown in Ramsey and Everitt's (2008) study of visitors to archeological sites in Belize, where the primary reason was focused on an enjoyable sightseeing day trip.

A marketing approach to product development

Thinking of cultural assets as products means they also need to be managed the same way as any other product. The most suitable way to do this is to adopt a marketing approach to asset management. Doing so provides a number of benefits, whereas the failure to do so presents a number of threats to the sustainability of the asset. Marketing involves more than sales. It is an overarching management philosophy that seeks to link consumers and products to provide appropriate experiences that satisfy both the needs of visitors and help the organization achieve its long-term financial and non-financial objectives (Sandhusen 2008). Non-financial objectives, such as conservation, preservation, education, and the creation of awareness of the cultural or heritage significance are often more important than financial goals, especially given that many cultural tourism products are owned by government agencies, trusts, or other not-for-profit organizations.

The ability to maintain control over how an asset is used is, arguably, the key benefit of adopting a marketing approach, by controlling how the product is shaped, what message is conveyed to the consumer, and who a desirable type of visitor is (McKercher and Ho 2003). Indeed, the most common impacts felt at cultural sites, including over-use, under-use, and inappropriate use, can be traced to the failure to adopt a marketing approach. Understanding why people visit and identifying who the desired type of visitor is enables the experience to be shaped to satisfy their needs in a manner that is compatible with the wider CM goals of the asset. While assets serve the needs of tourists, it does not mean that the tourist has an automatic right to do anything he or she wants. Nor does it mean that all tourists should have equal rights to visit. Indeed, quite the opposite is true.

The marketing approach enables the asset managers to define the core product in their own terms and, in doing so, identify and target the desired type of visitor. It may also involve prohibiting some activities or adopting a variety of pricing and other demand control measures to limit use. Indeed, demarketing, to reduce demand, transfer demand between seasons, or to shift pressure away from fragile areas to more robust ones, is as much an objective of marketing as increasing demand. Doing so can add value to the asset by signifying the experience is something that is truly unique. Explaining why something is not allowed may actually accentuate the experience being consumed. It has been our experience in Australia, for example, that most tourists respect the request of traditional Aboriginal owners not to visit sacred sites. Informing visitors why a site is closed to the public serves to enhance the overall experience, for it emphasizes the spiritual signifi-cance of the place being visited and also reinforces the desire of many cultural tourists to act in an appropriate manner.

It must also be appreciated that the same product can be presented in different ways to satisfy different market segments. This is because people can create differing images from each other of the same location (Ashworth 1999). A historic site can be presented in a more superficial way to appeal to the casual and incidental cultural tourist, while added interpretation and the opportunity to engage the site more deeply can appeal to the sightseeing and purposeful segments.

In other cases, though, the disparity between the needs of different users may be too great to be bridged. It may be an honourable goal to appeal to as many users as possible, and it may even be written into the mandate of publicly owned assets, but in practical terms no product can be all things to all people. In trying to satisfy everyone the danger is no one will be satisfied. It is better to target clearly defined, compatible users and to shape the experience around their needs. Others can visit but only under the terms set for the primary user. If a cultural or heritage asset exists primarily for the benefit of the local residents, for example, it cannot be easily transformed for tourism use without alienating the primary user.

Products as attractions

Hierarchy of attractions

Not all cultural tourists are the same. So too must it be recognized that not all cultural tourism products are the same. Some will be of great interest to the visitor and will draw visitors from great distances. Others will be of limited interest, while many more will have little or no appeal to tourists. Tourism theory recognizes that a clear hierarchy of attractions exists in most destinations and that this hierarchy is defined by the degree of compulsion felt to visit them (Leiper 1990). The more powerful the demand generation capacity of the attraction, the greater its ability to draw visitors from far away. Lesser attractions may provide activities for visitors while at a destination, but do little to draw them to it. Attractions can, therefore, be an intrinsic part of a trip and a major motivator for selecting a destination, or they can be an optional, discretionary activity engaged in while at a destination (Mill and Morrison 1985; Jordan 1999). (See Plates 10.1 and 10.2).

Attractions can be loosely classified into three groups: primary, secondary, and tertiary. Primary attractions are so important to most destinations that they play a critical role in shaping their image and in influencing visitation (Mill and Morrison 1985). The purchase decision becomes increasingly discretionary as one moves through the attractions' hierar-chy. Secondary attractions may be locally significant and worth going a little out of your

Plates 10.1 and 10.2 Great Wall of China

Many built heritage assets are so influential that they rise to the status of icon attractions that help define a destination. These attractions have such wide market appeal that visitation may have little to do with understanding their cultural significance but may be driven by the desire to capture an iconic site. Tourists are aware of their existence but may have limited or no specific knowledge of the site, its history, or meaning. Moreover, few will be interested in learning more about these sites. Creating a meaningful product is challenging because only a small number of visitors will be purposeful cultural tourists. Most tourists will be interested in a photographic experience. The Great Wall of China is one such attraction. The vast majority of visitors are not aware that the Great Wall is not one contiguous structure but a series of individual walls built over almost 2,000 years. Most people are also happy to visit the reconstructed sections that have been commodified for easy consumption. A chair lift brings people from the base parking lot to the start of the wall. Based on personal observation, the average length of stay is a few hours and includes a short walk along the parapets, shopping, and other sightseeing. Little or no interpretation is provided on the reconstructed section of the wall.

way to visit while in the destination, but they will rarely be the reason why people visit the destination. Instead they complement the tourism experience and may be very popular in their own right but do not influence the decision to visit the destination. Visits to tertiary or lowest order attractions are typified by convenience-based low involvement purchase decisions. Most cultural tourism attractions fall into the category of secondary or tertiary attractions.

The same attraction can function as a primary, secondary, and tertiary attraction simultaneously, depending on the centrality of the motive for visiting it. Barbieri and Mahoney (2010) discuss this issue in relation to performing arts. Arts may serve as the primary attraction for some who specifically travel to a destination to attend the theatre, arts, or special performances. Others may visit for a variety of reasons, including a night at the theatre as one of the many things they will engage in while on vacation. For these people, the performance is a secondary attraction. For others still, performance may be a tertiary attraction, whereby the performance did not play any role in the trip decision but they make a spur of the moment decision to purchase tickets.

Cultural tourism attractions embedded in the broader destination attraction mix

Cultural tourism attractions do not exist in isolation from the destination's other tourism products, possible activities, and overall destination image. Instead, they represent part of the product mix found in most destinations (Ashley et al. 2005; Munsters 2012). As such, the decision to visit involves more than simply choosing which of many temples or historic buildings to visit. It also involves a more basic decision whether to include any cultural site in the itinerary or to participate in something else. Cultural attractions, thus, need to offer something special that moves them up the choice set. Attractions or activities that are seen to be common, boring, or otherwise not appealing, will not be visited.

Moreover, the issue of serial monotony must also be considered, for after a while, similar attractions all begin to look the same. While tourists may be interested in sampling some cultural features, their interest in having the same type of experience over and over again is limited unless they are purposeful cultural tourists. Visiting one or two cathedrals or taking part in one historical walk may be appealing but the point of diminishing returns is reached quickly after that. While local custodians and asset managers may be aware of the subtleties of their places that make them unique, most tourists are not.

Interest in cultural products depends on compatibility with destination image

Whether or not the destination is associated with cultural tourism will influence both the volume and type of visitor. Cultural products located in places with a compatible destination image have a greater chance of succeeding while those located in destinations with incompatible images will struggle. The relationship between products, destination image, and tourist interest is shown in Figure 10.3.

Destinations invest heavily to create a desired image that will appeal to their target markets. The image conveys a number of messages about the type of experience tourists can expect when visiting and, just as importantly, defining what they will not experience. Products that complement the image tend to receive preferential treatment in marketing campaigns, while those that are inimical to it receive far less attention. At the same time,

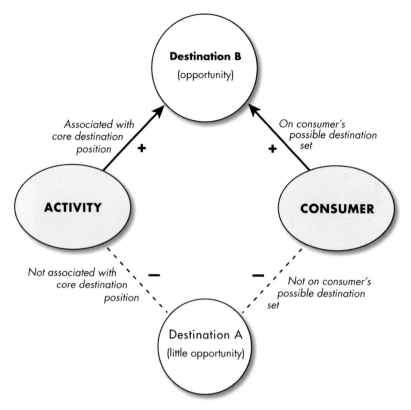

Figure 10.3 Compatibility with destination image

tourists look for destinations that can satisfy their needs. Again, the image portrayed will help place the destination on a possible choice set list, while a perception of an incompatible image will result in the destination being overlooked. (See Plates 10.3, 10.4, 10.5 and 10.6).

The combination of the consumer's predisposition to seek destinations that are compatible with his or her desired experiences, and the destination's propensity to promote activities that reflect its overall desired image, benefits those products that are congruent with both while also creating equally powerful barriers for those that satisfy neither. A place like Hong Kong has a clear image as a sophisticated urban destination. It supports this image through the promotion of shopping, dining, sightseeing, and festivals. Tourists thinking about an urban holiday would place Hong Kong on their choice set. Few people realize, though, that it also contains 10 percent of the world's identified soft coral species and that some businesses offer diving tours to see these corals. Why? Such nature-based experiences are not compatible with its urban image and, because of that urban image, few tourists would consider Hong Kong when thinking about a nature-based holiday. Thus, local operators offering such experiences face the dual challenge of offering a product that does not support the destination's image and operating in a destination that tourists simply do not see as a nature-based option.

Much the same situation occurs in cultural tourism. Some destinations have a clear image and market perception that is compatible with cultural products, while others do not. Melbourne and Edinburgh, for example, are seen as festival destinations. Other cities that are not will struggle to develop major festivals as attractions. London and New

Plate 10.3 Polynesian Cultural Centre, Western Samoa

Plate 10.4 Tjabukai Aboriginal Cultural Park, Australia

The volume of tourists visiting the destination will dictate the size of purpose-built attractions, especially if they function as secondary attractions. Hawaii, USA, and Cairns, Australia are popular destinations. The large number of visitors who come for holiday reasons provides a commercially viable market for the establishment of large, purpose-built cultural attractions, such as the Polynesian Cultural Centre (top) and the Tjabukai Aboriginal Cultural Park (bottom). These attractions complement the existing tourism product mix.

Plate 10.5 Cultural Park, Cook Islands

A destination like the Cook Islands attracts a much smaller number of tourists and, therefore, can support smaller scale attractions, in this case a much smaller family-owned attraction. The failure to consider tourist flows can lead to the development of facilities that are simply too large for the size of the market, resulting in their ultimate demise.

Plate 10.6 Tongan museum and amphitheatre

The island archipelago of Tonga received substantial foreign aid to build a cultural theme park, ideally rivalling the one in Hawaii. However, at the time, the entire country attracted fewer than 25,000 visitors, most of whom were former residents living overseas returning to visit family and friends. The volume of tourists simply could not sustain such an ambitious project and it failed.

York are theatre capitals. Other places have incompatible images. Las Vegas is seen as a gambling capital whose only cultural association is with stage shows. In other cases, the image is confused. Macau is now the world's largest casino destination and also one that happens to have a World Heritage designated core that reflects 500 years of Portuguese colonial settlement and the emergence of a unique Macanese culture. After a few years trying to please two completely different markets after the 2006 WHS inscription (du Cros 2009), Macau's heritage image is losing the battle with its gambling image. Gambling is more visible in residential areas (e.g. slot machines in coffee shops or 'Mochas') as well as those areas designated for casino mega-resorts.

Strangeness vs. familiarity, the environmental bubble, and the necessity of standardizing and commodifying products

The origins of the debate over the consumption of tourism experiences can be traced to tourism sociologists who were active in the 1960s. They felt people were no longer experiencing reality in their lives and instead they were being presented with a series of pseudo-events. Mass tourism was seen as being a prime example of how life had become overpowered by contrived experiences (Boorstin 1964). Tourists were portrayed as being passive onlookers who were isolated from the host environment and local residents. Some felt they were victims of an all powerful tourism industry who forced them to stay in tourist ghettos and who controlled their experiences. Others felt that tourists preferred to be ghettoized, choosing to disregard the real world around them. The end result was contrived tourism experiences that surrounded the visitor in a thicket of unreality (Boorstin 1964).

This work led Erik Cohen (1972) to explore tourist behaviour from the perspective of 'strangeness' by looking at the extent, variety, and degree of change tourists seek or are capable of seeking when they travel. He argued the degree to which strangeness prevails in the tourist's activities determines the nature of the tourism experience as well as the effects he or she has on the host society. While all tourists are, to some extent, strangers in the host community, different tourists have different abilities to engage with that strangeness. Some travel explicitly to engage themselves as fully as possible in the alien environment, while most want to experience the novelty of a destination but from the safety of their own environmental bubble. The environmental bubble is essentially a social or cultural safety blanket that surrounds the tourist with the known or familiar, enabling the person to sample the unfamiliar, while not being overwhelmed by it. Different tourists have different abilities to cope with strangeness and therefore require different sized environmental bubbles.

In essence, then, he argued that tourists seek strangeness only to the extent that it remains non-threatening. Tourists would choose different destinations if threat levels exceeded their comfort zones or, alternatively, would have to use the environmental bubble to reduce strangeness to an acceptable level. The environmental bubble within a cultural tourism context tends to address intellectual and emotional risk factors rather than physical concerns. (See Plates 10.7 and 10.8).

The process of tourism product development involves some form of strangeness reduction or environmental bubble creation that provides a number of benefits for the tourist, the tourism industry and the asset itself as summarized in Table 10.1. Reducing strangeness enhances touristic enjoyment, certainty about the experience, the ability to place the experience within a known cultural context and, ultimately, to provide greater confidence in the product being consumed. The tourism industry and the attraction itself benefit

Plates 10.7 and 10.8 Bangladesh

Sometimes a community's ICH is too 'raw' for most tourists. Intimidated tourists will not visit: instead they will seek other activities that are less threatening. Markets in the Bangladesh capital of Dhaka are a case in point. This major food market is located less than 200 metres from one of the city's major international hotels. Wandering through it provides a unique opportunity to understand the lifestyle of local residents. Moreover, stallholders and local shop-keepers welcome visitors. Yet few, if any, tourists feel comfortable enough to enter the market unaccompanied. An opportunity exists to provide a guided walking tour that will create a sufficiently large environmental bubble to reduce the strangeness to an acceptable level, while still providing guests with a highly rewarding experience. This type of idea has been used successfully in slum tours that take people through the barrios of Rio de Janiero.

Table 10.1 *Benefit of standardizing, modifying, and commodifying cultural tourism products for the tourist, the tourism industry and the asset itself*

Benefits to the tourist	Benefits to the tourism industry	Benefits to the cultural heritage asset
Safety/Risk reduction		
Increased safety, reduced physical risk while travelling	Control the actions of the visitor	Control the actions of the visitor
Greater personal and psychological security	Control experience which reduces real risk	Control experience which reduces real risk
Optimize use of time	Optimize limited time use by showing highlights	Optimize limited time use by showing highlights
Overcome inhibitions or distractions which may hinder participation	Make the product more accessible	Make the product more accessible
Thrill over skill (make it accessible)		Greater ability to manage the asset by controlling tourist actions
Highlight novelty of experience		
Observe without experiencing in an uncomfortable way		
Easier to consume – lower involvement purchase decision		
Satisfaction/Experience enhancement		
Explain key message or core benefit more easily	Explain key message or core benefit more easily	Explain key message or core benefit more easily
More confidence in buying a packaged, known product	Value add by being able to charge for knowledge and skill	Value add by being able to charge for knowledge and skill
Guarantee a quality experience as often as possible, thus enhancing customer satisfaction	Guarantee a quality experience as often as possible, thus enhancing customer satisfaction	Guarantee a quality experience as often as possible, thus enhancing customer satisfaction
Ease of consumption	Ease of consumption	Ease of consumption
Facilitate consumption of more experiences	Ordered predictable experience	Ordered predictable experience
Satisfy latent need by actualizing the product	Provide experiences demanded by the visitor	Provide experiences demanded by the visitor
Overcome cultural distance problems		
Ability to place the experience within the visitor's own frame of reference		

(Continued)

Benefits to the tourist	Benefits to the tourism industry	Benefits to the cultural heritage asset
Business considerations		
	Efficient processing of clients and the ability to process more clients	Efficient processing of clients and the ability to process more clients
Cheaper	Achieve economies of scale in product delivery	Achieve economies of scale in product delivery
Wider market appeal	Make the product accessible to more people	Make the product accessible to more people
	Enhanced profitability – increased income and reduced costs	Enhanced profitability – increased income and reduced costs

by the standardization, modification and commodification of its products to achieve efficiency in operations management, to reduce costs, and to provide some certainty of experience. Importantly, strangeness reduction broadens the market base, making it more accessible to a large number of consumers.

Minimal strangeness reduction may involve nothing more than signage or directional arrows. The provision of multilingual guides who can place the assets in context represents a stronger form of strangeness reduction. The creation of purpose-built spaces, such as museums, where the visitor can experience the society's past and form a sense of its cultural identity represents an even greater form of strangeness reduction. Purpose-built cultural theme parks, in particular, represent an extreme example of environmental bubble formation to reassure the more timid, pleasure-seeking tourists by creating themed spaces offering a safe, controlled, and controllable environment (Craik 1997). Hughes (1998) also observes the arts industries have standardized their product in order to satisfy consumer demand and enable effective signification to the consumer. Similarly, museums combine consumption activities with personal experiences that appeal to a larger number of people from different backgrounds (Prideaux and Kinnimot 1999; Tufts and Milne 1999).

The key here is fitness for purpose. The level of commodification must match the type of experience to be provided, the needs of the visitor, and the legitimate interests of stakeholders. It also involves balancing authenticity with practical product delivery concerns. Ashley et al. (2005) note maintaining sufficient authenticity in a cultural product that is packaged for tourists is one of the biggest challenges facing the sector. They comment that lack of authenticity can lead to tacky or mundane products and embarrassed or bored guests. But, at the same time, being too 'authentic' may not comply with tourist requirements for safety, accessibility and tight scheduling. They suggest, further, more authentic products are most feasible on a small scale, while higher volumes require standardization. In addition, heritage site managers and museum spokespeople discuss an extra ethical obligation they face, whereby they must balance edutainment with authenticity (McKercher et al. 2005). While theme parks may be able to be a little more flexible with the truth, museums have a professional obligation to present materials in a factual, culturally appropriate, and culturally sensitive manner (ICOM 2014). Theme parks aimed at providing a more superficial experience to the casual and incidental cultural tourist, for example, may employ costumed actors to perform certain roles. However, museums cannot do that.

Conclusion

Tourists are consumers of products. As such, any cultural tourism asset that is designed for tourist consumption must be thought of as a product and managed accordingly. The process begins with identifying the core need to want to be satisfied and then being able to actualize that need in a meaningful manner to ensure a high quality, consistent experience. This task is best accomplished through the standardization, modification, and commodification of cultural assets. This process provides a number of benefits for the tourist, the tourism industry that facilitates use, and the asset itself. Most tourists travel for pleasure to seek strange and different experiences, but only to the extent that they become non-threatening. Commodifying experiences encourages safe consumption. In doing so, it adds value to the tourism industry enabling products to be sold. Developing the asset around the tourists' needs enables the asset managers to control the experience and to better impart the desired message. Successful cultural tourism attractions share some common features and also adopt common strategies to present their products.

Key learning outcomes

- Products exist to satisfy consumers' needs and wants. As such, understanding the consumer is key to developing successful products.
- Products can be conceptualized as having three levels: a core product which specifies the benefits of use, a tangible product which transforms these benefits into something to be consumed, and an augmented produced that adds extra value.
- The product development process can be more challenging for some cultural assets because it begins with a tangible 'product' from which a core product must be defined and then a new 'tangible' product developed.
- Attractions fit into a clear hierarchy. The higher an attraction is in this hierarchy, the greater the obligation to visit. Visits to low order attractions are driven by convenience.
- Lower order attractions are also highly substitutable with attractions from different product classes.
- Successful products must also match the destination's overall image.
- Tourists' willingness to leave their environmental bubble will influence the type of product they seek.

11 Assessing product potential

Introduction

Previous chapters discussed products in a more generic nature, identifying the need to clarify the core product being offered, discussing the benefits of environmental bubble creation and the need for compatibility with the destination's image. Chapters 11 and 12 focus on the practical issues, consideration and options for product development at an asset specific level. This chapter reviews the broader issues that must be considered from both a tourism and CHM perspective, while the following chapter identifies an assessment audit tool to determine whether or not an asset has tourism potential and, if so, how that potential can be managed.

Considering the wider context

Tourism in general and cultural tourism in particular are linked closely to the broader social and political context in which they operate. If conditions are not favourable for cultural tourism development, regardless of how appealing the project may seem, its chances of success will be limited. No matter how good an idea is, if legislation prohibits certain types of development, it will not proceed. Likewise, if market conditions are not favourable or if the proposed product is incompatible with either the image of the destination or other products at the destination, then its chances of success are limited. Initially a broader or destination-wide assessment must be undertaken. Table 11.1 identifies many factors that must be considered. They are grouped under three broad areas: the political or legislative context, cultural or heritage assets, and tourism activity within the destination. Factors that are relevant to both CHM and tourism stakeholders are identified, as well as a wide range of sector specific concerns.

Legislative/political context

Any tourismification of cultural assets must work within a legislative or policy framework. The presence of international, national, and/or regional tourism master planning, cultural and heritage legislation, policy, charters of principles, and other frameworks can formally dictate, ultimately, if and how many assets can be developed for tourism. However, informal networks and collaborative opportunities will also play a significant role. A good test of how well integrated tourism and cultural aspirations are at any level is to look at the policies for tourism, culture, arts, and/or heritage and see how much cross-referencing occurs between these documents and how broad the reach is of public consultation involved in their creation. Too often tourism policy-making occurs in a very

Table 11.1 *Cultural tourism: looking at the broader context*

Theme	Common considerations	CHM considerations	Tourism considerations
Legislative/ political context	Existing legislative/ policy framework	Codes of ethics and conservation principles	Political importance of tourism
	Existence of conservation legislation	In-house heritage agency or departmental policies	Support for tourism in the community
	Zoning/use by-laws Development controls/guidelines	Heritage agreements with stakeholders	
Cultural/ Heritage assets	Quantum of cultural/ heritage assets	Robusticity – ability to withstand visitation pressures	Critical mass of assets
	Spatial distribution of assets	Resources available to manage the above	Ability to bundle awareness of cultural or heritage assets
	Importance/ uniqueness of these assets (local, regional, national, international)	Need to restrict access to certain assets for conservation or stakeholder related reasons	
	Icon assets		
Tourism activity at the destination	How the destination is positioned in the marketplace (and importance of cultural tourism in that positioning)	How the management policy or regime associated with conservation of the asset integrates tourism needs along with those of other users	Amount of tourism activity
			Level of infrastructure, superstructure
	Amount of other cultural or heritage tourism activity		Sources of tourists (domestic/international, cultural distance)
		Is an overall increase in visitation, if so, what planning and management is required?	Tourist profile (length of stay, trip purpose, first or repeat visitor, demographic profile, etc.)
			Psychographic profile
			Competing tourism products
			Complementarity of products
			Prices
			Synergies (bundling, nodes, etc.)

business orientated public forum with few other stakeholders invited to participate, and the same can happen with arts/heritage policy-making in return.

The debate about the merits of cultural tourism often has an overt political connotation. If tourism is supported politically and seen by the community as being beneficial, then support for projects will likely be forthcoming. If, on the other hand, animosity exists towards tourism, or if stakeholder groups object to the tourismification of assets, then it will be much more difficult to get proposals approved.

Cultural/heritage assets

Cataloguing serves a number of purposes. From a CHM perspective, it ensures that a representative sample of the region's tangible and intangible heritage is conserved for future generations. From a tourism perspective, cataloguing seeks to identify icon assets, determine if there is a critical mass of cultural assets at the destination to determine whether to promote it as a cultural tourism destination and what the theme might be for any promotion of that kind. In addition, the spatial distribution of these assets will offer insights into how they can be bundled into nodes, precincts, networks, or themed touring routes. While a critical mass of assets is important, it is even more important to be able to identify icon assets: those assets that are truly unique or outstanding that will draw people to the destination.

Tourism activity

As a discretionary activity, the success of most cultural tourism products or experiences is linked intrinsically to the overall performance of tourism at a destination. Therefore, a background study or situation analysis of tourism flows, the destination's current position in the marketplace, and an assessment of services and infrastructure plays an important role in determining whether opportunities exist to develop new products or expand existing ones. It is much easier to develop viable tourism products, cultural or otherwise, in recognized tourism destinations than in areas that have received little visitation. It is also important to consider how the destination is positioned in the marketplace and whether that positioning is compatible with the development of cultural tourism, as discussed in the last chapter.

Understanding the asset in its setting

The setting of the asset in its immediate surrounds, along with its developmental and socio-cultural context should be considered. Three factors come into play: the asset's physical setting within the region, physical access, and the social historical factors that have led to its creation (Table 11.2).

Socio-historical setting

It is important to understand the historical and social development that led to the creation of the asset. Producing a tourism product, which is divorced from the socio-historical context, is considered by the CHM community to be against the best interests of that asset. The setting that comprises its physical relationship to the surrounding landscape is also important to evoke associated cultural values. Hence, stories told by a storyteller are more evocative of continuity with the past if told by a tradition bearer in a 'cultural

Table 11.2 *The setting*

Theme	CHM considerations	Tourism considerations
Socio-historical setting	Historical context	Intact or fragmented
	Continuity	Contested or not
Physical setting within the region	Can the visitor still appreciate the cultural values?	Physical location within the destination
	Management and conservation considerations inherent in protecting the cultural values of the asset	Compatibility with surrounding facilities, structures
Access		Proximity to other cultural/heritage assets
		Location vis à vis tourism nodes
		Distance and market access

space' (such as a market or street) than if they are used as video presentation background in a site cafeteria.

Physical setting

The aesthetics of the setting need to be considered from both tourism and CHM perspectives. Attractive settings will enhance the quality of the experience, while an unattractive or unsafe setting may diminish the tourism appeal. A number of urban heritage buildings, including much industrial heritage, are located in unattractive or unsafe areas. These assets may have important intrinsic value but are of little interest for tourists if their safety needs are not met or if the setting is unappealing. Moreover, the compatibility of the tangible asset with its surroundings plays a role in enhancing the experience, helping to place the asset in context and assisting the visitor to better understand its meaning and significance. (See Plate 11.1).

Access

Ease of access will play a role in determining use levels. As a general rule, the easier, the more convenient and the more direct access is, the greater the potential for higher visitation. Conversely, inconvenient or awkward access may act as a de-motivator, unless the journey itself becomes part of the experience. Assets in close proximity and/or that are located conveniently close to tourism nodes are more appealing than solitary or remote assets. In the latter case, the tourist needs to overcome a perceived distance obstacle

Plate 11.1 Unsafe electrical wiring in historic building

Not only settings but also assets themselves may have safety issues. The wiring in this colonial building would need a lot of attention, along with any other conservation works on the structure prior to opening it to visitors.

before visitation can occur. If the visitor perceives that such a journey would consume too much time for too little reward, if more attractive alternatives are available, and/or if interest in the asset is not sufficiently high to force a visit, then visitor numbers will be limited. Both weak physical and market access will limit demand.

Asset specific considerations: place and cultural spaces

Once these broader issues have been considered, the next step is to look at the specific asset itself. Table 11.3 identities the types of issues that need to be examined. Tangible and intangible assets are identified in separate categories because the CHM community conceptualizes these assets differently. From a tourism perspective though, similar issues must be considered.

Tangible assets

The concept of 'place' is useful for identifying issues associated with the integrated management and development of tangible assets, including archaeological sites, historic buildings and precincts, as well as for movable cultural property or objects, such as artifacts, historic objects, or possessions. A place specific examination of tangible assets considers the physical state of the asset, its robusticity, physical state of repair, and integrity, as well as its cultural values and significance. Part of this assessment is undertaken to determine the asset's state of repair to assess what must be done to it if visitation is to occur. In addition, the assessment is undertaken to determine if visitation by non-traditional or non-local users will impinge upon the cultural values it evokes. Tourism considerations are much more pragmatic. The tourism assessment will determine if the asset will be appealing to tourists and, if so, where it could fit in the tourism attractions hierarchy (primary, secondary, or tertiary attraction). This assessment will also determine what needs to be done to the asset, if anything, to actualize its tourism potential.

Intangible assets

However, a somewhat different approach is required with intangible assets because the idea of 'cultural space' provides a useful means of examining this category of asset. The concept of cultural space allows all kinds of intangible assets to be associated with a traditional setting that enhances the interpretation and absorption of the asset's cultural values by the visitor. It also gives presenters of intangible assets a locus within which to control the visitors' experience and deal with any development and management issues. Again, the assessment will determine if tourism use is both acceptable and desirable, based on both a market perspective and a cultural analysis, and what can be done to the asset to convert it to a product.

Current and potential uses

The key point to be considered when looking at current and future users is to determine if tourism use and tourists are compatible with existing uses and user groups. If they are, then fewer problems are likely to occur when the asset is commodified. If, however, tourism represents an invasive or potentially incompatible activity, then the merits of tourism need to be reconsidered or plans to manage the actions of tourists need to be developed.

Table 11.3 *Focusing on 'place' and cultural space issues*

Theme	CHM considerations	Tourism considerations
Tangible assets	Physical state of asset and its robusticity	Uniqueness
	How much of it is still intact – integrity	Ability to shape, provide experience
		'Product' potential and ability to actualize that potential
	Cultural values it evokes	
	Visibility of the remains	Potential place on the attractions hierarchy
	Uniqueness	Commoditizing it sensitively to maximize visitor satisfaction without losing authenticity
	Good or bad example of its type	
	Overall cultural value	
Ownership/ Management	Presence/absence of a systematic management regime that allows for regular maintenance and monitoring of the asset at its most basic	Ownership structure (private, public, community)
		Purpose (private sector vs. public sector)
		Presence/Absence of a formal management structure and business plan
Intangible assets	Is tourism use of asset culturally appropriate? (e.g. access to sacred information)	Uniqueness
		Ability to shape, provide experience
	Marketing is conducted responsibly	'Product' potential and ability to actualize that potential
	Design of the tourism product does not include elements that go against preserving the asset's cultural values	Potential place on the attractions hierarchy
	Tradition bearers are not overwhelmed or adversely affected	How it complements or enhances the appeal of tangible assets being marketed
	Cultural values of the asset are not changed to accommodate tourism needs	Commoditizing it sensitively to maximize visitor satisfaction without losing authenticity
Current and potential uses	What is its current use – public space, private space?	Importance of tourism
	Who are its current users?	Number of similar/competing places and their level of development
	Education of the general public is the primary concern	Place on the attractions hierarchy and ability to shift places
	Use of asset to send a message about heritage conservation	

Stakeholder and consultation issues

Most cultural and heritage assets have multiple stakeholders, whose opinions need to be considered. Table 11.4 comprises the key issues for dealing with stakeholders in assessment and tourism planning. The failure to consider the needs of stakeholders, including even minor stakeholders, can lead to conflict situations that can endanger the effectiveness of any management structure put in place. The omission of stakeholders from the consultative process means that their concerns will not be heard, meaning that their legitimate concerns cannot be addressed from the outset. The consultative process is not a one-off process. For an asset to be truly sustainable, ongoing feedback from stakeholders must be encouraged so that emerging issues can be resolved.

Stakeholder identification and consultation

Three main challenges arise when considering stakeholders. The first is deciding who has a legitimate interest in the management of the asset. The second is to consider whether this interest is direct or indirect, while the third is to ensure that the consultation process is both fair and open. Depending on the size, significance, and political sensitivity of the tourism proposal, many potential stakeholders may claim an interest in it. Some will have an immediate and direct interest, such as tradition bearers, traditional owners, indigenous groups, ethnic minorities, or historical users, as well as tour operators and tour guides. Others will have an indirect, though still legitimate interest. Research facilities, heritage NGOs, international heritage agencies, other agencies associated with heritage management, historical organizations, and conservation groups, along with local, regional, and national tourism NGOs, the local travel trade, and public sector tourism bodies may all have some valid, though not direct, interest in the asset. However, if the proposed use is controversial, many other stakeholders who do not have a legitimate interest in the asset may also seek to assert their rights to become involved in its management. Sometimes, it is those with the least direct interest in the asset who are the most vocal.

Potential conflicts are much easier to resolve when dealing with stakeholders who have a direct interest in the asset, while they are much more difficult for a small project when stakeholders with no direct interests become involved. Those people with direct interests usually know each other, usually recognize the legitimacy of each other's interests and, normally, will strive to find a pragmatic solution. Sometimes stakeholders with direct interests may have intractable differences (as discussed in the next chapter), which makes the successful transformation of a cultural asset into a product impossible. Stakeholders with an indirect interest tend to treat issues at a more philosophical and political level. Ideals are often entrenched, leading indirect stakeholders to view potential outcomes as win/lose situations. While their needs should be considered, too heavy an involvement can result in unnecessary delays that do not necessarily contribute to the best interests of all the direct stakeholders involved.

Having said this, the line between direct and indirect stakeholders is sometimes blurred, for some direct stakeholders may be physically distant from the asset in question, while indirect ones may be situated in close proximity to the asset. For example, UNESCO is a physically remote stakeholder that has a direct interest in all World Heritage areas. As a direct stakeholder with the power to potentially delist sites for a variety of reasons including rapid tourist development, its views must be considered.

Ensuring that the consultation exercise is both fair and transparent represents the third issue. In some places, consultation is undertaken as a rather cynical exercise aimed at being seen to involve the public rather than genuinely seeking input into the planning and management process. Ideally consultation should seek to involve all legitimate stakeholders in the entire planning process. Further, consultation seeks to have stakeholders with different viewpoints listen to and understand other stakeholders' concerns with a view to seeking a mutually agreeable resolution of any real or imagined problems.

Stakeholder issues

Consultation must commence from the outset and continue as a regular part of the ongoing management of the asset, especially when indigenous stakeholders, local community user groups, and tradition bearers may be asked to sacrifice something in order to achieve the asset's tourism potential. Consultation must be conducted in an open and transparent manner that allows the process to be fully participatory. The identification of leading stakeholders, key spokespeople, and main controllers of the asset (where they differ) early in the process will make the entire planning process operate more smoothly. It is important, as well, that the process be managed effectively to ensure that it does not break down into a series of autonomous parallel processes. A management framework needs to be designed and agreed upon that allows for continual and regular communication to continue between task-holders. (See Plate 11.2).

Plate 11.2 Stakeholder consultation meeting, Yunnan, China

Consultation with local tradition bearers can be an important part of the process. These stakeholders are often key to accessing ICH assets and need to have their views included in planning and management exercises. This tourism master-planning project in Yunnan, China, highlighted the importance of consulting such stakeholders, although some later projects have not.

Stakeholders generally have a long history with each other. It is important to understand such issues as the power alliances that have formed between and among groups, which stakeholders have assumed the mantle of leadership, the past history between stakeholders, whether there have been any major conflicts or if they have worked towards mutual solutions, when commencing the consultative process. In addition, tourism often represents a powerful new stakeholder that can alter the power balance. Care must be used when discussing tourism issues to ensure that all stakeholders recognize tourism's true power position in case they develop unrealistic expectations. Table 11.4 lists a range of stakeholder issues.

People, skills and financial resources

Finally no assessment is complete without assessing the skills, resources, and capabilities of the people involved and the resources available to them. Some of the considerations are identified in Table 11.5. The ability to deliver on visions and to manage cultural assets as tourism attractions in a sustainable manner is directly related to the skills of the people directly involved in any project. The human element can be a fatal flaw that turns good ideas into failed projects with significant management problems. Issues relating to the ability of the people involved delivering on a project's goals and an assessment of their motives for becoming involved needs to be considered. If the skills are not present, does the person have the ability to acquire them him or herself or the resources to buy them?

Buying skills raises a second fundamental question and that is, does the proponent have sufficient financial resources to deliver on the idea? In general, it is difficult to acquire monies for conservation work. But it is generally easier to source funding for one-off development projects or site stabilization than it is for ongoing maintenance. Tourism assets, however, require ongoing maintenance. Where will the resources come from? Further questions must be asked about the financial viability of proposals. Business plans need to be developed and scrutinized closely to assess their reliability.

Finally there are two more crucial questions that need to be answered. Why is tourism being proposed? Is tourism an end in itself or is it a means to another end? Tourism reasons must be the only reasons a cultural asset is developed for tourism. By this, the authors mean that only assets with strong appeal to tourists, that are robust enough to cater for visitors, and that can be positioned uniquely and attractively in the marketplace should be developed as tourism attractions. Caution must be used if tourism is used as a justification for the pursuit of other objectives, such as a desire to conserve assets further, to protect them from demolition or as a means of getting assets listed on a heritage registry.

Conclusion

Now that this information has been gathered, it must be assessed in a meaningful manner. While all the information is important, clearly some details (such as legislative context, values at stake, and financial resources) are more important than others. Likewise, more critical issues emerge from an asset specific perspective as the evaluation process moves from the general to the specific. Chapter 12 discusses one means available to use this information to direct the management process.

Table 11.4 *Stakeholders*

Theme	Common considerations	CM/CHM considerations	Tourism considerations
Stakeholder identification and consultation	Identifying all relevant stakeholders as early as possible in the process Inviting their participation throughout the process Being aware that there are dominant stakeholders with controlling interests Understanding their different involvement expectations and capabilities Noting any history of conflict or collaboration	Listening to stakeholders' concerns and incorporating feedback into day to day management once the asset has been fully developed as an attraction Understanding the perspective and agenda of the tourism sector and associated stakeholders	Listening to stakeholders' concerns and incorporating feedback into product development, marketing, and business strategies Understanding the perspective and agenda of the CHM and conservation sector and associated stakeholders
Types of stakeholders		Educational institutions, arts, conservation and heritage NGOs, government agencies, museums, indigenous groups/ethnic minorities, religious groups, others	Local, national, state government tourism organizations, tour operators, local guides and others
Key stakeholder issues	Power and power relationships between stakeholders Agreement by controlling stakeholder(s) to allow the asset to be presented to visitors Awareness of impacts of tourism Ownership and copyright issues are addressed Commitment to an ongoing conservation	Controlling stakeholders and owners agree to visitation and conservation measures Designing interpretation that is culturally appropriate and suits visitors' needs Community arts or CH manager understands and takes into account the role of volunteers and sponsors Robusticity and physical capacity of the asset	Controlling stakeholders and owners support visitation and development Design and marketing of a viable product that is culturally appropriate and sustainable Ongoing costs of stakeholder consultation Potential of a long lead time to approvals given by other stakeholders to tourism ventures

Table 11.5 *People, skills, and financial resources*

Theme	CM/CHM considerations	Tourism considerations
People	Skills of individuals involved	Skills of individuals involved
	Skill gaps	Skill gaps
	Ability to fill skill gaps	Ability to fill skill gaps
	Motives for being involved	Motives for being involved
Resources	Amount of money/resources available	Amount of money/resources available
	Amount of money/resources needed	Amount of money/resources needed
	Desired use for money and resources (maintenance, development, etc.)	Possible sources of money/resources
	Possible sources of money/resources	Tourism as a means to an end or as an end in itself
	Tourism as a means to an end or as an end in itself	

Key learning outcomes

- Tourism and cultural heritage stakeholders both have a legitimate role to play in product development but each is guided by different considerations relating to:
  - legislation;
  - the asset itself;
  - the response to tourism activity in the destination.
- Consideration of place and cultural space will influence product potential.
- Stakeholder consultation is essential prior to entering tourism and must be considered as an ongoing part of asset management even after entering this sector.
- The ability to deliver on potential is influenced by the people involved and the financial and non-financial resources available.

12 Market Appeal/ Robusticity Matrix
A site specific auditing tool

Introduction

Cataloguing represents the first small step in the road to successful product development: it helps to narrow the selection as not all cultural assets have the potential to become products. As a case in point, Sakharchuk et al. (2013) indicated that Moscow alone has more than 400 museums, 200 galleries and exhibition halls, 129 theatres, 60 architectural and park ensembles, 14 theme parks, and more than 300 objects of cultural interest and, when extended to the region in its immediate environs, there are more than 6,400 sites of cultural and historical heritage, including 2,600 monuments, 1,400 churches, chapels and monasteries, 341 homesteads, and 350 monuments of military glory. They suggest this volume of cultural assets results in significant potential for the development of cultural tourism. But such a conclusion is naive for, in reality, few of these assets likely have much real tourism potential. Documenting helps, but documenting without a goal in mind accomplishes little other than building impressive lists. The question now becomes what to do with this information? A systematic evaluation protocol is needed to distinguish potential tourism products from the vast array of cultural assets. (See Plate 12.1).

This chapter presents a two-step evaluation model. The first step assesses whether assets satisfy a progressive set of criteria that are necessary to be considered as products. Failure at any one stage precludes progression to the next stage unless and until the cause of the failure can be resolved. The second step then evaluates this information in a more holistic manner to identify if and where candidate assets fit into the tourism product hierarchy, and offer insights into the level of appropriate use for tourism, while also helping to identify management actions.

The Market Appeal/Robusticity Matrix

The Market Appeal/Robusticity Matrix (du Cros 2001) as shown in Figure 12.1 is a proven assessment tool that can be applied in a proactive manner to assess potential and identify management options prior to tourismification or, reactively, to evaluate existing tourism products to identify issues that need resolution. It is predicated on the integration of different elements that constitute its two axes. The Robusticity Axis focuses on issues relating to cultural and physical values, while the Market Appeal Axis reflects product and experiential values. A series of indicators for each value dimension is shown in Box 12.1.

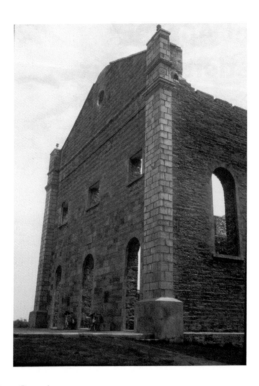

Plate 12.1 Ruin in eastern Canada

Most heritage sites are not known and valued beyond the local community and therefore have limited ability to draw tourists from far away. Lack of knowledge means few tourists can relate to the site. As a result, few places have significant tourism potential. They may create attractive photo opportunities for people who pass by them by happenstance, but stand-alone structures that are locally significant, such as this church ruin in eastern Canada, are not tourist attractions.

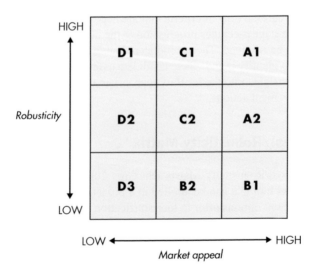

Figure 12.1 Market Appeal/Robusticity Matrix of tourism potential

Box 12.1 Cultural heritage tourism sub-indicators

Robusticity

Cultural values

Does it have:

- aesthetic value (including architectural value)?
- historical value?
- educational value?
- social value?
- scientific value?

Is it:

- rare or common (locally, regionally, nationally)?
- representative of a community's heritage?
- locally, regionally, nationally, or internationally significant?
- reflective of a unique cultural tradition (living or disappeared)?

Do:

- stakeholders want tourism/tourists?

Can:

- tourism occur without compromising its intrinsic meaning to stakeholders, custodians, and tradition bearers?

Physical values

What is the:

- state of repair?
- fragility of the asset (social and physical)?

Does it have:

- management plans or policies in place?
- regular monitoring and maintenance?

Can it be:

- modified for increased use (legislative, zoning restrictions)?
- modified without compromising its cultural values?

What is the:

- potential for ongoing involvement and consultation of key stakeholders?
- potential for negative impacts of high visitation on:
    - the fabric of the asset(s)?
    - lifestyle and cultural traditions of local community(ies)?

Market appeal

Tourism values

What is its:

- ambience and setting?
- proximity to other attractions?
- complementarity with other attractions?

Is it:

- well known outside the local area?
- a national icon or symbol?
- unique, rare, or unusual?
- big enough to attract tourists and retain them for a sufficiently long time to justify the journey?

Can it:

- be accessed easily?

Does it:

- tell a good story that is evocative of place?
- have some aspect that distinguishes it from nearby attractions?
- appeal to special needs or uses (e.g. pilgrimages, festivals, sports)?

Are:

- suitable amenity needs nearby, including toilets, parking, pathways, refreshments, availability of information?

Is the broader destination area:

- associated with culture or heritage?
- politically supportive of tourism?

Experiential values

Does the asset have the potential to:

- tell a good story?
- offer interesting experiences to tourists?
- provide a participatory, engaging, educational, or edutainment experience?
- provide an authentic experience?

Can tourists:

- relate to the asset from their own frame of reference?
- create an emotional connection with the asset?

Is it:

- capable of meeting different tourists' expectations (ranging from the incidental through to the purposeful cultural tourist)?

Are:

- appealing markers present to entice visitation?
- suitable and sufficient pieces of collateral information available?

Plate 12.2 Kyrgyzstan

Conservation must proceed before tourism development can occur. In many parts of the world, no management plans exist for heritage sites, as is the case in Kyrgyzstan where petroglyph carved boulders can be found scattered throughout a field. Site management plans and visitor management strategies will need to be developed to ensure the sustainable use of this site and its conservation for generations to come.

Robusticity

The two values sets that constitute the robusticity dimension determine whether the asset is culturally significant and whether it can cope with the pressures brought by increased visitors. The cultural values element, for example, assesses its social, historic, scientific, or educational significance, and further seeks to determine if it is a rare or common example of the type of asset under consideration. Importantly, as well, issues relating to social impacts and the desires of stakeholders have to be considered. (See Plate 12.2).

The physical values element focuses primarily on issues relating to the state of repair, fragility of the asset, and the existence of formal plans of management or legislative controls designed to conserve its unique values. This evaluation will answer pragmatic questions about the ability of the site to cope with tourists and whether its fabric can be modified without compromising its cultural values. (See Plates 12.3, 12.4, and 12.5).

Market appeal

The market appeal dimensions focus on whether the asset has the necessary attributes to function as a product. The product values element considers the asset and its surrounding area. On-site considerations relate to existing awareness levels, whether the place offers enough activities to justify the journey time, and whether it can be positioned uniquely in the marketplace either as a product or for specific market segments. Finally, issues relating to amenity provision and the broader context of the destination must also be considered. Off-site considerations relate to the appeal of the surrounding area and whether it is conducive to tourism. Experiential values focus exclusively on the ability of the asset to provide a high quality experience for visitors. It examines how well it is presented currently and how it could be presented in the future. Importantly, the goal is to determine if the tourists can engage with the place.

A qualitative tool

This matrix is qualitative in nature, even though it was envisioned initially as a quantitative tool. Attempts have been made to apply it in a quantifiable manner (Li and Lo 2004; Stamenkovic and Jaksic 2013) with mixed results, primarily because it was difficult to develop absolute weighting measures for context specific issues that may have different impacts. For example, the issue of stakeholder willingness to enter tourism may be a paramount concern in some assets but irrelevant in others. Likewise, amenities may be critical in remote assets but not particularly relevant in cultural items located in well-established tourism nodes.

However, a qualitative approach relies on the professional judgement of the person or people doing the assessment, making it potentially open to personal bias, where the individual's own interests may either cloud their judgement or lead to differing interpretations of the results. It has been our experience that pro-tourism stakeholders tend to minimize the potential risks tourism can post heritage assets while heritage managers often fail to evaluate effectively the experiential elements of a product. Local stakeholders also tend to overestimate the significance and market appeal of common assets.

It is for this reason that training, pre-testing, and teamwork is encouraged. Cultural heritage managers need to be informed about tourism practicalities and the tourism sector must learn the principles of cultural heritage managers. Pre-testing is encouraged to ensure consistency in application, especially if multiple teams are collecting information for the assessment. Practitioners and others using the matrix can also develop additional

Plate 12.3 Honge Hani Rice Terraces, China

Plate 12.4 Honge Hani village, China

Plate 12.5 Typical activities Honge Hani, China

Assessment of robusticity takes many forms. The Honghe Hani Rice Terraces area in western China was inscribed as a World Heritage cultural landscape in 2013. Local community leaders and provincial politicians are hoping to be able to use its designation as a catalyst for successful tourism development, as part of a broader strategy to help conserve the assets of the area, revitalize the local culture, generate employment, and retain young people. Clearly, the asset itself is impressive, covering some 16,600 ha, reflecting over 1,300 years of continuous habitation and representing the home of two minority ethnic groups. But can it withstand increased visitation? A number of issues arise. First, access is by a narrow, often single-track road with no safety barriers along exposed cliff faces and hillsides. It is currently suitable for the low volume of traffic it receives but is not appropriate for increased traffic including buses. Substantial improvement to the road system will be required to make the journey safe. Second, the villages themselves are small, have limited water and electricity, and no public sewage system. No parking facilities are provided. The villages' infrastructure at present is barely capable of meeting the needs of local residents and certainly cannot meet the needs of tourists. Third, while community leaders hope the local community will become involved in small-scale enterprises, facilities are not up to international standards, hygiene conditions are poor, and the area suffers from a lack of human capital. Fourth, and most significantly, it is unclear how and to what extent tourism will affect the cultural integrity of the resident minority groups that live in the area.

sub-indicators to suit their local situation. Ideally assessors should have an arm's length relationship with the asset under consideration to ensure objectivity. Finally, the framework seems to work most effectively when small teams are deployed to assess assets. Each team member will bring his or her own perspective, bias, and interests. By working collaboratively, a small team is likely to come up with a more reliable recommendation than if an individual works independently.

A wide array of background information can be gathered prior to starting any evaluation. Details of ownership structure, management history, known cultural significance, available resources for interpreting the information, level of accessibility to the public, the existence of tourism products or nearby attractions, and an identification and evaluation of stakeholders who are likely to be involved in tourism, heritage conservation, and planning will help familiarize assessors with the asset in question, identify information gaps, and also help identify issues to be verified by the site visit. Information about cultural heritage values can be collated from government supported heritage agencies, public records offices, and libraries, and informants can help speed up the process. Information on the tourism sector sub-indicators can be collected from tourism association publications, tourism product information, guidebooks, and tourism sector reports. Site inspections fill information gaps and are essential to the completion of the assessment process.

Operationalization: a two step process

Operationalization involves two steps: an initial sequential audit using each dimension separately and an integrative review combining all value sets.

Step 1: sequential audit

Step 1 involves a sequential hierarchical evaluation of the asset according to each of the four dimensions, beginning with cultural values, and followed by physical values, tourism values, and experiential values (Figure 12.2). Criteria for each value set must be met in order to confirm tourism potential. For example, sites need to satisfy the cultural dimension first before physical values can be considered, pass the physical values dimension before tourism values become relevant, and then meet the product criteria before experiential values can be assessed

Failure at any stage indicates structural obstacles to the successful transformation of the asset to a product and therefore must be resolved before other elements can be met. The purpose of this initial assessment is therefore twofold. On the one hand, it will enable evaluators to identify fatal flaws that preclude the tourismification of the asset. On the other hand, it will help identify non-fatal but still fundamental deficiencies or issues that must be resolved before the asset has a chance of successfully appealing to tourists. For example, if unresolved stakeholder issues emerge in the cultural values stage, then they must be resolved or else the subsequent tourismification of the asset will lead to conflict and consumer dissonance. Likewise, if the asset does not possess the necessary product attributes required to be successful, then the quality of the experiential attributes becomes meaningless because tourists simply will not visit.

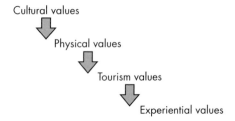

Figure 12.2 Sequential assessment tool

Application of this matrix among a number of smaller cultural heritage attractions yielded two important findings that affect the ability of most heritage assets to function as successful tourism products (McKercher and Ho 2006; Bjeljac et al. 2012). Most places satisfy the robusticity requirements of being culturally significant and able to withstand some increased visitation, with or without minor site modifications. However, the vast majority failed at the market appeal stage, due to either poor product or experiential values. (See Plate 12.6).

Indeed, most attractions had multiple tourism value flaws that collectively represented fatal flaws which effectively negated any potential for successful transformation into products, regardless of the amount of time, money, or effort invested. Remoteness (isolated from either tourism nodes or other attractions), weak access (infrequent public transit, poor signage, often needed/closed for use by other user groups and so on), lack of uniqueness (common), poor market access (many similar or better quality examples exist closer to tourism nodes), poor setting (in industrial parks), incompatible neighbouring land uses (in one case a piggery), and unresolved stakeholder issues (where tourism was imposed on unwilling custodians), individually, but more often in combination, were identified as fundamental structural obstacles that could not be overcome. (See Plate 12.7).

Plate 12.6 Tung Chung Gun Battery, China

Much built heritage satisfies the robusticity dimensions of possessing significant cultural values and being capable of withstanding increased visitation, as is the case of this 200-year-old gun battery in China that has been designated as a declared monument. However, many, if not most, of these places do not satisfy the market appeal dimensions of product and experiential values, limiting their appeal as attractions. In fact, many places have a combination of fatal flaws that render them non-attractions. Small scale, physical isolation, poor access, lack of complementary products or services, and limited ability to create an experience are among the range of fatal flaws that have been identified. In the end, the experience offered is too low to warrant the effort required to visit the site, especially if other more rewarding opportunities exist that are more readily accessible. Hence, success at the robusticity phase was negated by fatal flaws discovered later.

Plate 12.7 Crown Point Fort, USA

Many culturally significant buildings that satisfy the significance and robusticity criteria to be considered as cultural tourism products fail at the product level. Physical isolation, small scale, lack of surrounding tourism facilities, or perceived lack of uniqueness in the face of other more competitive structures hinder their success as tourism products. Crown Point Fort, located in upstate New York, is a case in point. Crown Point was the largest fort built by the British in North America. It was destroyed in the early 1800s when cinders from the fort's bakery ignited ammunition stored in the powder magazine, destroying part of the defensive wall. It was abandoned soon afterwards. While representing a magnificent piece of architecture, the fort never saw action, reducing its perceived significance. In addition, the nearby Fort Ticonderoga was the site of numerous battles between the English and the French, and later in the Revolutionary War. While Crown Point has been designated as a New York State historic site and has a museum with an award-winning multimedia presentation, it attracts relatively few tourists who are most likely to correspond to the profile of purposeful cultural tourists.

In addition, the relative competitiveness of small attractions proved to be challenging, again limiting their appeal (Laing et al. 2014). Significant experiential weaknesses were identified at smaller and more remote heritage assets compared to better known, better developed, and more accessible attractions, making it difficult for tourists to see the benefits of visiting. At best, they could be classified as supporting experiences that on their own do not have the ability to entice visitors but, if properly packaged and bundled, could complement higher order attractions. Improving product and experiential values by the introduction of thematic interpretation, better transport links to peripheral areas, the creation of self-guided trails to connect sites, and allowing public access on a regular basis to excavations might improve their appeal (Laing et al. 2014). (See Plates 12.8 and 12.9).

Step 2: integration

Completion of Step 1 will narrow down the full set of cultural assets into a smaller sub-set of those that have some tourism potential. Step 2 determines what that potential is and identifies a range of development and management actions to actualize that potential in a sustainable manner. In this step the Four elements are aggregated into their two core axes of market appeal and robusticity to classify each asset according to its potential. (See Figure 12.1).

'A' grade assets are heritage places with moderate to high market appeal and high (A1) to moderate (A2) robusticity. They are ideally suited for significant tourism activity because they possess features that appeal to tourists and also can withstand significant

Plate 12.8 Fort, Tung Chung, Hong Kong

The ability to provide a quality experience is the last element required before a cultural asset can be transformed successfully into a tourism product. Tung Chung Fort, located in Hong Kong, is culturally significant, robust, and has some features of interest to warrant a visit, yet offers little in terms of experience to entice tourists to engage with the attraction. There is no interpretation, the grounds are unkempt, and little of its story is presented.

Plate 12.9 Monte Fortress, Macau

By contrast, the Monte Fortress in Macau is a vibrant successful attraction. Interpretation is provided, tourists are encouraged to wander throughout the fort, a museum is located inside it, and various shopping and dining opportunities exist.

use levels. Only minimal to moderate conservation measures are required to protect the cultural values from the impact of heavy visitation.

'B' grade assets have high (B1) to moderate (B2) market appeal but are low in robusticity. Low robusticity may mean that the physical fabric of the asset is fragile or that its cultural values are sensitive to significant impacts by visitors. Tourists may show strong interest in visiting these places but because of their fragility the sites have limited ability to cope with intense use. Some tourism use will likely occur regardless of management activity. As such, the management challenge becomes one of ensuring that visitation does not damage the intrinsic values of the asset. In some cases visitation may need to be restricted or discouraged, while in other cases it may be possible to put conservation and visitor management measures in place that will allow greater tourism use to occur. Extreme options may also be considered for assets with exceptionally strong tourism appeal that are also exceptionally fragile. Tourism may be actively discouraged if it is felt the asset or its key non-tourism stakeholders could not cope with visitation. Alternatively purpose-built facilities located some distance from the asset may be considered, as has been done by the reconstruction of rock paintings at a visitors centre near the original Pleistocene rock art site at Lascaux in France. Rapidly evolving digital technology also may offer exciting alternatives to the real experience and may become the preferred option to present such assets to tourists in the future, for fragile assets with high market appeal.

'C' grade assets have moderate tourism appeal and have high (C1) to moderate (C2) robusticity. Two management options exist. Because these assets are robust, they may be able to withstand greater visitation levels than their current market appeal would suggest. A management approach to develop the asset's potential fully or to enhance the experience in order to widen its market appeal may be adopted. Alternatively, management plans may strive to maintain the status quo, with the recognition that tourism numbers will be limited.

'D' grade assets have low market appeal and are unlikely to attract significant visitation unless the asset is commodified to such an extent that its intrinsic values would be almost totally sacrificed. This type of assets should be managed for reasons other than tourism, other than perhaps for the small number of purposeful cultural tourists. The hard challenge may be to convince asset managers of their limited appeal.

The application of the matrix also offers guidance as to whether tourism or CHM should be the lead consideration in management decisions. Where the tourism potential is high and the asset is robust (A grade assets), perhaps tourism can take a leading role in the setting of management objectives. When the asset is fragile, however, CHM considerations must dominate, regardless of the tourism potential (B grade). Similarly, when tourism potential is low (D grade), there is little merit in identifying tourism as the lead management consideration, regardless of the level of robusticity. Where there is some tourism appeal and the asset is moderately to highly robust, opportunities exist for a more equal relationship between tourism and CHM objectives. Clarifying the objectives of assets will also help address stakeholder issues.

Conclusion: a precursor to site and experience management

The audit process also facilitates a community wide approach to facilitate the identification of key issues and the selection of possible management directions that will form the basis of the development of subsequent management plans. This issue is the focus of the next part of the book but is worth mentioning here. Application of the audit tools identifies five main options:

1   deciding not to identify tourism as an objective as the asset has insufficient market appeal;
2   selecting another asset for tourism use that is less costly to conserve or commodify;
3   continuing the development process with the original asset with a higher priority on conservation measures to better manage its cultural values in face of projected visitation;
4   continuing the development process with the original asset with a higher priority on commodification and tourism product design needs to boost or enhance market appeal;
5   continuing the development process with the original asset with equal emphasis on conservation measures and commodification/product design needs.

Key learning outcomes

- Not all cultural assets have what it takes to become successful cultural products. The Market Appeal/Robusticity Matrix provides a useful tool to assess tourism potential.
- Successful products must satisfy four criteria in order. They must be culturally significant, able to withstand increased visitation, have the attributes to attract and retain tourists, and provide a quality experience. If any element is missing, it must be resolved before other elements can be considered.
- Many heritage assets satisfy the robusticity requirements but few satisfy the product requirements. In fact, many have multiple fatal flaws.
- Once assets satisfy the criteria, then the matrix can be applied to identify where a product is likely to sit on the product hierarchy and what type of management actions are required.

Part E
Operationalization

13 Framework for understanding what is necessary for a successful attraction

Introduction

Chapters 10–12 identified what products are and how to evaluate product potential. A first step before planning a product or attraction at the destination level is to understand what is going to make it successful. This chapter reviews some of the factors that have been identified in successful attractions and discusses some of the development options available and proven tactics that lead to quality experiences.

Success factors

Government agencies have been publishing a variety of 'how to' manuals for more than 20 years to help communities, community groups, custodians, non-profit organizations, and nascent entrepreneurs become involved in cultural tourism. However, at the time of writing there has been relatively little research published critically reviewing the key factors that lead to successful product development. A Canadian-based consultancy group that specializes in cultural tourism has written about a 'willing-ready-able' continuum for product development (Lord 2002). An eight-point checklist was identified to help cultural tourism products determine their own level of readiness to enter the sector. These items include:

- perceived high quality of the product relative to other products;
- creation of awareness to draw attention to the product;
- creating a customer service culture by establishing policies and procedures that put the customer first and ensuring adequate training for front-line staff so that they are capable of delivering on that service promise;
- a long-term orientation towards sustainability, which is in harmony with the community's values and also has a commitment to maintain its own heritage and environment;
- an element of uniqueness or something special to enable tourists to do something different while on vacation;
- being convenient for tourists, including ease of purchase, adequate safe parking particularly for cars and buses, providing accessible washroom facilities, and offering advanced scheduling of events, exhibits and shows, etc.;
- ensuring strong community support for both the human and financial resources to ensure the community is a strong ally in reaching the tourist market, generating positive word of mouth publicity and influencing the choices of people visiting friends and relatives;

- a commitment to sound management and the ability to live to that commitment including the ability to develop marketing/business plans specific to target markets, source funding, and have the necessary human capital.

Jansen-Verbeke and Lievois (1999) identified three factors they deemed to be necessary for consideration for a successful transformation process for heritage assets to be successful tourist attractions. The spatial concentration of a cultural heritage asset is a key concern: the higher the spatial concentration the more attractive it is. In addition, they identify accessibility and tourist functions performed by the asset, where the tourist function depends largely on the accessibility for tourists as gauged by public access and opening hours and on the present use and function of the assets. Lastly, interaction and synergy between the tourist attraction and other tourism activities and supporting infrastructure, such as shops, restaurants, festivals, events, etc., are important to the successful transformation process.

Carlsen et al. (2008) and Hughes and Carlsen (2010) identified a total of nine factors focused primarily on commercial objectives, whose importance varied depending on the level of commercial focus of the enterprise. Critical success factors are identified in Table 13.1. In particular, the need for clear objectives, which are agreed upon and supported by the majority of stakeholders, emerged as a key consideration. This point reflects a number of related themes. First, the agreement on clear objectives ensures that all stakeholders buy into the decision to pursue tourism. In addition, it means that all are working towards the same outcomes. Carlsen et al. (2008) highlight the risk of failing to agree upon core objectives, for differences may lead to developments that are conceptually diverse, waste scarce resources and lead to internal conflict. It can also result in the delivery of a confusing experience for visitors, leaving them dissatisfied.

Table 13.1 *Critical success factors for cultural tourism products*

Business Focus	Agreed objectives & clear concepts	Financial planning	Marketing strategies	Monitoring markets & flows	HR management	Planning life cycle & value adding	Quality and authenticity	Expertise-conservation & promotion	Integrated interpretation
Strong Commercial Focus	X	X	X	X	X	X	X	X	X
Significant Commercial Focus	X	X	X	X	X	X	X	X	X
Moderate Commercial Focus		X	X			X	X		
Minimal Commercial Focus							X		

Source: adapted from Hughes and Carlsen (2010).

Financial issues also emerged strongly. Sufficient capital is required for conservation, needed maintenance, and ongoing operations. In addition, assets will have difficulty delivering quality experiences if adequate funding is not secured. Adequate funding, in turn, underscores two other core issues: the need to clearly understand the size of the potential market and its willingness to pay. Ultimately, the success of any business, even a not-for profit business, relies on balancing income with expenses. Assuming too high fixed costs through overbuilding for the actual market size is a sure recipe for failure. The second issue is price setting. Price has two dimensions. On the one hand, the price will dictate how much revenue is generated. On the other hand, price also reflects perceived quality. A price that is too low indicates the experience is poor and likely not worth participating in. But if the price is too high for the quality offered, tourists will complain.

Lynch et al. (2010) identified a further financial matter if funding to make up financial shortfalls comes from multiple sources. The case in question is specific to Aboriginal communities but it can also apply to other attractions where ongoing seed funding comes from multiple sources. In this case, the community relied on a combination of fundings from federal, provincial, and local sources but it appears there was little coordination among the three groups. The net result was financial uncertainty.

Hughes and Carlsen (2010) determined that cultural attractions with a strong commercial focus were most successful in achieving both financial and non-financial critical success factors and in ensuring their profitability over time. In particular, purpose-built attractions with clearly defined business plans, marketing strategies, and product development plans to renew the attraction on a regular basis were successful. Interestingly they were also able to maintain high quality authentic products, could bring in expertise in both conservation and promotion, and were most effective in presenting an integrated interpretive programme that focused on both education and entertainment. Calver and Page (2013) further remind us that entertainment and conservation priorities are not mutually exclusive but are complementary and with the active involvement of the visitor help co-create a desired experience. The traditional curatorial management approach to historic properties has evolved into a much more visitor-focused approach which seeks to actively attract, entertain, inspire, and in the process, perhaps, inform visitors.

Identification and achievement of financial goals become increasingly less important as the focus of the attraction moves towards the 'minimal commercial' end of the spectrum. Places with a moderate commercial focus still have to identify financial plans and establish product renewal policies. However, the emphasis on an overall master plan, marketing strategies, and the delivery of an integrated interpretive experience become less important. It seems that delivery of an authentic experience was the only factor that was important for those assets with minimal or no commercial focus. However, the ability of non-commercial attractions to achieve this goal may be limited, as minimally commercialized heritage experiences are also associated with low visitation levels and low to non-existent on the ground management. Indeed, one could argue that the ability of a cultural asset to attract tourists valorizes that attraction and, in doing so, stimulates ongoing management and conservation.

McKercher et al. (2004) also conducted an analysis of the attributes to popular built cultural attractions. As shown in Table 13.2, five interrelated factors – product, experience, marketing, cultural values, and leadership – emerged. In this study of issues relating to cultural tourism product supply, cultural heritage managers identified experience and marketing most frequently, with accessibility and the provision of a commodified experience playing the most important roles. This study found that the most popular attractions were readily accessible by public transit, were located in existing tourism nodes, and were sufficiently large to attract visitors. Purpose-built facilities were especially popular,

Table 13.2 *Attributes of popular cultural tourism attractions*

Category	Attribute
Product	Site
	Setting
	Scale
	Access
	Purpose-built or extant facility
	Complementary adaptive re-use
Experiential	Uniqueness
	Relevance to tourist
	Ease of consumption
	Focus on 'edutainment'
Marketing	Position
	Does the asset have tourism potential?
	Identification of viable market segments
	Place in attraction's hierarchy
	Product life cycle stage and ability to rejuvenate product life cycle
Cultural	Local vs. international social values
Leadership	Attitude to tourism
	Vision
	Ability to assess tourism potential realistically
	Ability to adopt a marketing management philosophy to the management of the asset

as the design of the facility could be built around the desired experience. Small remote attractions tended to be less popular. Edutainment emerged as the critical experiential factor where attractions that present themselves in an entertaining and educational manner proved popular. Indeed, one museum curator felt that attractions needed to incorporate elements of theme parks in their design, along with a greater moral obligation to ensure presentation was accurate and culturally sympathetic.

Marketing was another key factor, for the ability to clearly define target markets and to shape the experience to match the audience's needs was a major factor, especially if resources were limited. In particular, the need to dovetail the product's markets into the existing marketing mix of the destination was a key success criterion. As with Hughes and Carlsen (2010), the issue of product lifecycle also arose. Tourists may go to a museum or heritage asset once but are unlikely to return unless something different is offered on repeat visits. Again, like theme parks, the product mix needs to be continually upgraded. Lynch et al. (2010) identified awareness building as a further marketing consideration. Much native culture is invisible to the travelling public, with the lack of awareness exacerbated among small remote communities. More advertising is often called for to increase awareness. However, if fatal flaws exist that restrict the ability to deliver a product (and isolation and scale are two of the most important fatal flaws), no amount of advertising will reverse this situation.

Interestingly, local cultural significance seems to have less to do with success than the ability to shape the product in such a way that tourists can identify familiar factors from their home cultural background. Popular attractions need to transcend the local to have broad appeal. In many ways, this observation builds on Timothy's (1997) recognition of different levels of connectivity to cultural heritage. Assets with a very small, but deeply personal connection will draw relatively few visitors, while those that can touch on broader regional, national, or global themes have the potential to attract more people.

Finally, leadership is critical but it emerged rarely in the literature. While leadership can take many forms, the key feature here seems to be the willingness of key decision-makers to engage with tourism and to see tourists as a valued and highly sought-after visitor group. Leaders who expressed that view tended to adopt a stronger service orientation and ensured that the places they managed provided additional information and amenities to visitors.

Development options

The suite of potential cultural tourism products seems to be ever increasing as more and more destinations, non-profit organizations, custodians, and entrepreneurs enter the sector. A number of strategies exist to develop cultural heritage assets into cultural tourism attractions. They include:

* building a primary attraction (new or through adaptive re-use);
* packaging and bundling;
* clustering through the creation of tourism precincts;
* developing linear touring routes or heritage networks;
* rebranding/creating a specific cultural tourism area or network;
* events.

Building

Building a primary attraction is the dream of most community leaders. Some communities will do it successfully but many do not have the resources, innate tourism appeal, and proximity to major markets or themes around which an attraction can be built. Purpose-built primary cultural tourism attractions tend to be built along one of two themes: tourismification of the extant yet previously undeveloped heritage assets or building of purpose-built cultural or heritage theme parks. Opportunities exist to develop extant heritage assets, such as forts, penal colonies, abandoned mines, ghost towns, historic precincts of cities, and abandoned industrial assets into attractions. This strategy has certainly been used to great effect in many parts of the world (UNWTO 1995; Sletvold 1996; Costa and Ferrone 1998; Rudd and Davis 1998). Where such extant assets do not exist, an opportunity exists to purpose build heritage theme parks.

The costs associated with converting extant assets into tourism attractions and then securing ongoing funding for essential conservation work, coupled with the marginal economic returns if the location is isolated, are often prohibitive for the private sector. In such cases, the public sector is forced often to assume the role of developer and asset manager. This action is justified because of the broader community benefits derived (attachment to the past, educational opportunities, employment, economic stimulus) or because the attraction can act as a catalyst to stimulate private sector tourism development, including accommodation, shopping, and food services.

The private sector is more likely to invest in purpose-built theme parks that have a heritage flavour. The decision to enter this sector is based on business reasons, with profit and financial viability driving most decisions. Developers can choose an ideal location, rather than having to work with an extant structure. They can purpose build facilities to cater for the tourist's needs and, importantly, structure the experience in such as way as to maximize its appeal and optimize revenue generation opportunities. In many ways, purpose-built attractions provide a better quality, though clearly less authentic, tourist experience than extant facilities.

Packaging and bundling

Packaging is defined as a themed experience with two or more components that are sold formally by one vendor via one transaction for a fixed price (Failte Ireland 2012). Thorne (2008), for example, suggests that packages can include a hotel and admission to a special event, performance, or art exhibit to create an appealing one-off product. Their appeal lies in the one-stop shop approach, whereby the consumer can purchase all components in a simple single step. They are also appealing to the travel trade, for such packages usually include a commissionable component, enabling third parties (tour operators, travel agents, online retailers) to profit from their sale. In doing so, the package can be distributed more widely in the marketplace.

Clustering and precincts

The development of cultural tourism precincts represents an extreme form of bundling. Theatre, museum, historical, and ethnic districts provide a number of direct benefits to both the consumer and the provider. Concentration creates a critical mass of products that facilitates easier use by the tourist. In turn, larger tourist numbers provide enhanced business opportunities for ancillary attractions and service providers. In addition, strong consumer demand provides a powerful economic reason to protect and conserve heritage areas.

Clustering offers a number of benefits to consumers (MTC 2009). Tourists on limited time budgets appreciate the convenience of being able to visit many places or to experience many activities in close proximity to each other. The creation of a critical mass of attractions justifies travel time. In addition, most clusters or precincts are anchored by a primary or icon attraction that in and of itself will generate business. The presence of a large number of visitors creates opportunities for smaller complementary attractions and experiences. In doing so, clustering maximizes a range of individual attractions to create an overall cultural experience that serves as a destination motivator for the cultural tourist. (See Plate 13.1).

Linear or circular tours and networks

Increasingly, regional communities are realizing that, collectively, the sum of their cultural assets has greater tourism appeal than the individual assets alone (Rosenbaum 1995a; Stocks 1996). Opportunities also exist for destinations with similar or complementary cultural assets to work cooperatively for their mutual benefit (Morrison 1998). The creation of linear or circular touring routes linking different communities provides another low cost option for many destinations. Möller and Deckert (2009) indicate that successful cultural routes follow a geographically fixed course, focus on a defined theme or topic, and ensure that all components of the tour are compatible with that theme. They are then packaged to develop tourism offers that can encourage people to prolong their stay or travel more widely throughout a destination.

Tours can vary in format, type of provider, and scale. They include either guided or self-guided tours. Self-guided tours are easier to provide because the individual tourist can participate at his or her convenience and does not require other travel companions.

Plate 13.1 Kaiping *diaolou* (fortified houses), China

The clustering of assets can result in the creation of a tourism product where the value of the sum of the assets is much greater than the value of any individual asset. Clustering works best when clusters are in close geographic proximity. Kaiping, in southern China has over 1,700 *diaolou* (fortified houses) spread throughout the county. They were built mostly in the latter part of the nineteenth century and early part of the twentieth century when many of the men migrated overseas to work in gold mines or to build railways. The remnant population consisted largely of women, children, and seniors. This era in China coincided with the final years of the Qing Dynasty in the early years of the First Republic and was typified by lawlessness. In particular, warlords and gang leaders terrorized many citizens in southern China. In response, individual families or groups of families built fortified houses. The cultural significance of the Kaiping *diaolou* was recognized in 2007 when the area received World Heritage designation. Rather than listing all 1,700 structures, four clusters, each with individual characteristics (a streetscape, an abandoned village, a farming village, and an affluent family's compound), were identified that have since been developed as unique tourist nodes.

They can take a number of forms. For some, the tourist simply follows a map or interpretative guide that leads them from site to site. In other cases, the tourist can use a pre-recorded audio guide (Lade 2010), while in other instances still, they use their mobile devices to tag sites and gain an interpretive message. Alternatively, guided tours employ a docent or guide to lead the group. They are more costly and somewhat less convenient for the tourist, for guided tours have to depart at specific times. Travel agents and licenced tour guides provide these services on a commercial basis. But, as Snowden (2008) notes, many historical societies offer some form of heritage walk or tour as part of their promotional activities. (See Plates 13.2 and 13.3).

The scale varies depending on both the geographic configuration of the place being visited and the mode of transport used. Self-guided and guided tours are common in museums and art galleries. Walking tours usually lead people through interesting neighbourhoods or sites of historical interest. Bus day tours are usually confined to urban destination areas or their immediate hinterlands. Self-drive tours, on the other hand, can cover vast areas (Hardy 2003) and, in extreme cases, may involve multinational trips (Messineo 2012). Hardy (2003) has identified 10 'Ps' of successful touring routes. They include:

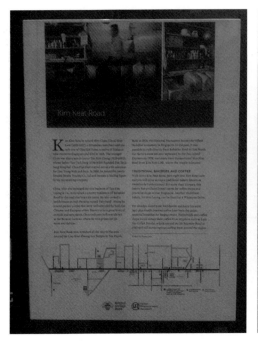

Plates 13.2 Singapore's Balestier Road Heritage Trail

Plate 13.3 Rickshaw puller refreshment stall on Heritage Trail

Heritage trails work best when they have good interpretative signage (Plate 13.2) and actual physical examples remaining of that heritage (Plate 13.3), not just so-and-so lived/was born in this place, which is now the site of a high-rise building. Taxi drivers still sometimes use the rickshaw pullers' refreshment stall pictured (Plate 13.3) because it offers free and fresh water supplied by a local charity.

1 Place: routes and their associated attractions must be interesting to the visitor.
2 Product: product development should focus on visitor satisfaction.
3 Promotion: promotional materials must be developed that are compatible with the target audience's needs.
4 People: stakeholders from the area must be involved right from the conception of the project through to its ongoing management.
5 Paraphernalia: sufficient information must be provided prior to and during the drive tourism holidays.
6 Path: a clearly defined path and clear signage along the route must be provided to enable the tourist to follow the path.
7 Presentation: since the touring routes are presented as a whole product, presentation must be consistent. Importantly, attractions must be compatible both in theme and quality to ensure visitor satisfaction
8 Principles of interpretation: consumers need interpretative material that not only informs the person of the features of the tour but also encourages them to become engaged in it. Interpretation should be enjoyable, relevant, organized, and, most importantly, thematic.
9 Price: tours must be cost effective for both those in charge of the ongoing maintenance and management of the route and the visitor.

10   Protection: a core principle for the development of themed touring routes is protection of natural and cultural heritage. Touring routes must have a reason to attract people and this will usually be either natural or built heritage.

Rebranding/creating a specific cultural tourism product area or network

This phenomenon is now becoming a more recognized strategy as online marketing and other Internet manifestations make it easier to operationalize. It is often more than just creating or bundling experiences, setting up a linear route or network in that the product takes on a whole new brand identity and image through strategic marketing. Even though this has been evident for other areas of tourism (e.g. Gold coast for sun and surf tourism in Queensland, Australia), it is just starting to become common in cultural tourism. The earliest examples known to the authors for cultural tourism are the US NHAs (see Plate 4.6 earlier) and the rebranding of Deqen Autonomous Prefecture as 'Shangri-la' in Yunnan, China.

The creation of the new cultural tourism branded area of 'Shangri-la' was the result of a clever and strategic marketing proposal made by Sri Lankan marketing consultant, Renton de Alwis, who was part of a UNWTO master planning team in 2000 (UNWTO 2001). The idea came about initially to solve a problem with Yunnan's overall destination brand image internationally for tourism. It achieved this aim by taking the existing concept of Shangri-la as a mythical Tibetan mountain paradise in western popular culture and then suggesting through strategic destination marketing promotion that it might be somewhere in the general area of Zhongdian city in Deqen Autonomous Prefecture (with a largely Tibetan population and heritage attractions). It may well be the case that it was not in this area, however, no better heirs to the title have been proposed. As no other area has been able to make a stronger claim, it has since positioned itself as being one of the strongest cultural tourism brands in China, putting the Prefecture and Yunnan on the map for tourism investors as well as tourists.

The Silk Road has also grown beyond its initial designated cultural connotations to evince a particular cultural tourism experience thanks to strategic marketing. Like many of the NHAs in America, it is also receiving a large amount of domestic self-drive tourism (du Cros and Ong 2011). Self-drive tourism together with strategic marketing often underpins the success of these large-scale cultural tourism product areas. It is likely that they can only become more prevalent as more people in emerging economies purchase cars and travel independently. Again, strategic online marketing can affect travel decisions both before and during these car trips. An array of new apps and ways to facilitate easy trans-border crossings are already being devised in developed countries, which will no doubt spread to others.

Artsipelago is an example of a cross-border arts heritage network that was developed for tourism for Eastport, Maine, and New Brunswick, Canada. It was developed to stimulate economic growth and arrest outmigration, while showcasing arts and indigenous heritage practices (Bowman 2013). Artsipelago is made up of many small arts and heritage attractions along the peninsula and coast of Maine (USA) and New Brunswick (Canada). By joining together into one larger product, more marketing and promotion is possible from which all players can benefit.

Through partnerships and working with other organizations like StudioWorks and Cultural Pass, new ideas are being developed to expand Artsipelago by the key facilitator, the Tides Institute and Museum of Art. There is still space for this product to grow in the cultural tourism marketplace, especially since it is the only funded arts product in Maine and the only network of its kind in the region. More is being done to facilitate easier border crossings and explore what kinds of experiences tourists from either side desire. Meanwhile, Artsipelago is perceived as having a lot to offer and has attracted substantial sponsorship and support from a diverse range of sponsors from both sides of the border (Tides Institute and Museum of Art 2012).

Accordingly, these products also need the support of extensive and strong partnerships between sectors and between destinations to succeed. Marketing is not enough if the supply of experiences does not meet demand, and that requires careful implementation to satisfy the needs of all stakeholders. Even so, this strategy can create a product category with lots of potential for sustainable cultural tourism.

Festivals and events

Festivals and events are de facto short duration primary attractions. Festivals serve to concentrate a wide array of activities into a condensed time frame, creating a critical mass of products for tourist consumption. Moreover, festivals and events enjoy a strong opportunity of becoming de facto branded products or of linking into well-known de facto brands and, in doing so, fostering positive brand associations. A jazz festival is branded as a jazz festival and will appeal to jazz lovers. Accordingly, interactive arts festivals with opportunities for hands-on experiences are important to destinations wanting to attract creative tourists as well as being seen as 'creative cities' or the like, as has been discussed in Chapter 7. (See Plates 13.4 and 13.5).

Plate 13.4 Swedish costumed performers

Mega events, including such sporting events as the world ice hockey championships held in Sweden, can be a catalyst for the provision of associated cultural activities and events. These events have the ability to draw international tourists because of their very nature, whereas events of a more local nature are unlikely to do so.

Plate 13.5 New Orleans Heritage and Jazz Festival children's mask workshop

At the festival, visual arts and local culture are promoted alongside performing arts. Children's art workshops, such as this voodoo mask painting one, are a useful way to engage non-local children in aspects of other cultures.

Categories for successful and sustainable arts events and activities include *inspirational events* for building creative (social, cultural, and human) capital; *affirming events* for encouraging links to cultural identity or heritage; *pleasurable events* that offer enjoyable recreational, leisure, and touristic experiences; *enriching events* that create opportunities for personal growth and/or to sell products or experiences and, finally, *celebratory events* that encourage cultural diversity. Monitoring the success of contemporary arts attractions requires us to be honest about what their intended market or orientation is likely to be. Table 13.3 positions certain types of arts events and activities in a grid in relation to four types of foci that are commonly found in the marketing and planning of most events. The grid allows for some overlap between those orientations that allow insiders as well as tourists and the public to participate. Accordingly some participants will have to pay to attend and others can attend for free depending on the key orientation of the event, namely, private sector that invests in/profits from the arts, arts industry professionals (non-producers), public, tourists or artist/performers. Finally, understanding more about an event's orientation or focus will help with identifying where the event is seeking its highest impact in terms of attracting the private sector, appealing to tourists, professional networking, artistic or community affirmation or building public awareness.

Assessing the performance, sustainability, and generation of creative capital of arts events is essential for both short-term and longitudinal monitoring of their success. Du Cros and Jolliffe (2014) have devised a framework for understanding how creative capital can be kept fresh and appealing to the key market or orientation for an event/activity.

Table 13.3 *Four main orientations of arts events and activities*

Commercial/private sector		Arts Industry
Investment, promotion, sponsorship, tourism opportunities, merchandising	International art fairs, award ceremonies, auctions	Networking, benchmarking/arts criticism, promotion, branding
International travelling exhibitions, city arts festivals, gallery hops, affordable arts fairs, popups, community arts events	Events with broad appeal that successfully balance all four focuses	Some international film festivals, biennales/biennials, graduating exhibitions/ performances
Appreciation, awareness, cultural exchange, education, cultural identity, community affirmation	Most fringe festivals, arts seminars/conferences, studio openings, creative tourism workshops and activities	Knowledge transfer, acknowledgement, networking, inspiration, artistic affirmation
Public/Tourists/public sector		Artist

Source: based on du Cros and Joliffe 2014.

The sustainable creative advantage of an event/activity is different from a sustainable competitive advantage found in most marketing literature. Arts attractions are not really the same as other attractions because of the way creative processes and capital are drawn. Arts ecologies work together in a way that is crucial to their success.

Overall creative advantage in this context is a two-way street. You have to be creative and consistent in helping others to help yourself. Asking questions about flow on effect, such as, 'how does or will the event provide benefits that flow onto the community and other sectors?' is important in understanding where to build mutual goodwill and important social capital in terms of connectivity with arts/cultural ecologies. Mapping or identifying multiple pathways of potential connections stemming from the event is important for finding potential partners and participants and ways to engage the latter, whilst offering something in return. Needless to say, this is more evident in community arts styled events that are free to the public and tourists than in events that are heavily orientated towards industry or commerce or artists and/or performers only. However, arts event organizers trying to focus on all four orientations must consciously examine these relationships and connections on a regular basis in order to ensure balance is maintained.

Creating memorable experiences

Successful cultural tourism attractions seem to share the features that are outlined in Box 13.1. Indeed, the Canadian Tourism Commission (CTC 2004) stresses the need to adopt these six features when transforming cultural and heritage assets into tourism products.

Tell a story

Cultural and heritage tourism places have been described as destinations with a story, with cultural tourism described as the process of telling that story (Cass and Jahrig 1998). Sometimes attractions are quite blunt or forthright about telling the story associated with

> ## Box 13.1 Features of successful cultural tourism attractions
>
> • Tell a story;
> • Make the asset come alive;
> • Make the experience participatory;
> • Focus on quality;
> • Make the experience relevant to the tourist;
> • Make it relevant to the tourist.

their product and sometimes they allow tourists to construct much of the story themselves from information presented (Latvia 2006). This is an oversimplification of cultural tourism, of course, but it illustrates the importance of interpretation and shaping the experience around a story that relates to the tourist's reference points. The story may be told in many ways and at many levels, through interpretation, signage, performance, interactive sites, technology, and the like, so that the consumer can choose how deeply to engage with the place.

Cultural assets have little meaning on their own unless their context or, for want of a better word, their story can be conveyed. The world is full old buildings. The world is full of museums. The world is full of evidence of historical or prehistoric occupation by ancient peoples. For the most part, these have little meaning to tourists whose knowledge of local history and culture may be minimal. Weaving a story around a place, a tangible asset, or an intangible asset instills that asset with some meaning, bringing it to life and making it relevant. It also creates consumer interest in hearing that story first-hand. Telling a story also provides signals as to how the tourist should interpret or use the asset. The choice of stories selected to be told also provides signals about what activities are acceptable or unacceptable at that asset.

Make the asset come alive

Telling a story makes the asset come alive and this makes discovering it more exciting for the tourist. The United States National Trust for Heritage Preservation states in its excellent little booklet about how to succeed in heritage tourism (NTHP 1999: 13) "the human drama of a history is what visitors want to discover not just names or dates. Interpreting assets is important, but so is making the message creative and exciting." Being entertained is an important part of most experiences. Having an enjoyable experience enhances visitor satisfaction but also, importantly, creates opportunities for learning either directly or indirectly. If the tourism experience is enjoyable and engrossing, the visitor will be motivated to spend more time at the attraction which will enhance his or her chance of consuming it at a deeper level. If, on the other hand, the presentation is dry and alienating, the visitor will not engage with the asset in any meaningful manner. (See Plate 13.6).

Make the experience participatory

Tourism by its very nature is an active, participatory experiential activity. The very nature of the physical plant of most cultural tourism attractions, such as museums, festivals,

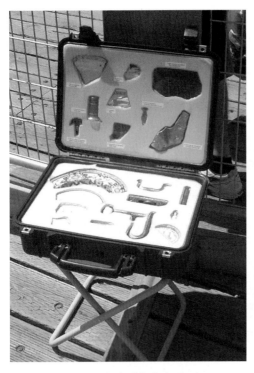

Plate 13.6 Archaeological finds in Quebec

Simple displays can make history come alive. Archaeological artifacts excavated at Quebec City, Canada are presented in a suitcase to provide a portable educational experience that can be relocated to different parts of the destination throughout the day. The "archaeological chest of drawers" from Fort Chambly, Quebec (right) and similar interpretative devices can be used to convey archaeological concepts to visitors.

historic assets, cultural assets, arts centres, should encourage participation. These experiences can be enjoyed best by wandering through the attraction and by engaging with it on a personal level. Providing opportunities to do so enhances the experience for the visitor. Lerkplien et al. (2013) note many monuments in Thailand that are open to tourists have little interpretation and on-site management. As a consequence, they are presented in a rather staid manner that encourages superficial consumption, rather than an opportunity to educate. By making the experience of the attraction or event participatory, managers/organizers also enhance the message absorption process.

Focus on quality

While quality has been assumed to be a critical element of any successful tourism product, it has emerged as an explicit theme among many government agencies that have prepared 'how to' manuals. Irish agencies encourage creating memorable moments (Failte Ireland 2012). Lord (2002) writes about developing experiences that satisfy the needs of the new emerging creative class, while Ashley et al. (2005) write about the need to think laterally to create added value in touristic experiences. Indeed, the whole idea of co-creation focuses on quality to produce experiential learning opportunities that meet the needs of tourists (Pedrotti 2012). Lack of perceived quality in the form of boring or tired exhibits, poor interpretation, amateurish presentation, has been identified as one of the many reasons why some places struggle to survive (Lade 2010).

Make it relevant to the tourist

Few people would argue with the first four features. However, it is important to appreciate who the story is being told to, for whom the asset is made to come alive, and who will engage with the asset. Cultural tourism attractions are first and foremost tourism products, and products exist to satisfy the needs, wants, and desires of consumers. As such, they must be made relevant to the person who will be consuming the attraction. That is, they must be presented in such a way that they relate to the tourists' knowledge and frame of reference. (See Plate 13.7).

Plate 13.7 Ibn Battuta Shopping Mall, Dubai, UAE

The Ibn Battuta Shopping Mall in Dubai is themed around the discoveries of this famous Muslim explorer and the technological discoveries that were made around the time of his travels. Each wing of the mall covers a different country he visited, which is also reflected in high quality interior design and handiwork. The mall was constructed with the regional Arab market in mind, although other tourists often find it fascinating.

The challenge is both to control the message and also to foster an image that will appeal to the desired type of visitor. Because of their status in the tourism hierarchy, and because of the nature of the tourism distribution system linking the consumer to the product, many cultural tourism attractions are many steps removed from the tourist when the decision is made to visit a destination. The result is that the message the tourist receives may be quite different from the message the attraction owners or managers would like the tourist to receive. This issue is explored in greater detail in Chapter 15.

Key learning outcomes

- Attractions need one or more of the factors discussed to be successful. In particular, attractions must give the tourist a reason to visit and in doing so offer a high quality experience.
- Although different success criteria have been identified for commercial and non-commercial attractions, adopting some commercial objectives (specific goals and so on) can be beneficial, even if the asset does not generate revenue.
- Six options exist to develop cultural tourism attractions including:
  - building;
  - packaging and bundling;
  - clustering;
  - rebranding;
  - developing touring routes or heritage networks;
  - events.
- Regardless of the type of cultural heritage asset considered, any successful attraction must:
  - tell a story;
  - make the asset come alive;
  - make the experience participatory;
  - focus on quality;
  - make it relevant to the tourist.

⟨14⟩ Applying planning and management frameworks

Introduction

So far, this book has discussed what cultural tourism is, how both CHM and tourism work, how to assess whether cultural assets have the potential to function as tourism products and, considering both robusticity and market appeal, where an asset fits into the attractions hierarchy. The task now is how to transform this information to create sustainable products that deliver high quality experiences. This task involves three final steps: planning for tourism, marketing the product in such a way that a suitable audience is attracted for the core experience provided, and delivering experiences. Chapters 14 and 15 address these topics. Since each asset is unique, each will require different planning, marketing, and experienced management treatments. However, the core principles remain the same.

Three operationalization scenarios exist, of which only one is sustainable. In one unsustainable scenario, the transformation of assets to products occurs organically. Subsequent management is reactive in nature. Small numbers of tourists discover places and begin to consume them. Word of mouth publicity spreads and more tourists begin to visit. The travel trade and local destination marketing organization observe this pattern and see an opportunity to develop the product further. Typically as well, the first group of tourists shapes the experience for later tourists. The travel trade and/or the DMO then further define or refine the core product and promote its benefits to potential consumers. The asset manager, if one exists, is then placed in a reactive position of having to cope with both increased visitation and associated unplanned impacts. In many instances, no formal manager exists, especially when cultural assets are seen as common property used by traditional stakeholders, creating an even greater challenge of how to manage the asset and control the experience. The end result is often a loss of control over the site, the message conveyed about the expected experience and how the place is consumed.

A second, also unsustainable scenario is more proactive in nature. Asset managers, local custodians, NGOs, and business people feel an asset has tourist potential but grossly overestimate the size of the market, the asset's position in the attractions hierarchy, and its competitive advantages. Large sums of money are invested to develop it. However, insufficient visitor numbers are generated to cover day-to-day operational and longer-term maintenance costs, resulting in either bankruptcy or the need for ongoing public funding to keep the product operational. Scarce resources are spent promoting this asset, to little avail, because its fundamental flaws mean that it will never succeed. Worse still, resources may be diverted from other areas to prop up this asset. And, as discussed previously, lack of resources means necessary maintenance and conservation works cannot be undertaken, resulting in the progressive deterioration of the asset.

The third, sustainable scenario involves a realistic assessment of the asset's tourism potential, as considered from both a robusticity and market appeal perspective. From here, management plans are developed that include both conservation and use. A core product is identified that is compatible with the asset's values and target markets are identified that can appreciate the asset. A quality experience is then shaped to reflect both the core product and the market's needs. The development of formal management plans are often mandated as part of the CHM process at larger sites, or those sites that are designated in the global or national heritage list. Management plans, also referred to as business plans, are also usually developed at larger purpose-built cultural tourist attractions, and also for many festivals and events, especially if funding from public sector organizations is sought. Many successful smaller attractions may not have formal plans per se, but that does not mean they have not undertaken a planning process. The individual business person, asset manager, or traditional custodian may have developed informal plans that mirror more formalized ones, even if they are not written down.

Planning

Planning by its nature is an iterative process, which often requires revisiting certain elements as the plan changes or initial conditions change. In a cultural tourism context, especially, effective planning is a consensus building exercise that seeks to include and assuage as many stakeholder concerns as possible, while also building partnerships between previously disparate groups. It is for this reason that cultural tourism planning is such a challenging task. However, by identifying CM and tourism concerns at an early stage, a balance can be created that can be maintained throughout the development and management of the attraction.

Embarking on the planning process can happen at any time during the life of an asset, however it is of most use and is most likely to be endorsed by all parties during the initial lifecycle stage, when it is in the process of being converted from its 'raw state' to the 'cooked' as an attraction. It is at this stage that some fundamental questions need to be resolved, such as: What options should be examined before converting the asset into a sustainable tourism attraction?; Who should lead the planning and management process?; and, How should the key stakeholder group that actually controls the asset work with the rest to reach an acceptable balance between tourism and conservation concerns?

Many approaches to planning exist and many different terms are used but, ultimately, planning should have one main goal: to move a place/asset/business/event/destination from its current position to a more favourable position in terms of sustainability, experience, financial rewards, community acceptance, or whatever other goals have been identified. A strategic approach adopts a longer-term orientation to achieve specific goals, by answering three questions: Where are we now?; Where do we want to be in the future?; and, How do we get there? (Donohoe 2012). This course of action is rare in the cultural tourism sector, as numerous studies have identified 'short-termism' as a significant barrier to the development of the field (Baker and Cameron 2008; Chhabra 2009; Mansor et al. 2011, Failte Ireland 2012). Kotler and Armstrong (2003: 23) add that applying a marketing management perspective involves the analysis, planning, implementation, and control of programmes designed to create, build, and maintain beneficial exchanges with target buyers for the purpose of achieving organizational objectives. Within the context of cultural tourism, organizational objectives can include financial and non-financial goals to differing degrees, depending on the nature of the asset in question, ownership, and overall objectives.

McKercher and Ho (2003) conclude that adopting a marketing approach enables cultural heritage asset managers to:

- develop a deep knowledge of the factors that can adversely affect the sustainable use of the asset;
- use this knowledge to identify broad goals for managing the asset in a sustainable manner;
- develop assets as products to achieve these goals;
- identify and implement a range of tactics to ensure the goals are met;
- identify optimum visitation levels that will allow the asset to be used sustainably (not too low, not too high);
- identify the preferred type of visitor for the type of experience offered;
- establish a clear market position to reach these target audiences;
- signal the desired message about the asset to potential users and communicate the desired message clearly to the target audience;
- set expectations of appropriate behaviour;
- control the tourist's movement on site.

Likewise, many different planning models have been devised, some with a stronger commercial focus and others with a stronger conservation focus (see, for example, Pedersen 2002; DEA 2004; English Heritage 2011; Bandarin and van Oers 2012; UNWTO 2012; UNESCO et al. 2013; Heritage Preservation 2014). They all share a number of features in common. Simplified, the planning process involves the following steps:

- background research and documentation;
- a realistic assessment of the current situation, including an internal and external analysis;
- stakeholder consultation (undertaken at all stages);
- specialist studies, as needed;
- a realistic assessment of the asset's potential to function as a tourism product and what measures are needed to achieve that potential;
- identification of options and the selection of the most feasible;
- establishment of a mission or vision;
- establishment of quantifiable and assessable goals and objectives;
- creation of specific action plans to achieve the goals and objectives;
- establishment of an evaluation and feedback mechanism to monitor achievement of the plans' objectives.

The first five steps have been addressed in detail, culminating in the application of the Market Appeal/Robusticity Matrix that should set broad management parameters and identify possible use strategies. However, many development opportunities present themselves within these broad parameters. The next step is to identify the possible options and then select the one that is in the best interests of the asset and its stakeholders. At this stage, social and physical capacity, the willingness and ability of both the asset and its current users to cope with increased visitation, and their willingness and ability to accept some change to the current use to meet the tourists' needs must be of paramount consideration. In particular, consideration of the total visitor numbers, visitor flows, and the impacts of seasonal or daily peaks in visitor numbers must be considered. When assets have a clear financial orientation, the ability to generate sufficient income and an acceptable return on investment must also be considered. This step may involve presenting and evaluating a number of use scenarios for consideration. Typically, scenarios represent low, medium, and high use, or low, moderate, and high commodification. Each is assessed against the likely positive and negative impacts. (See Box 14.1).

Box 14.1 Online planning resources

- Alliance for National Heritage Areas, USA: http://www.nationalheritageareas. us/sustainability
- Department of Environment Australia (DEA), Steps to Sustainable Tourism: http://www.environment.gov.au/resource/steps-sustainable-tourism
- European Union Cultural Heritage Management research agenda network: http://www.jpi-culturalheritage.eu/2014/02/strategic-research-agenda-sra
- Getty Conservation Institute: http://www.getty.edu/conservation
- Heritage Preservation, USA: http://www.heritagepreservation.org/CAP/index. html
- Heritage Victoria, Protecting Local Places: http://www.dpcd.vic.gov.au/__data/ assets/pdf_file/0005/44474/Protecting-Local-Heritage-Places.pdf
- ICOMOS bibliography: http://www.icomos.org/en/the-researcher-s-corner/ thematic-bibliographies
- ICOMOS and UNESCO manuals, see reference list and websites such as: http:// whc.unesco.org/en/tourism
- National Park Service, USA: http://www.nps.gov/index.htm
- Organization of World Heritage Cities: http://www.ovpm.org/en/ compilation_case_studies_conservation_and_management_historic_cities
- Sustainable Preservation (archaeology): http://sustainablepreservation.org/ about-us
- Sustainable Tourism Online: http://www.sustainabletourismonline.com/ parks-and-culture

Many social media pages can also provide a useful link to access free and useful information on current principles and practices, such as ICCROM's Conserving Culture: Promoting Diversity: https://www.facebook.com/iccrom

Good case studies of conservation planning and implementationcan be found at UNESCO Asia-Pacific Awards for Cultural Heritage Conservation at: http://culture360. org/news/unesco-asia-pacific-awards-for-cultural-heritage-conservation-call-and-special-publication/#sthash.XSj4dM0L.dpuf

---

Situation analysis

Once consensus has been reached about the desired uses of the asset, then more detailed strategic marketing decisions need to be made about whether and how the asset can compete in a crowded tourism marketplace to deliver these desired goals. Conducting such a situation analysis is an important, but often neglected step in the planning process (Chhabra 2009). As Colbert (2013) notes, in order to succeed, an organization must have a clear understanding of the structure of its market and then adapt to that structure. It is important to understand how the product is perceived by consumers, as well as how it is perceived in relation to competitors' products and, finally, how it is understood relative to its target market segments. In addition, it is important to have a clear understanding of its own internal strengths, weaknesses, and limitations. The failure to acquire this fundamental knowledge heightens the risk of inefficient allocation of resources, over or underestimating the size of the market and, importantly, failing to shape the experience in a sustainable manner. Much of what has been discussed in this book relates directly to the ability to conduct effective situation analyses.

In essence, the situation analysis should be able to answer the following six questions:

- Which products do I choose to offer?
- Which products do I choose not to offer?
- Which markets do I choose to target?
- Which markets do I choose not to target?
- Which competitors do I choose to compete against?
- Which competitors do I choose to avoid?

No product, asset or destination can be everything to everyone. Instead, hard decisions must be made as to how to shape the product and position it in the most favourable way in the marketplace. The first two questions above go to the heart of this issue by forcing stakeholders to consider the core product to be offered and, by extension, the core products not to be offered. As a general rule of thumb the deeper the experience represented by the core product, the smaller the market, while the shallower the experience, the potentially broader the appeal of the asset. But also remember that toothpaste analogy, where essentially similar products can be positioned uniquely in the marketplace by identifying different core attributes.

The decisions made here will influence the next two sets of questions, defining which markets to pursue and which competitors to compete against. These decisions, in turn, will be informed by the position of the product in the attraction's hierarchy, its geographic location within the destination in general, and in proximity to other products in particular, and the resources available to achieve the desired goals.

Ultimately, scenario development and market analysis will identify the optimal or most feasible option available. This task may be time-consuming and controversial as different stakeholders may have different views but it is an essential step for it ensures consensus, buy-in from stakeholders and, most importantly, it will set the course of action for the development of subsequent business, management, marketing, and experience delivery plans.

Establishment of an overall mission or vision and goal getting

Elucidating a clear mission or vision for the asset is much more easily said than done, but until it is achieved the rest of the planning process cannot proceed. The mission or vision must be compatible with the nature of the asset. It is as important to decide what the asset is not, what it will not offer in terms of experience, and what type of tourist it will not be shaped for, as it is to decide what its core product, market, and message are. This phase will require input from the previous ones – particularly any value-based or use assessment, the audit of its tourism potential, and situation analysis.

The vision, in turn, needs to be formalized into a set of goals and/or objectives that can then be used to evaluate if the vision has been achieved. Goals must be SMART: specific, measurable, attainable, realistic, and timely. Goals are the benchmarks by which the success or failure of a cultural tourism product will be assessed. Unless they are specific and their attainment measurable, it will be impossible to determine how well the asset is performing. In addition, it is recommended that interim or milestone goals be identified so that organizations can assess how well they are performing during the life of the plan and how likely they are to achieve their targets. The failure to meet milestone goals may necessitate a revision of the plan. Likewise, exceeding milestones may not necessarily be good news, especially if they relate to visitor numbers at sensitive attractions. Again, if milestones are exceeded, the plan will need to be modified.

Goals can include but are not limited to:

- financial goals, such as return on investment, income, gate receipts, ancillary sales receipts, net profit, reserves for conservation work, etc.;
- non-financial goals relating to social well-being, conservation of the asset, capacity building, etc.;
- experiential goals relating to desired learning outcomes, and so on;
- asset management goals relating to setting ongoing maintenance schedules and levels of use, and whether a broader social responsibility role will be fulfilled.

Creation of action plans

Once goals are established, action plans can be developed to ensure they can be achieved. Such plans may include conservation and monitoring of assets during development, actions for presenting an asset, marketing responsibly, accommodating key or special users other than tourism, avoiding or mitigating negative impacts, and continued consultation and involvement of key stakeholders. Clearly all of these plans work towards the accomplishment of the same sets of goals and so care must be taken to ensure that they are integrated and compatible. As has been identified earlier in the book, marketing is an important management tool and has to be closely linked to the overall planning of the attraction in relation to use patterns, supply, and demand. This integration of all the work undertaken for a planning study should reflect a balanced and strategic view in the creation of action plans and their measures without duplication or gaps.

Action plans can take many forms but usually involve the creation of some type of master plan. While the names may vary (management plan, conservation plan, business plan, etc.), each should have a number of component parts developed in a holistic manner that work towards the achievement of the broader goals. Much has been written about business plan development and many fine resources are available on this topic. As this book is not a small and medium business planning manual; business plans will not be discussed here formally. However, some attention will be placed on marketing, since the ability to manage the market is critical to the ability to manage the experience.

Marketing

Marketing is defined as a social and managerial process by which individuals and groups obtain what they need and want through creating and exchanging products and value with others (Kotler and Armstrong 2003). Hsu et al. (2008) note organizations that adopt a marketing orientation must understand and meet the real needs of customers and be able to create customer value in order to survive and succeed in a competitive environment. In essence, marketing is all about matching markets with products or matching products with appropriate markets to enable organizations to achieve their financial and non-financial goals.

Many people equate it with sales when in reality sales and marketing are quite different. Sales essentially involves pushing products onto consumers with the goal of maximizing revenue. Marketing, on the other hand, begins with an understanding of the consumer's needs and then shapes products or experiences to satisfy those needs. Importantly, a marketing orientation is something that must be coordinated throughout the entire organization so that everyone involved is working towards common goals. Marketing is, therefore, or should be, an integral part of the overall management process used to develop facilities and services as tourism products, identify potential travellers and their needs and wants, price their products, communicate their appeal to target markets, and deliver them to their customers' satisfaction, in compliance with organizational goals (American Marketing Association as modified by Richardson 1996).

While adopting a marketing approach means considering assets as products, it also means acknowledging that some types of visitors are more desirable than others. Indeed, managing demand is one of the key goals of marketing (Colbert 2013). Many of the adverse impacts noted in cultural tourism are a direct result of the failure to adopt a marketing management perspective, rather than because of adopting one. As a result of failure to identify clearly the core product, the target market, financial and non-financial objectives, and a plan of action to achieve them, mixed messages can be sent to the travelling public. Consequently the 'wrong' type of person expecting the 'wrong' type of experience is likely to be attracted to the asset, which in turn forces asset managers to present their products in an inappropriate manner to satisfy consumer demand.

However, this task is more easily said than done. Sangpikul (2010) and Mansor et al. (2011) identify the lack of marketing skills among small to medium operators in developing Asian economies. The Irish tourism body, Failte Ireland (2012), adds that most providers of cultural products are either small businesses or operate on a not-for-profit basis. They have limited staff, often tasked with multiple challenges including marketing, and even more limited budgets. A second problem is that few cultural tourism attractions have formalized marketing plans with clearly stated goals and objectives, and when they do they usually fail to include external environmental (Chhabra 2009) or competitor analyses (Failte Ireland 2012; Snowden 2008) to evaluate their position in the marketplace. Snowden (2008) and Tracy (2004) add that for any product to be viable, it needs to be competitive, especially given that there are many possible destinations to choose from and, within a given destination, many possible activities are available. A third factor is that destinations are obsessed with visitor numbers, rather than providing quality experiences. While they talk about quality experiences, the volume of visitors and its subsequent economic impact are usually indicators by which they measure success. Quality of experience falls somewhat lower on the list. Thus, at a macro level, much marketing activity is directed at maximizing visitation.

Cultural tourism has a number of unique features that both pose challenges to marketers and also highlight the importance of considering marketing in the planning process. Non-financial objectives often have an equal or stronger role in the overall set of objectives than financial goals. Conservation, education, awareness building, creating pride in one's past or even religious contemplation may be more important objectives than visitor numbers or financial gain. In fact, increased visitor numbers may actually work against the achievement of non-financial goals. Further, when considering the entire spectrum of cultural tourism attractions, only a small number are operated as viable business concerns. Most either generate no direct revenue from tourism or charge a nominal entry fee as a means of trying to recover some costs to augment private and public sector operating grants.

A second feature is that tourists and local residents share the asset, creating the need to be cognizant of both external (tourist) and internal (local residents) markets. Part of the balancing act in developing cultural tourism products from extant cultural heritage assets is to gain community support for the tourismification of the asset, while at the same time ensuring that tourism use does not compromise the needs of local user. Baker and Cameron (2008) identify stakeholder involvement as one of four key elements in successful destination marketing and stress the importance of meaningful involvement of the local residential and business communities. Yet Chhabra (2009) concludes that most heritage tourism plans fail to emphasize the need to build relationships with the community as a core objective.

The third unique element is that many cultural or heritage asset managers fail to appreciate that their facilities are, indeed, tourist attractions and, therefore, must be managed, at least in part for tourism use. This circumstance is especially true if the asset is open to the public at no charge (such as historic houses, churches, temples) or is operated as a non-profit community service (community museums, historic buildings). Management must be convinced of the asset's role in the tourism hierarchy before marketing issues can be considered.

A word on demarketing

Demarketing is a term that appears in debates about managing demand. It can be a critical function of marketing and the ongoing management of an attraction (Colbert 2013). A range of management actions can be introduced to control the volume of visitors so that the physical or experiential thresholds are not exceeded. Price, obviously, is one option available, where the price charged can reflect the scarcity value of the place being visited. High prices may deter some people from visiting. Variable pricing may encourage visitation at some times of day, days of the week, or seasons, while discouraging visitation during peak times. But other less dramatic options exist, including setting daily or hourly quotas, admitting people on a lottery system, managing behaviour in the site to ensure that existing tourists do not damage the fabric, etc. Even such actions as purposefully limiting the size of car parks and limiting bus parking spaces may reduce the volume of visitors.

These and other actions fall into the broad category of demarketing, Fullerton et al. (2010) reviewing the literature identify three different types of demarketing. General demarketing seeks to reduce the level of total demand; selective demarketing seeks to reduce demand from certain market segments; while ostensible demarketing gives the appearance of wishing to reduce demand as a result of scarcity, which actually stimulates greater demand based on increased scarcity value. Essentially demarketing seeks to discourage consumption or encourage people to stay away from certain places or at certain times of day (Donohoe 2010). Boddy (2013) discusses how destination marketing organizations have adopted demarketing to dissuade rowdy tourists from visiting Mediterranean destinations and how the organizers of the 2012 London Olympics tried to dissuade domestic tourists from visiting London during the games in order to ease congestion worries.

Reverend Canon Brett adopts such a marketing approach with Canterbury Cathedral in England. He indicates that careful and accurate description of the character of the site and of the desired message site managers wish to promote will do much to attract the visitor who has the right kind of interest in the cathedral (Brett 1999). He holds that "good marketing can be a useful means of selection [of appropriate visitors] which can help with problems of sustainability at high-profile attractions". The Department of Canadian Heritage in Parks Canada has also used marketing to try to influence demand for services and to direct the message conveyed by the travel trade to the consumer (Whytock 1999).

While it is a legitimate management strategy, demarketing is often difficult to put into practice given the mixed mandate of many publicly funded cultural assets, the fact that many are offered free of charge, thus negating pricing as an option, and the fact that many people feel a legitimate right to access their shared collective heritage. One example would be the specially reconstructed Baroque period theatre in Cesky Krumlov, Czech Republic, where visits can only be made by appointment and by providing evidence of expertise in this area of the performing arts (see Plate 14.1). Tourists can visit it on the national heritage open day once a year. Likewise, the government house in Hong Kong is only open once a year to visitors, and locals are preferred over tour groups. In these cases, the potential demand is likely to be high and beyond what the assets' managers feel able to deal with given these places are not purpose-built for tourism. In such situations, Cochrane and Tapper (2006: 99) have observed, "the presence of visitors can threaten the integrity of ecosystems, of fragile buildings or other cultural artifacts, or the 'spirit of place', which is often a hugely significant element of the site".

Plate 14.1 Cesky Krumlov Theatre, Czech Republic

This Baroque period theatre is actually an intricate reconstruction of the type of facility that would have been in the town's castle during that time. It is quite fragile in nature (for instance, some of the theatre props, such as the one pictured) so that the theatre managers only open it to tourists if they make a special appointment and show that they have a background in Baroque theatre. Alternatively, tourists can wait for the town's annual heritage day when all private and restricted buildings are open to the public.

Evaluation and feedback mechanisms

Evaluation and feedback mechanisms form the last step of the current planning process and the first of the next planning round. These devices enable the asset managers to track success towards the achievement of stated goals. All aspects of the attraction's performance can be measured. Which ones are selected will depend on the core needs of the asset and the resources available. As a minimum, the effectiveness of the experiential aspects of the attraction should be assessed through visitor satisfaction surveys, monitoring of social media, or other mechanisms. As well, tourism impacts should be monitored by employing longitudinal studies of the kind described in Chapter 3 and sections in this book on marketing analysis.

Finally, it should be noted that the work does not stop once an asset is developed to its full potential for cultural tourism. Business models and budgetary planning should take into account the behind-the-scenes costs of maintenance, improvements to interpretation, asset presentation, staff training, and other ongoing expenses. Most responsible professionals recognize this fact, but it should be emphasized clearly in the master plan that management and care of an attraction is an ongoing process.

Key learning objectives

- The planning process involves ten steps.
- A range of options needs to be developed from which the best or most suitable can be chosen.
- Once selected, SMART goals need to be defined that include both financial and non-financial considerations.
- Action plans will deliver on these goals, with clear benchmarks set to monitor success.
- Marketing is a powerful tool to manage demand. In some cases, demarketing is a useful and desired management action.

15 Experience creation

Introduction

Why is it important to talk about experience creation rather than interpretation of cultural values? Interpretation has not become any less important, but it forms just one aspect of the total experience delivered to the visitor. Hopefully that experience is special enough for messages about cultural values to have been conveyed, creating the opportunity for further self-reflection after the visit. It has been suggested that creating an overall favourable experience and engaging visitors with educational/thought provoking messages is achieved through the provision of a series of positive micro-experiences from the beginning to the end of the visit (Law 1999). Brett (1999) indicates micro-experiences that add up to a 'Golden Memory' should be a key objective in planning and management frameworks. Hence, service encounters, the nature of facilities and their management, ambience, lighting, personal comfort and safety, and so on all play a role in visitor engagement. Tactics that take into account the nature of visitor experience, as well as an understanding of basic human nature, are more likely to be successful with tourists. This chapter outlines such tactics first and then deals with interpretation issues and techniques for conveying messages for this reason.

Tactics to create peak experiences

Box 15.1 identifies a number of tactics that are available to create peak experiences. The tactic or tactics chosen will depend on a combination of factors relating to the physical and emotional characteristics of the asset, the desired CHM goals, the desired experience to be provided, and the existing knowledge or level of awareness of the asset and the tourist. These factors are interrelated. Accordingly the existing knowledge or level of awareness of visitors influences their behaviour, which may directly or indirectly influence management activities. Well-known assets, or assets that have a strong position in the consumer's mind, will predispose the visitor to an expected experience and thus to expected behaviour. The expectations for the known assets will be much lower, while tourist behaviour will be less predictable at places that fall outside visitors' normal frames of reference.

Mythologize the asset

Mythologizing an asset transforms it from the mundane to the extraordinary and converts a physical asset into a place of spiritual or secular significance. Two tactics are available when mythologizing an asset: tying it to existing myths, or creating a new myth. The first

> ### Box 15.1 Tactics available to create cultural tourism attractions
>
> - Mythologize the asset;
> - Build a story around the asset;
> - Emphasize its otherness;
> - Show a direct link from the past to the present;
> - Make it triumphant;
> - Make it a spectacle;
> - Make it a fantasy;
> - Make it fun, light and entertaining;
> - Make it unique.

option is easier, for national myths tend to be known and are often focused around precise geographic locations. It is, therefore, easier to create an association between a place and an existing strong myth. Creating new myths is difficult unless there is some form of mass media promotion of the myth or the destination has undergone a paradigmatic social or political shift away from existing myths. One example is the way the daily military exercise of taking down the flags on both sides of the border between India and Pakistan has been turned into a successful tourism attraction.

Plate 15.1 Robin Hood, Nottingham, UK

The legend of Robin Hood plays a key role in the marketing of Nottingham, UK.

Build a story around the asset

Alternatively, if the asset does not have the potential to be mythologized, yet is interesting nonetheless, it is possible to build a story around it that will make a visit enjoyable. The story may be based on historic fact or may be based on a fictional character known from popular culture. It matters little, just as long as it is a good enduring story. One attraction that presents a particular narrative about a married couple in politics that want to leave a certain kind of legacy is the William J. Clinton Presidential Library and Museum, Little Rock, Arkansas (Clinton Library 2014).

The library and museum are part of a tradition of valourizing American presidents with titular cultural facilities as a service to history, the community, and mostly domestic tourism. The library has temporary exhibitions on a range of political topics or more personal topics (e.g. presidential pets), as well as the permanent exhibition on the Clintons that includes a reconstruction of the Oval Office in the White House and a display of political memorabilia. The basic story told about the couple is very different from what appeared in popular media during the Clinton presidency, and is popular with pro-Democrat visitors, with some aspects that even appeal to children. Hence, the narrative tries to incorporate some informal as well as formal moments from the presidency in the experience. (See Plates 15.2 and 15.3).

Plate 15.2 Reproduction Oval Office, William J. Clinton Presidential Library and Museum, Little Rock, Arkansas, USA

Plate 15.3 Intentionally humorous audio-visual presentation, William J. Clinton Presidential Library and Museum, Little Rock, Arkansas, USA

The library's highlights are a reconstruction of the White House's presidential Oval Office (Plate 15.2) and a video of Hillary Clinton undertaking a humorous self-portrayal in an audio-visual display (Plate 15.3).

Emphasize its otherness

A third tactic available is to emphasize the otherness of a place in terms of the tourist's frame of reference. This tactic is used in domestic tourism destinations to highlight differences from the core culture. It has proven to be especially effective when promoting the cultural diversity of ethnic minority groups (Cave et al. 2003) or diasporic neighbourhoods (Conforti 1996). Darling Harbour, Sydney, is a purpose-built tourism attraction and leisurescape within the remains of a historic dockland. Close to Sydney's Chinatown area is a section given over to the Chinese Garden of Friendship (see Plate15.4) (Darling Harbour Authority 2014).

Show a direct link from the past to the present

History comes alive when a direct link between the past and present can be established. Heritage theme parks are popular tourist destinations because they show a direct link from a region's historic origins to its current status. The presentation is often idealized or fictionalized, concentrating different historical eras or events into a confined space. But they are popular because they allow tourists to consume a wide array of experiences designed specifically for them at one venue. (See Plate 15.5).

Plate 15.4 Chinese Garden of Friendship, Darling Harbour, Australia

Chinese people were the earliest Asian immigrants to Australia post-European settlement in the nineteenth century and have a long-standing relationship with Sydney. The Garden is popular with international tourists who also visit other cultural attractions in Darling Harbour, Sydney, such as the Powerhouse Museum of Arts and Design and the Maritime Museum. The appeal of this purpose-built garden is that it showcases the Chinese tradition of landscaped water gardens in an Australian context, while allowing a shared space for tourists and the local Chinese who enjoy and are encouraged to add to its ambience by holding weddings there.

Plate 15.5 Artifact display, Jerusalem

Sometimes opportunistic learning experiences present themselves, as in the case of this display of artifacts found when a convention centre in Jerusalem was being built. The site is located over a former Roman garrison. The foundations of the garrison can be viewed from above through a glass floor in the convention centre, or from below by entering the basement. Selected artifacts of interest are hung on the walls.

Make it triumphant

Making a place triumphant or extraordinary sets it apart from other, more common places. If the place can be made triumphant, then visiting it assumes more importance than if it is seen to be common. There are literally hundreds and thousands of battlefield sites around the world. The ones that stand out tend to be those places where turning points in wars ensued (Waterloo, Hastings, Quebec, Bull Run, Bunker Hill). The assets people are aware of and therefore want to visit are those that are most spectacular, either in terms of their historical impact or in terms of sheer human carnage (see Plate 15.6). Parks Canada, for example, commemorates certain historical events as part of the act of presenting the cultural values associated with its historic parks.

Ironically, places of defeat, failure or incredible human suffering can achieve a similar status providing its scale is exceptional. Here size or historical significance does seem to count. Little Big Horn is spectacular because of the sheer scale of the defeat suffered by General Custer. Nazi death camps have achieved status as cultural tourism attractions partly because of the scale of the atrocities committed by Hitler but also because of the triumph of the human spirit in surviving such horrendous conditions. To succeed, though, these places have to be presented in a manner that conveys the horror of the past within a contemporary context that is peaceful and hopeful. Thus, for example, battlefield sites are presented in a peaceful park-like manner even though they were the scene of mass death.

Plate 15.6 Great War Memorial, Vimy Ridge, France

This WW1 memorial at Vimy Ridge, France, commemorates human suffering. The memorial is located on the site of the most famous battle fought by Canadian soldiers during the War. Its base is inscribed with the names of over 11,000 soldiers who died and have no known grave.

Make it a spectacle

Cultural festivals succeed because they create a spectacle. Festivals and events serve the purpose of both concentrating attention into a finite time frame as well as creating a critical mass of activities to convert the event into a spectacle. Making something a spectacle implies that the person is going to have a special experience while attending and also, importantly, that those who do not attend will be missing out on something special (see Plate 15.7). Live music is available in most large cities every night of the week. Yet a music festival turns attendance at a live concert into a special event.

Make it a fantasy

The popularity of castles and stately homes as cultural tourist attractions has as much to do with the fantasy element as it does with physical presence of magnificent buildings. Transforming fantasy into reality, even if that reality is experienced in a fleeting and vicarious manner, is an important element in the cultural tourism experience of a large number of people who are motivated to participate for entertainment and escapist reasons. Some existing historical attractions have accommodated the needs of film-induced and literary tourists who thrive on finding locations to provide a place-based as well as a liminal space for such escapism (Beeton 2005). Increasingly there are purpose-built theme parks, historic assets and and reconstructions of the historic events (regularly or as special occasion) to allow people to speculate what it was like to live back then or enter a fictional world. If it is overdone, it could attract negative comments or even become the subject of a satirical novel or film itself (e.g. *Austenland*, Hale 2010).

Plate 15.7 Suitman at K11 Art Mall, Hong Kong

The spectacle of a large inflatable artwork in a temporary arts event attracts tourists to an art themed shopping mall. Suitman is the creation of Young Kim, an artist from South Korea. He and other artists were featured by the Art Mall at a special and much hyped event promoted as 'Public Fair No 1' in 2012 (suitman.org 2012).

Make it fun, light, and entertaining

Cultural tourism does not have to be oppressive. We have already shown that the majority of people who visit cultural and heritage tourism attractions are not seeking a deep learning experience. Many are looking to be entertained; many others may simply be looking for something interesting to do as an incidental activity in their vacation. Making the cultural experience fun, light, and entertaining is important for many tourists. It is still possible to get some important points across about the asset's importance or cultural significance. (See Plate 15.8).

Make it unique

Above all else, though, a tactic could be deployed to make the attraction unique: make it something the person feels he or she must see. Cultural attractions excel when they achieve a level of distinction that motivates travellers to seek them out 'against all odds' (MTC 2009). Uniqueness can take on many forms, whether it is a one-of-a-kind building, an unusual exhibit, a rare type of intangible heritage, or just something that cannot be experienced anywhere else. The challenge is that few cultural assets are truly unique and, as a result, few have the potential to be converted into successful products. However, historic sites or arts events that have pioneered some new art form or technology can later appeal to tourists interested in its origin, despite many imitators.

Plate 15.8 Jerusalem Segways

Technology is transforming the delivery of the tourist experience. Here, outside of the walls of the Old City of Jerusalem, tourists are using Segways to enable them to consume more experiences in a limited amount of time.

Interpreting the values of the asset

Some cultural assets have a more complicated message than others to convey to tourists who may not know much about their cultural values or context. In some instances, assets may be visually and historically complex as in the case of the Roman Baths in Bath, England. Potentially a confusing site, it has been clearly labelled, and the remains and their histories are carefully pointed out. For the most part, Tilden's (1977) principles for site interpretation are still as relevant. He was the first to recognize that the visitor should be able to recognize the familiar within the unfamiliar, otherwise the information will not engage them and therefore seem sterile. Hence the chief aim is for information to be more than just instruction. He also made the important distinction between what is simply information and what is interpretation (a particular viewpoint on the asset based on information available about it). Tilden (1977) also asserted that interpretation should aim to present a version that was as complete as possible and not restrict itself to a particular phase or part of the story.

With some other approaches, though, visitors are asked to choose between more than one historical narrative of historical events, especially if the interpretation programme is attempting to present controversial or contested heritage. History is usually written by the winners but, increasingly, others too are demanding their voices be heard, hence postmodernist pluralism in the narratives presented is sometimes popular for certain kinds of cultural attractions (e.g. the range of viewpoints provided about the First Fleet arrival in Australia in 1788 at the Museum of Sydney; MOS 2014). The postmodernist approach of 'constructivism' also relies on the visitor working a little harder intellectually to understand an asset. Often this approach is the key to interpreting dark tourism cultural attractions successfully and appropriately, when they have a confronting aspect of history to present. Visitors often want to understand why such awful things have happened the way they have and information should be provided in a form that allows them to construct a meaning from the experience that will resolve this question for them in some way.

Box 15.2 Online interpretation planning resources

Manuals and other resources:

- A Sense of Place Manual: http://www.jamescarter.cc/files/place.PDF
- Heritage Destination Consulting Interpretative Resource Library: http://www.heritagedestination.com/resource-centre.aspx
- Heritage Interpretative Centres Network Handbook: http://www.diba.cat/c/document_library/get_file?uuid=63952a92-928c-4eb9-a698-587bea5cf637&groupId=99058
- Distilling the Essence, New Zealand Interpretative Manual: http://www.doc.govt.nz/about-doc/policies-and-plans/visitor-management/interpretation-handbook-and-standard
- Basic Interpretive Skills Manual: http://www.interp.de/dokumente/topas_course_manual.pdf

Professional organizations:

- Association for Heritage Interpretation (UK): http://www.ahi.org.uk
- Interpretation Australia: http://www.interpretationaustralia.asn.au
- Interpretation Canada (Interpscan): http://www.interpscan.ca/new
- Interpret-Europe: http://www.interpret-europe.net
- National Association for Interpretation (US): http://www.interpnet.com

---

Effective ways of conveying messages

A variety of techniques are available to bring assets to life. They include: the provision of signage (locational, advisory, and interpretative); incorporation of new communication and virtual technologies and existing audio-visual ones; interactive and participatory activities; and the role of human interlocutors.

Signage

First, providing good interpretative signage is an art in itself. There are three general rules for readability. The sign should allow for one-third image, one-third text, and one-third blank space. Most attractions elect to provide multiple language signs, which means that there is less space for a particular message. Hence, supporting resources (e.g. pamphlets, tours, and audio-visual aids) are frequently provided to supplement the information or as an alternative if a particular language option is not available. Most signage designers aim at a pre-teens reading age (11 or 12 years-old) with simpler/more information sometimes available where there is space to provide it for younger visitors or enthusiasts.

Most importantly, the signage should fulfil an intended purpose in the way it conveys information. Sometimes it is just facts, while at other times it interprets events or underlines the cultural or intrinsic values inherent within the asset. The approach taken to the latter over the years has varied and may vary with the asset or intended market for the attraction.

Messages about visitor etiquette are also part of the experience whether they intend to be or not. However, there are other ways of conveying information about etiquette as well. The Laos government has produced an illustrated pamphlet in collaboration with a famous Lao cartoonist which tries to engage backpacker tourists humorously about respecting Lao living culture and its traditions while travelling. The pamphlet outlines particular practices that tourists should avoid in order not to cause offence and ones they should adopt to show respect (MICT 2009).

As can be seen from Plate 15.9 signage is also an important part of experience management. Signage as an area of visitor management and cultural tourism product development has grown beyond simply signs to locations or content-based signage about history and value of the asset.

New media and technology

A new area of digital technology that has great potential to bring many sites to life is that which can be termed 'immersive' or 'immersive virtual environments' (IVEs). Often these projects integrate high resolution digital datasets from archaeological sites (photography

Plate 15.9 Museum entrance sign

Cultural tourism should be experiential. This sign at the entry to the children's area of a museum in Nottingham, England, captures what experiential learning should be all about. More places need to encourage people to become actively involved in the experience.

and 3D models) with immersive and interactive display systems (Kenderdine 2013). Previously used for architectural design or research on astronomy, their application to experiencing heritage assets and cultural space in new ways is becoming more common in museums, visitor centres, and at special arts events.

The *PLACE*-Hampi project created specially for the Kaladham Museum near the Vijayanagar WHS, Hampi, India, which features animation as part of the 3D immersive imagery. It is presented in an interactive installation that projects 3D imagery onto a 9-metre diameter circular screen from a rotating platform which can be controlled by one viewer at a time. The animation superimposed on the 3D images is of Indian mythological characters and events associated with the cultures that produced the ruins of the WHS (ICOM Australia 2013; AliVE 2014).

Another innovative IVE project is one that uses images of ancient Buddhist religious art as a basis for the 'Pure Land: Augmented Reality Edition' application, resulting in presentations such as 'Pure Land. Inside the Mogao Grottoes at Dunhuang, 2012.' It used data and images recorded by various Dunhuang Caves conservation project teams in China over the years to create a set of interactive virtual tour presentations for the visitors. The presentations allow visitors to see more of Dunhuang's art in greater detail and help to conserve the wall paintings inside the caves, as fewer and shorter trips to the caves by tourists are now possible (CityU and Dunhuang Academy 2012) (see Plate 15.10).

Plate 15.10 'Pure Land' at Hong Kong Art Fair 2012

The 'Pure Land' IVE application was demonstrated at the Hong Kong Art Fair in 2012 allowing fairgoers to use iPads to view the Buddhist wall frescoes from Mogao Grottoes at Dunhuang, China. This is a different version to the 360-degree installation mentioned above, but one that works well in small temporary spaces.

These kinds of technologies may eventually replace the actual visit as large crowds are increasingly pressuring fragile assets. Digital tools such as laser scanning and high resolution photography occupy crucial roles in providing experiences to offset these impacts, while allowing some kind of continuing access for tourists to sites under threat. More photographic projects are being established in a race to 'capture' and preserve the caves before any more degradation occurs. They also provide an experience of the asset in a way that is fun and interesting to visitors, particularly those used to virtual technology and video games.

Audio-visual options

Audio-visual techniques of a more modest nature are viable options to convey messages and experience an attraction. These options include audio-tours, video installations, and increasingly, iPad tours/presentations of items in cultural institutions and heritage attractions (see Plate 15.11). Gibson (2012: 1) observed "once perfected communication technologies rarely die out entirely; rather, they shrink to fit particular niches in the global info-structure'. Hence it is still worth considering whether older or simpler techniques. Content, budget, potential market, and many other considerations should be taken into account when deciding the answer to this question. Often tourism plans of the kind discussed earlier will outline a range of potential options and possibly some phasing and/or actions to be implemented over a series of phases, but will leave it to the attraction's developers or managers to make the executive decision.

Plate 15.11 Audio guides

Audio guides are a very effective communication tool that appeals to sightseeing and purposeful cultural tourists and may even convert some casual and incidental cultural tourists into serendipitous ones. Their appeal lies in their ability to reach different senses and, in doing so, to provide more information that enhances the experience. The person's gaze can be firmly fixed on the item being interpreted, while the audio commentary explains the observed attraction in much more detail. Unlike fixed interpretive signs, people are free to wander around and get different perspectives while still listening to the commentary. More detailed information can be provided to add depth to the experience. The use of mobile technology, wifi, phones, and tablets further allows the freedom to select individual stops and bypass others that are less appealing.

Interactive and participatory activities

Meanwhile other new non-digital interactive activities are being devised to distract tourists from over-using popular sites and channel their energies in more productive directions. One such project is a 'fake tomb' as an alternative to visiting a real tomb in the Valley of the Kings, Luxor. The physical replica of Tutankhamun's tomb was made possible by using high resolution recording and is a part of a major initiative by the Ministry of State for Antiquities to preserve the tombs in the Valley of the Kings. The project was launched in collaboration with a wide array of stakeholders including the University of Basel, the Friends of the Royal Tombs of Egypt, the Foundation for Digital Technology in Conservation, the European Union, and the Ministry of Tourism. The facsimile is almost identical to the original tomb from a normal viewing distance (Past Preservers 2014).

Archaeological voluntourism also has been growing in popularity to the point that it is not uncommon for archaeological excavations to be fully or partly funded by non-specialist participants. More recently, some excavations can also be followed online which gives prospective voluntourists an idea of what is involved in digging in different regions, and where current research is being undertaken (AIA 2014). Activities for archaeological voluntourists are not just limited to excavation. It is also possible to work directly with artifacts in a laboratory setting, for example, the Montpelier project run by a not-for-profit trust in the US (James Madison's Montpelier 2014).

Creative tourism and gastronomic tourism products are also highly participatory. Creative tourism provides learning experiences alongside creative ones as tourists can opt to master a skill or just get an inkling of what is involved under the supervision of a professional artist. Participating in food preparation can assist in conveying an understanding of the cultural values of different cultures as there are strong cultural reasons why certain ingredients are used and certain techniques are preferred. Even small restaurants can give instances of providing participatory experiences for tourists. (See Plate 15.12 and 15.13).

People

People are a very important aspect of information provision and making an attraction a great experience. To start with, one of the best aspects of having human interlocutors (docents, community derived caretakers, artists, performers, and so on) at an attraction is that they can show more empathy to tourist needs and can embody the storytelling tactic discussed earlier so that a range of stories, of their own experiences or traditional ones, which can provide an extra dimension of experience for the tourist. They can also personally demonstrate arts and crafts in a way that feels more authentic than watching a video, particularly if they contextualize these demonstrations with information and stories. Both volunteers from a particular community or cultural group, as well as on-site guides (who may feel the need to be more formal or authourative). Accordingly most participatory activities of the kind described above require a human presence or human supervision. (See Plate 15.14).

Attractions and communities have little influence over what off-site guides choose to say, unless they are part of a local community to start with and have worked closely with that community in order to know what and how to convey cultural information to tourists. Hence the deeper experience or fuller message may need to be conveyed on-site. Other people who are employed by the attraction should also show willingness to supply information in a clear and polite way, if they know it, or if they cannot, at least be willing to redirect tourists to someone who can. Politeness and responding quickly to tourists' requests can often cement a memorable experience.

 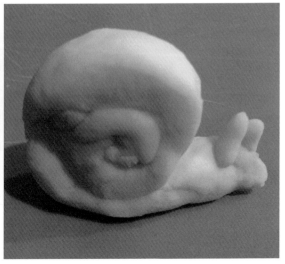

Plates 15.12 Dough ball rolling, Katoomba,   **Plate 15.13** Moulding dough balls, culinary meets creative
Australia

Dough ball rolling is how the restaurateur of Pappadino's Pizza Restaurant, Katoomba, Australia, encourages children to show interest in the culinary practices behind what they eat. The children are given small dobs of pizza dough to roll and/or create little sculptures that are then baked and handed back to them with their pizzas to eat or keep (Plate 15.12). This participatory activity helps them to think about pizzas as more than just food but also an artistic medium (Plate 15.13).

Plate 15.14 Guide interpreting a temple, Thailand

A professional guide provides some additional information by contextualizing the site with a visual aid. Often simple methods work best, such as having some historic photos or plans to hand that can be used to show change over time.

Key learning outcomes

- Experiences should be engaging, stimulating, and pleasant for tourists to consider them 'great' and 'golden memories'.
- Great experiences should lead tourists to respect the assets and develop some understanding of the cultures behind them and their values.
- Interpretation tactics and techniques are not an end in themselves and should be carefully selected to support the overall experience of the asset.

 **Epilogue**

Much has changed since the first edition of this book was published more than 12 years ago. Much is also likely to change in the future as cultural tourism continues to evolve. This chapter outlines some key improvements in outlook, where the challenges still lie, a few general observations, and where researchers may look next. It also provides points of discussion for professionals, teachers, and students.

Improvements needed

While much progress has been made in the past 12 years, some improvements are still needed, including:

- greater awareness that tourism planning and management need to be inclusive and integrated into CHM plans;
- the need to incorporate tourism considerations in other forms of planning and management (as, for example, the HUL Approach does);
- continued maturation of ICH management in relation to tourism: it is a work in progress but at least more anthropologists are showing an interest, as are museums, UNESCO and UNWTO;
- more case studies highlighting positive examples of full partnerships to complement those already developed from Croatia, Canada, and South Korea;
- more direct communication between tourists and asset managers by means of social networking/media popularity to facilitate greater collaboration;
- the rise of social media and promotion of new travel concepts such as slow travel and questing deeper cultural tourism experiences have implications for enhancing sustainable development and cultural diversity, respectively.

Challenges still remain

However, many challenges still remain including the need for:

- more awareness of sustainable tourism from all sectors, including more joint meetings, conferences, and seminars between key sectors;
- more inclusive policy-making that closely links arts/culture public policy with tourism with input from a greater variety of stakeholders in many places;
- more codes and planning/management tools to help intangible heritage asset managers and tourism sector types and other stakeholders to collaborate on culturally sensitive yet lucrative ICH tourism projects;

- new ways of attracting corporate social responsibility and corporate funding to the table to safeguard and protect cultural assets and encourage cultural tourism enterprises in developing countries;
- more research into the opportunities provided by crowdsourcing and other forms of seed funding to assist in the creation of community-based tourism products;
- destination marketers to develop a realistic understanding of their cultural assets true potential for cultural tourism.

Some general observations

Finally some general observations:

- The mass market will still dominate but more niches within cultural tourism will emerge.
- The rise of large-scale cultural tourism products, such as specifically branded cultural tourism areas, purpose-built cultural hubs and leisurescapes in Asia, which are meant as tourism attractions foremost (e.g West Kowloon Cultural Hub).
- The increasing commodification of long transnational pilgrimage or trade routes (the way of St James, Spain/France, and the Silk Road) for religious and sightseeing cultural tourism is also part of this trend.

A few possible research areas

We need more research on:

- identifying if discrete sub-niches exist and whether they are truly different or simply variations on a theme;
- documenting the size and motivations for sub-niches in cultural tourism;
- understanding emerging markets, especially in the BRICS area (Brazil, Russia, India, China, and South Africa) whose values are different and who may be seeking different experiences;
- the way in which the market will evolve and what the cultural tourists of 30 years time will be like;
- what more can be done to improve ICH products for domestic tourists in developing countries and for better managing impacts;
- how social media is influencing not just tourists motivations but also blending of products, e.g. film-induced touring mixed with heritage tourism;
- the impact new virtual technologies are having on cultural tourism experiences;
- the potential of crowdsourcing for being a new kind of seed funding to add to that of microcredit to help small heritage and creative tourism projects get started.

We need less research on:

- activity-based market studies that conflate participation with trip motivation;
- sub-niches that do not exist.

⬤ Glossary

arts/cultural ecologies   A term to describe either a local or an international arts community in terms of describing the health of linkages and interdependent relationships between key stakeholders in a similar way to that of natural ecologies. One of the uses of the term is in presenting the relationships between an arts-funding body and its funded organizations, artists, and society in general. The healthier the spread and growth of benefits, the more vibrant the ecology.

authenticity   The appearance and experience of what is perceived as being a true or genuine activity, item, or setting based on the cultural understanding of the observer.

best practice   The best the world has to offer. Most arts and heritage professionals use the various charters of principles or codes of ethics produced by ICOM or ICOMOS and so on.

commodification   The process by which cultural expressions and aspects of heritage become 'cultural goods' because they have been transformed into commodities to be consumed easily by tourists. Most ICH assets require some level of commodification to make their cultural values easily understandable to outsiders.

conservation of materials   Conservation changes meaning a little when used in the context of chemical preservation or special works carried out by specialists such as conservators (for objects) or conservation architects (for buildings).

conservation plan   A document that is produced to outline what is significant about a tangible heritage asset to enable that significance to be retained in its future use and development.

conservation/preservation   Warning: these terms basically mean the same to North Americans, Australians, and the British. That is, the practice of caring for assets for the enjoyment of present and future generations. Some Americans now seem to prefer 'stewardship' instead.

creatives   Arts professionals who are increasingly describing themselves as more than just artists, inventors, communications or IT types, becoming 'creatives' in some debates and literature.

creative class   This is usually people who have absorbed the message of Florida's (2002) work on the 'Creative Class' and want to be acknowledged as part of that group. Basically 'creatives' who are based at a particular place most of the time comprise its 'Creative Class'.

cultural assets   Cultural assets are everything from historic buildings to works of artistic expression that reflect different aspects of a culture. Sometimes, they are attractive to tourists or are used by a destination to attract tourists.

cultural heritage   The record of a people manifest in the tangible (cultural relics, handicrafts, monuments, historic towns, and villages) and intangible (literature, theatre, music, folk customs) heritage of their culture.

cultural heritage management (CHM)   Cultural heritage management is the systematic practice of implementing elements of established codes and charters of conservation principles to preserve cultural heritage assets for present and future generations.

cultural heritage trails   Walking tracks meant to offer the user a first-hand view of the surrounding environment. Walking trails can be found in natural and urban areas and vary in length and degrees of difficulty, depending on location.

cultural identity   Each individual, community, or nationality has some core cultural values which are shared and which provide a basis for their social behaviour in a wider context.

cultural landscape   A landscape that has tangible and/or intangible heritage assets that need to be seen as a sum of the individual parts.

cultural space   A space that can act as a setting for intangible heritage assets that require some kind of staging or location. Examples include open spaces in public squares, historic gardens, streets, and forecourts of temples.

cultural values   The value of cultural assets at a tourist destination in terms of their intrinsic significance of historical, aesthetic, social, scientific, or spiritual value evident in a tangible or intangible form.

environmental impact assessment (EIA)   An environmental impact assessment is an assessment of the possible impact – positive or negative – that a proposed development project may have on the environment, which incorporates more than just the natural environment. It also includes the socio-political and economic context within which the proposed development is placed. When only dealing with the cultural heritage of an area, it is known as a cultural heritage impact assessment.

globalization   It involves the movement of people, goods, capital and ideas due to increased economic integration, which in turn is propelled by increased trade and investment. It is like moving towards living in a borderless world and can also include the process whereby aspects of one particular culture are adopted worldwide.

host community   It is a general concept that encompasses all of the people who inhabit a defined geographical area, ranging from a continent, country, region, town, to a village or historic site.

intangible cultural heritage (ICH)   Heritage assets that are a culture's non-physical legacy. Special or local kinds of 'soft' culture, such as stories, customs, knowledge and expertise, needed to make handicrafts, visual, and performing arts (see also *tangible heritage*).

interpretation strategy   A strategy that enables the communication of the importance and cultural significance of a heritage asset to the tourist in an interesting, stimulating, and engaging way.

limits of acceptable change   A broader concept than that of 'carrying capacity' for sites. Instead it concerns all cultural and heritage assets and deals with managing the absorption of new influences by them and negative impacts of tourism on them.

limits of growth   A similar concept to the above for understanding when important thresholds have been reached for negative tourism development impacts.

over-commodification   A condition that occurs when an asset has been unsympathetically transformed into a product and much of authenticity and original meaning has been lost or trivialised.

revitalization   The process by which disappearing cultural traits, activities, or practices are given new life to continue in a dynamic way within a culture.

stakeholders   Those people or groups who have a specific interest in or are likely to be affected by any changes to a heritage asset.

social and cultural impacts   Positive and/or negative impacts or changes the introduction of tourism and other factors from outside have upon a society and its culture.

sustainable creative advantage   This umbrella term tries to encompass at least four kinds of capital (social, cultural, human and economic) as well as the creative spark that makes a really good arts event appeal to participants.

tangible heritage   Physical manifestations of culture, which include buildings, archaeological sites, cultural landscapes, gardens, and all categories of movable cultural property considered to be of cultural significance (see also intangible heritage).

tourist precinct or area   Precincts or areas that draw tourists as a result of incorporated attractions, food and beverage outlets, entertainment, and historic buildings converted into merchandizing centres.

References

!Khwa ttu (2014) San cultural and educational centre. Available at: http://www.khwattu.org (accessed 8 April 2014).

AHC (Australian Heritage Commission) (1997) *Australia's National Heritage. Options for Identifying Heritage Places of National Significance. A Discussion Paper*, Canberra: Australian Heritage Commission.

AIA (Archaeological Institute of America) (2014) Archaeology's interactive dig. Available at: http://interactive.archaeology.org/index.html (accessed 8 April 2014).

Akehurst, G. (2009) User generated content: the use of blogs for tourism organisations and tourism consumers, *Service Business* 3(1): 51–61.

ALiVE (2014) Related projects. Available at: http://alive.scm.cityu.edu.hk/projects/related (accessed 7 April 2014).

Allcock, J. B. (1995) International tourism and the appropriation of history in the Balkans. In Lanfant, Marie-Françoise, Allcock, John B. and Bruner, Edward M. (eds) *International Tourism: Identity and Change*, London Sage Publications, pp. 100–112.

Altman, J. (1992) Tourism and aboriginal communities. In Faulkner, B. and Kennedy, M. (eds) *Australian Tourism Outlook Forum 1992*, Canberra: BTR, pp. 79–88.

Ambrose, T. and Paine, C. (1993) *Museum Basics*, London: ICOM and Routledge.

ANHA (Alliance of National Heritage Areas) (2014) Celebrating 30 years of powerful partnership. Available at: http://www.nationalheritageareas.us (accessed 20 May 2014).

Antolovic, J. (1999) Immovable cultural monuments and tourism. In ICOMOS (ed.) *Cultural Tourism Session Notes XII Assembly ICOMOS*, Mexico: ICOMOS, pp. 103–118.

Ap, J. (1999) Arts/Cultural tourism position paper, unpublished report prepared for the Arts/Cultural Tourism Working Group, Hong Kong Tourist Association and Hong Kong Arts Development Council, Hong Kong Polytechnic University.

Arlt, W. (2006) *China's Outbound Tourism*, London and New York: Routledge.

Ashley C., Boyd, C. and Goodwin, H. (2000) Pro-poor tourism: putting poverty at the heart of the tourism agenda, *Natural Resource Perspectives* 51: 1–6.

Ashley, C., Poultney, C., Haysom, G., McNab, D. and Harris, A. (2005) Brief 2: stimulating local cultural and heritage products. Overseas Development Institute Business Linkages in Tourism. Available at: http://www.odi.org.uk/sites/odi.org.uk/files/odi-assets/publications-opinion-files/2257.pdf (accessed 5 May 2014).

Ashworth, G. (1999) Tourism in the communication of senses of place displacement in New Mexico, *Tourism Culture and Communications* 1(2): 115–128.

Asian Art Museum (2009a) Matcha Japanese Tattoo at Asian Art Museum of San Francisco. Available at: http://www.youtube.com/watch?v=a7zEwCtA_T0 (accessed 3 April 2014).

Asian Art Museum (2009b) Samurai invades SF. Available at: http://www.youtube.com/watch?v=de8ReTWmF9g (accessed 3 April 2014).

Australia ICOMOS (2013) Australia ICOMOS *Burra Charter*. Available at: http://australia.icomos.org/publications/charters (accessed 14 May 2014).

Bachleitner, R. and Zins, A. H. (1999) Cultural tourism in rural communities: the resident's perspective, *Journal of Business Research* 44(3): 199–209.

Baker, M. and Cameron, E. (2008) Critical success factors in destination marketing, *Tourism and Hospitality Research* 8: 79–97.

Bandarin, F. and van Oers, R. (2012) *The Historic Urban Landscape. Managing Heritage in an Urban Century*, Oxford: Wiley-Blackwell.

Barbieri, C. and Mahoney, E. (2010) Cultural tourism behaviour and preferences among the live-performing arts audience: an application of the univorous–omnivorous framework, *International Journal of Tourism Research* 12: 481–496.

Baxter, I. (2010) Global heritage tourism. In Smith, G. S., Messenger, P. M. and Soderland, H. A. (eds) *Heritage Values in Contemporary Society*, Walnut Creek, CA: Left Coast Press, pp. 241–254.

BBC News (2013) Glastonbury 2014 tickets sell out in record time. Available at: http://www.bbc.co.uk/news/entertainment-arts-24418582 (accessed 3 April 2014).

Beesley, L. (2005) The potential role of cultural tourism on the Gold Coast. Melbourne: CRC for Sustainable Tourism. Available at: http://www.crctourism.com.au/wms/upload/resources/bookshop/Beesley63015_culturalTourism.pdf (accessed 7 March 2014).

Beeton, S. (2005) *Film-induced Tourism*, Clevedon, OH: Channel View Publications.

Bennett, E., Neiland, A., Anang, E., Bannerman, P., Atiq Rahman, A., Huq, S., Bhuiya, S., Day, M., Fulford-Gardiner, M. and Clerveaux, W. (2001) Towards a better understanding of conflict management in tropical fisheries: evidence from Ghana, Bangladesh and the Caribbean, *Marine Policy* 25: 365–376.

Besculides, A., Lee, M. and McCormick, P. (2002) Residents' perceptions of the cultural benefits of tourism, *Annals of Tourism Research* 29(2): 303–319.

Best in Heritage (2014) What is Best in Heritage in museums? Available at: http://www.thebestinheritage.com/presentations/search/what-is-the-best-in-museums,44.html (accessed 7 April 2014).

Best in Heritage (2011) Heart for people's cafés, Ghent, Belgium. Available at: http://www.thebestinheritage.com/presentations/search/heart-for-peoples-cafes,200.html (accessed 7 April 2014).

Bjeljac, Ž., Ćurčić, Z. and Brankov, J. (2012) Tourism evaluation of IBA areas in the Serbian part of Banat, *Forum Geographic* 11(2): 161–167.

Blackwell, C. (1997) Tourism and cultural tourism: some basic facts, *Preservation Issues* 7(3). Available at: http://www.umsl.edu/services/library/blackstudies/culttour.htm (accessed 14 May 2014).

Boddy, C. (2013) Counter-marketing case studies. In Bradley, N. and Blythe, J. (eds) *Demarketing*, Abingdon: Routledge, pp. 65–81.

Boniface, P. (1998) Tourism culture, *Annals of Tourism Research* 25(3): 746–749.

Boorstin, D. (1964) *The Image: A Guide to Pseudo Events in America,* New York: Harper and Row.

Bossen, C. (2000) Festival mania, tourism and nation building in Fiji: the case of the Hibiscus Festival, 1956–1970, *The Contemporary Pacific* 12(1): 123–154.

Bowes, B. (1994) Cultural tourism: are we on the brink? *ICOMOS Canada* 3(3). Available at: http://www.icomos.org/canada/bulletin/vol3_no3_bowes_e.html (accessed 6 May 2014).

Bowman, L. (2013) Eastport projected to lose almost half of residents by 2030. Available at: http://www.workingwaterfront.com/articles/Eastport-projected-to-lose-almost-half-of-residents-by-2030/15353 (accessed 20 May 2014).

Boylan, P. J. (2006) The intangible heritage: a challenge and an opportunity for museums and museum professional training, *International Journal of Intangible Heritage* 1: 54–65.

Boylan, P. J. (1994) Europe's built environment and movable heritage, *Research Paper for the Council of Europe's Task Force on Culture and Development.* Available at: http://www.city.ac/artspol/coe-dev.html (accessed 20 May 2014).

Brett, Reverend P. C. (1999) Principles of visitor management and care for historical sites, with special reference to Canterbury Cathedral. In *Cultural Tourism Session Notes XII Assembly ICOMOS,* Mexico: ICOMOS, pp. 83–92.

Brooks, G. (2003) *Heritage at Risk from Tourism*, Paris: ICOMOS. Available at: http://www.international.icomos.org/risk/2001/tourism.htm (accessed 11 May 2014).

Brooks, G. (1993) Visitation to major heritage sites – some essential planning considerations. In ICOMOS (ed.) *Archaeological Heritage Management, Cultural Tourism and Conservation Economics Proceedings of the ICOMOS 10th General Assembly*, Columbo: ICOMOS, pp. 14–17.

Buckley, R., Bramwell, B. and Lane, B. (2004) The effects of World Heritage listing on tourism to Australian National Parks, *Journal of Sustainable Tourism* 12(1): 70–84.

Bull, Adrian (1991) *The Economics of Travel and Tourism*, Melbourne: Pitman.

Bullen, P. A. (2007) Adaptive reuse and sustainability of commercial buildings, *Facilities*, 25(1/2): 20–31.

Burgess, L., Limb, M. and Harrison, C. M. (1988) Exploring environmental values through the medium of small groups, *Environmental and Planning Analysis* 20: 457–476.

Byrne, D. (1991) Western hegemony in archaeological heritage management, *History and Anthropology* 5: 269–276.

Caffyn, A. and Lutz, J. (1999) Developing the heritage tourism product in multi-ethnic cities, *Tourism Management* 20: 213–221.

Calver, S. and Page, S. (2013) Enlightened hedonism: exploring the relationship of service value, visitor knowledge and interest to visitor enjoyment at heritage attractions, *Tourism Management* 39: 23–36.

Cameron, C. and Rössler, M. (2013) *Many Voices, One Vision: The Early Years of the World Heritage Convention*, London: Ashgate.

Cameron, J. I. (1997) Applying socio-economics: a case study of contingent valuation and integration catchment management, *Ecological Economics* 23: 155–165.

Campbell, E. (2008) The double mystery of Ankgor. Available at: http://www.abc.net.au/foreign/content/oldcontent/s2464937.htm (accessed 26 April 2014).

Carlsen, J., Hughes, M., Frost, W., Pocock, C. and Peel, V. (2008) *The Old and the New: Success Factors in Cultural Heritage Tourism Enterprise Management*, Canberra: CRC Sustainable Tourism, p. 24.

Carpenter, G. (2008a) Overview of arts and cultural programming. In Carpenter, G. and Blandy, D. (eds) *Arts and Cultural Programming. A Leisure Perspective*, Champagne, IL: Human Kinetics, pp. 3–22.

Carpenter, G. (2008b) Special events. In Carpenter, G. and Blandy, D. (eds) *Arts and Cultural Programming. A Leisure Perspective,* Champagne, IL: Human Kinetics, pp. 143–157.

Carson, D. (2008) The 'blogosphere' as a market research tool for tourism destination: a case study of Australia's Northern Territory, *Journal of Vacation Marketing* 14(2): 111–119.

Cass, G. and Jahrig, S. (1998) Heritage tourism: Montana's hottest travel trend, *Montana Business Quarterly* 36(2): 8–18.

Cave, J., Ryan, C. and Panakera, C. (2003) Residents' perceptions, migrant groups and culture as an attraction—the case of a proposed Pacific Island cultural centre in New Zealand, *Tourism Management* 24(4): 371–385.

CBI (Centre for the Promotion of Imports from Developing Countries Belgium) (2014) *CBI Product Factsheet: Cultural Heritage and Colonial Tourism from France, the Netherlands, Italy and Spain to Latin America,* The Netherlands: Netherlands Ministry of Foreign Affairs. Available at: http://www.cbi.eu/system/files/marketintel_documents/2014_pfs_cultural_heritage_and_colonial_tourism_from_france_the_netherlands_italy_and_spain_to_latin_america_0.pdf (accessed 7 March 2014).

CBI (Centre for the Promotion of Imports from Developing Countries Belgium) (nd) *Cultural Tourism in Belgium*, Brussels: Ministry of Foreign Affairs. Available at: http://www.cbi.eu/system/files/marketintel/cultural_tourism_in_belgium.pdf (accessed 7 March 2014).

Chang, T. C. (2000) Singapore's little India: a tourist attraction as a contested landscape, *Urban Studies* 37(2): 343–366.

Chang, T. C. and Teo, P. (2009) The Shophouse Hotel: vernacular heritage in a creative city, *Urban Studies* 46(2): 341–367.

Chapagain, N. K. (2013) Introduction. Contexts and concerns in Asian heritage management. In Silva, K. de and Chapagain, N. K. (eds) *Asian Heritage Management: Contexts, Concerns, and Prospects*, New York: Routledge, pp.1–19.

Cheer, J., Reeves, K. and Laing, J. (2013) Tourism and traditional culture: land diving in Vanuatu, *Annals of Tourism Research* 43: 435–455.

Cheon, J. (2012) Foreword, *International Journal of Intangible Heritage* 7: 6.

Cheong, S. M. and Miller, M. L. (2000) Power and tourism: a Foucauldian observation, *Annals of Tourism Research* 27(2): 371–390.

Cheung, S. C. H. (1999) The meanings of a heritage trail in Hong Kong, *Annals of Tourism Research* 26(3): 570–588.

Chhabra, D. (2009) Proposing a sustainable marketing framework for heritage tourism, *Journal of Sustainable Tourism* 17(3): 303–320.

Chhabra, D. (2008) Positioning museums on an authenticity continuum, *Annals of Tourism Research* 32(2): 427–447.

Chong, D. (2009) *Arts Management*, London: Routledge.

Chow, J. (2014) Getting locals to rediscover Singapore charms, *The Straits Times*, 5 March 2014. Available at: http://www.straitstimes.com/breaking-news/singapore/story/getting-locals-rediscover-singapore-charms-20140305 (accessed 5 March 2014).

CityU and Dunhuang Academy (2012) *Pure Land. Inside the Mogao Grottoes at Dunhuang* (pamphlet), Hong Kong: CityU and Dunhuang Academy.

Clark, I. (2009) Naming sites: names as management tools in indigenous tourism sites – an Australian case study, *Tourism Management* 30(1): 109–111.

Clinton Library (2014) William J. Clinton Presidential Library and Museum. Available at: http://www.clintonlibrary.gov (accessed 1 May 2014).

Cochrane, J. and Tapper, R. (2006) Tourism's contribution to World Heritage site management. In Leask, A. and Fyall, A. *Managing World Heritage Sites*, Oxford: Butterworth-Heinemann, pp. 97–109.

COE (Council of Europe) (nd) Impact of European cultural routes on SMEs' innovation and competitiveness: provisional edition. European Commission's Competitiveness and Innovation Framework programme (CIP). Available at: http://www.coe.int/t/dg4/cultureheritage/culture/routes/StudyCR_en.pdf (accessed 7 March 2014).

Cohen, E. (1988) Authenticity and commoditization in tourism, *Annals of Tourism Research* 15(3): 371–386.

Cohen, E. (1972) Toward a sociology of international tourism, *Social Research* 39: 164–182.

Cohen, E. and Cohen, S. (2012) Authentication: hot and cool, *Annals of Tourism Research* 39(3): 1295–1314.

Colbert, F. (2013) The marketing of heritage venues or destinations. In Rizzo, I. and Mignosa, A. (eds) *Handbook on the Economics of Cultural Heritage*, Cheltenham: Edward Elgar, pp. 231–250.

Conforti, J. M. (1996) Ghettos as tourism attractions, *Annals of Tourism Research* 23(4): 830–842.

Cooper, H. (2014) Anzac landing at Gallipoli anniversary to be marked by 10,000 Australians in Turkey. Available at: http://www.abc.net.au/news/2014-04-24/australians-flock-to-gallipoli-to-mark-anniversary-of-landing/5407982 (accessed 5 May 2014).

Cooper, M. J. M., Ogata, M. and Eades, J. S. (2008) Heritage tourism in Japan. A synthesis and comment. In Prideaux, B., Dallen, J. T. and Chon, K. (eds) *Cultural and Heritage Tourism in Asian and the Pacific*, London: Routledge, pp. 107–117.

Copley, P. and Robson, I. (1996) Tourism, arts marketing and the modernist paradox. In Robinson, M., Evans, N. and Callaghan, P. (eds) *Tourism and Culture: Image, Identity and Marketing,* Sunderland, UK: The Centre for Travel and Tourism/British Education Publishers, pp. 15–34.

Corsane, G. and Bowers, J. (2012) Sense of place in sustainable tourism: a case study of the rainforest and savannahs in Guyana. In Convery, I., Corsane, G. and Davis, P. (eds) *Making Sense of Place: Multidisciplinary Perspectives*, Woodbridge: Boydell Press, pp. 249–260.

Costa and Feronne (1998) *Sociocultural Perspectives on Tourism Planning and Development,* Virtual Conference Centre, MCB Press. Available at: http://www.mcb.co.uk/services/conferenc/jan98/eit/paper4-3.htm (accessed 24 April 2014).

Craik, J. (1999) Interpretive mismatch in cultural tourism, *Tourism Culture and Communications* 1(2): 115–128.

Craik, J. (1997) The culture of tourism sites. In Rojek, Chris and Urry, John (eds) *Touring Cultures: Transformations of Travel and Theory*, London: Routledge, pp. 113–136.

Croes, R. and Semrad, K. (2013) The relevance of cultural tourism as the next frontier for small island destinations, *Journal of Hospitality and Tourism Research* DOI: 1096348013491599.

CTC (Canadian Tourism Commission) (2013) Building cultural tourism in New Anglia. Creative tourism consultants. Available at: http://www.newanglia.co.uk/wp-content/uploads/2013/11/CTC-New-Anglia-final-report-Jan13-Web.pdf (accessed 7 March 2014).

CTC (Canadian Tourism Commission) (2004) *Canada: Destination Culture. A Symposium on Cultural and Heritage Tourism Products. A Discussion Paper*, Canadian Tourism Commission. Available at: http://torc.linkbc.ca/torc/downs1/Destination_Culture_ENG.pdf (accessed 14 May 2014).

Cuattingguis, N. (1993) Cultural tourism in Sweden. In ICOMOS *International Scientific Symposium on Cultural Tourism, ICOMOS 10th General Assembly*, Sri Lanka, Paris: ICOMOS, pp. 43–50.

Culler, J. (1988) The semiotics of tourism. In Culler, J. *Framing The Sign: Criticism and Its Institutions*, Norman: University of Oklahoma Press, pp. 1–10.

Dahles, H. (2002) The politics of tour guiding: image management in Indonesia, *Annals of Tourism Research* 29(3): 783–800.

Dante, E. (2013) Re-enactment of a traditional Korean wedding in San Francisco's Asian Art Museum. Available at: http://www.youtube.com/watch?v=hhZGJevBKNU (accessed 3 April 2014).

Darling Harbour Authority (2014) The Chinese Garden of Friendship, Darling Harbour. Available at: https://www.darlingharbour.com (accessed 14 May 2014).

Dauner, B. (nd) On cultural tourism: how embracing an important market segment can sell more room nights. *Hotel Business Review*. Available at: https://hotelexecutive.com/business_review/1917/on-cultural-tourism-how-embracing-an-important-market-segment-can-sell-more-room-nights (accessed 7 March 2014).

David, B. and Oliver, C. (2006) Contested identities: the dissonant heritage of European town walls and walled towns, *International Journal of Heritage Studies* 12(3): 234–254.

DCMS (Department of Culture, Media and Sport) (2011) State of the Environment Report 2011: heritage. Available at: http://www.environment.gov.au/science/soe/2011-report/9-heritage/contents (accessed 8 April 2014).

DCMS (Department of Culture, Media and Sport) (2008) World heritage for the nation: identifying, protecting and promoting our world heritage. A consultation paper. Available at: http://www.culture.gov.uk/images/publications/whconsultation_engversion.pdf (accessed 11 May 2009).

DEA (Department of Environment, Australia) (2014) *Australia's World Heritage*. Canberra: Department of the Environment. Available at: http://www.environment.gov.au/topics/heritage/about-australias-heritage/world-heritage (accessed 17 April 2014).

DEA (Department of Environment, Australia) (2011) State of the Environment Report 2011: heritage. Available at: http//www.environment.gov.au.science/soc/2011-report/9-heritage/contents (accessed 8 April 2014).

DEA (Department of Environment, Australia) (2004) Steps to sustainable tourism. Available at: http://www.environment.gov.au/resurce/steps-sustainable-tourism (accessed 30 April 2014).

Deacon, H. (2004) *The Subtle Power of Intangible Heritage. Legal and Financial Instruments for Safeguarding Intangible Heritage*, Johannesburg, South Africa: Social Cohesion and Integration Programme.

Deacon, J. (2006) Rock art conservation and tourism, *Journal of Archaeological Method and Theory* 13(4): 379–399.

De Bres, K. and David, J. (2001) Celebrating groups and place identity: a case study of a new regional festival, *Tourism Geographies: An International Journal of Tourism, Space and Environment* 3(3): 326–337.

Deery, M., Jago, L., Mistilis, N., D'Ambra, J., Richards, F. and Carson, D. (2007) *Visitor Information Centers: Best Practice in Information Dissemination*. Queensland, Australia: Sustainable Tourism CRC. Available at: http://crctourism.com.au/WMS/Upload/Resources/bookshop/Deery_VICs%20Best%20practice.pdf (accessed 15 March 2014).

De Kadt, E. (1979) *Tourism: Passport to Development*, New York: Oxford University Press.

De Simon, E. (2012) Non-residents' attitudes towards heritage: exploring tourist typologies by cultural consumption, *Acta Turistica* 24(2): 177–208.

Dewar, K., du Cros, H. and Li, W. (2012) The search for World Heritage brand awareness beyond the iconic heritage: a case study of the Historic Centre of Macao, *Journal of Heritage Tourism* 7(4): 323–339.

Dicks, B. (2003) *Culture on Display. The Production of Contemporary Visitability*, Maidenhead, UK: Open University Press.

Discover Saint John (2013) Gallery hop. Available at: http://discoversaintjohn.com/event/gallery-hop-2 (accessed 20 March 2014).

DKS (1999) Pennsylvania heritage tourism study, D. K. Shifflet and Associates, prepared for Pennsylvania Department of Conservation and Natural Resources, 63 pp. plus appendices.

Dolnicar, S. (2007) Market segmentation in tourism. In Woodside, A. G. and Martin, D. (eds), *Tourism Management: Analysis, Behaviour and Strategy*, Cambridge: CAB International, pp. 129–150.

Domicelj, J. (1994) A question of authenticity: cultural diversity. In Larsen, K. (ed.) *Proceedings of the Nara Conference on Authenticity in relation to the World Heritage Convention,* Nara, Japan: UNESCO World Heritage Centre (France), Agency for Cultural Affairs (Japan), ICCROM (Italy) and ICOMOS (France), pp. 301–304.

Donohoe, H. (2012) Sustainable heritage tourism marketing and Canada's Rideau Canal World Heritage site, *Journal of Sustainable Tourism* 20(1): 121–142.

D'Sa, E. (1999) Wanted: tourists with a social conscience, *International Journal of Contemporary Hospitality Management* 11 (2/3): 64–68.

du Cros, H. (2014) New models of travel behavior for independent Asian youth urban cultural tourists, *Asia Research Institute Working Paper Series 217*, Singapore: Asia Research Institute, National University of Singapore. Available at: http://www.ari.nus.edu.sg/publications.asp?pubtypeid=WP (accessed 23 March 2014).

du Cros, H. (2013) World Heritage-themed souvenirs for Asian tourists in Macau. In Cave, J., Jolliffe, L. and Baum, T. (eds) *Tourism and Souvenirs: Glocal Perspectives from the Margins*, London: Channel View Publications, pp. 176–189.

du Cros, H. (2009) Emerging issues for cultural tourism in Macau, *Journal of Current Chinese Affairs* 38(1): 73–99.

du Cros, H. (2007a) Too much of a good thing? Visitor congestion management issues for popular World Heritage tourist attractions, *Journal of Heritage Tourism* 2(3): 225–238.

du Cros, H. (2007b) China's tea and horse trade route and its potential for tourism. In Jolliffe, L. (ed.) *Tea Tourism: Tourists, Traditions and Transformations. Tourism and Cultural Change Book Series 11*, London: Channel View Publications, pp. 167–179.

du Cros, H. (2006a) Managing visitor impacts in Lijiang, China. In Leask, A. and Fyall, A. (eds) *Managing World Heritage Sites*, London: Butterworth-Heinemann, pp. 205–214.

du Cros, H. (2006b) The 'Romantic European Culture Island' with a turbulent history: the intrinsic and extrinsic values of Shamian Island, Guangzhou, *China Tourism Research* 1(2&3) (Chinese and English): 193–220.

du Cros, H. (2004) Postcolonial conflict inherent in the involvement of cultural tourism in creating new national myths in Hong Kong. In Hall, C. M. and Tucker, H. (eds) *Tourism and Postcolonialism: Contested Discourses, Identities and Representations*, New York: Routledge, pp. 153–168.

du Cros, H. (2002) *Much more than Stones and Bones. Australian Archaeology in the Late Twentieth Century*. Melbourne: Melbourne University Press.

du Cros, H. (2001) A new model to assist in planning for sustainable cultural heritage tourism, *International Journal of Tourism Research* 3(2): 165–170.

du Cros, H. (2000) Planning for sustainable cultural heritage tourism in Hong Kong, unpublished report to the Lord Wilson Heritage Trust, Hong Kong.

du Cros, H., Bauer, T., Lo, C. and Song, R. (2005) Cultural heritage assets in China as sustainable tourism products: case studies of the Hutongs and the Huanghua section of the Great Wall, *Journal of Sustainable Tourism* 13(2): 171–194.

du Cros, H. and du Cros, D. (2003) Romance, retsina and reality in Crete. In Bauer, T. and McKercher, B. (eds) *Romance, Sex and Tourism*, Binghamton, NY: Haworth Press, pp. 42–56.

du Cros, H. and Johnston, C. (2002) Tourism tracks and sacred places. Two case studies from Australia and Nepal, *Historic Environment* 16(2): 38–42.

du Cros, H. and Jolliffe, L. (2014) *The Arts and Events*, Abingdon: Routledge.

du Cros, H. and Jolliffe, L. (2011) Bundling the arts for tourism to complement urban heritage experiences in Asia, *Journal of Heritage Tourism* 6(3): 181–195.

du Cros, H. and Kong, W. H. (2006) A preliminary study of factors influencing congestion at popular World Heritage tourist attractions in Macao, unpublished report to the Office of the Secretary of Social and Cultural Affairs, Macao SAR Government.

du Cros, H. and Lee, Y. S. F. (2007) *Cultural Heritage Management in China: Preserving the Pearl River Delta Cities*, London: Routledge.

du Cros, H. and Liu, J. (2013) Chinese youth tourists' views on local culture, *Tourism, Planning and Development* 10(2): 187–204.

du Cros, H. and Ong, C. (2011) Self-drive tourism in China. In Prideaux, B. and Carson, D. (eds) *Drive Tourism: Trends and Emerging Markets*, Abingdon: Routledge, pp. 103–118.

Dwyer, L. and Edwards, D. (2013) Ecotourism and the triple bottom line. In Ballantyne, R. and J. Packer (eds) *International Handbook on Ecotourism*, Cheltenham: Edward Elgar, pp. 245–263.

Edventures (2013) Vision/Schedule. Available at: http://www.edventures.ca/en (accessed 3 May 2014).

Elkington, J. (2004) Enter the triple bottom line. In Henriques, A. and Richardson, J. (eds) *The Triple Bottom Line: Does It All Add Up?*, London: Earthscan, pp. 26–34.

Eller, J. D. (2009) *Cultural Anthropology. Global Forces Local Lives*, New York and London: Routledge.

Ename Charter (2014) The Ename Charter ratified. Available at: http://www.enamecharter.org (accessed 26 March 2014).

English Heritage (2011) *Valuing Places. Good Practice in Conservation Areas*, London: English Heritage.

Enz, C. (2010) *Hospitality Strategic Management: Concepts and Cases* (2nd Edition), Hoboken, NJ: John Wiley and Sons.

EPGC (1995) *Packaging and Selling to the United States,* Ottawa: Economic Planning Group of Canada for Tourism Canada.

ETC (European Tourism Commission) (2005) *City Tourism and Culture: The European Experience*, Brussels: European Tourism Commission.

EU (European Union) (2009) *Sustainable Tourism Based on Natural and Cultural Heritage?* Brussels: European Union.

Evans, G. (2003) Hard-branding the cultural city – from Prado to Prada, *International Journal of Urban and Regional Research* 27(2): 417–440.

Failte Ireland (2012) *A Tourism Toolkit for Ireland's Cultural Experiences: How to Develop & Communicate Cultural Experiences for Visitors*, Dublin: Failte Ireland. Available at: http://www.failteireland.ie/FailteIreland/media/WebsiteStructure/Documents/2_Develop_Your_Business/3_Marketing_Toolkit/5_Cultural_Tourism/Culture_Tourism_Toolkit.pdf (accessed 7 March 2014).

Falk, J. H. and Dierking, L. Y. (2000) *Learning from Museums: Visitor Experiences and the Making of Meaning*, Walnut Creek, CA: Altamira Press.

Fastfoward 17 (2007) The story. Available at: http://www.youtube.com/watch?v=6wC_YDKupho (accessed 20 March 2014).

Faulkner, B. and Russell, R. (1997) Chaos and complexity in tourism: in search of a new perspective, *Pacific Tourism Review* 1(2): 93–102.

Felsenstein, D. and Fleischer, A. (2003) Local festivals and tourism promotion: the role of public assistance and visitor expenditure, *Journal of Travel Research* 41: 3–392.

Ferrucci, S. (2012) *UNESCO's World Heritage Regime and Its International Influence* (Electronic Edition), Hamburg: Tradition.

Fesenmaier, D. R., Vogt, C. A. and Stewart, W. P. (1993) Investigating the influence of welcome centre information on travel behaviour, *Journal of Travel Research* 50: 154–170.

Florida, R. (2002) *The Rise of the Creative Class: And How It's Transforming Work, Leisure, Community and Everyday Life*, New York: Basic Books.

France, R. L. (2011) *Veniceland Atlantis. The Bleak Future of the World's Favourite City,* UK: Libri Publishing.

Francioni, F., Bakker, C. and Lenzerini, F. (2014) Evaluation of UNESCO's standard setting work of the culture sector. Part III – 1972 Convention Concerning the Protection of the World Cultural and Natural Heritage. Draft report to UNESCO. Available at: http://unesdoc.unesco.org/images/0022/002269/226922e.pdf (accessed 2 April 2014).

Frangialli, F. (2009) Creativity: a key for the 21st-century tourism. In APC Forum (ed.) *From Cultural Tourism to Creative Tourism*, Seoul: APC Forum, pp. 6–18.

Franklin, A. and Crang, M. (2001) The trouble with tourism and travel theory?, *Tourist Studies* 1(1): 5–22.

Fullerton, L., McGettigan, K. and Stephens, S. (2010) Integrating management and marketing strategies at heritage sites, *International Journal of Culture, Tourism and Hospitality Research* 4(2): 108–117.

Fyall, A. and Garrod, B. (1996) Sustainable heritage tourism: achievable goal or elusive ideal? In Robinson, M., Evans, N. and Callaghan, P. (eds) *Managing Cultural Resources for Tourism*, Sunderland, UK: Business Education Publishers, pp. 50–76.

Galla, A. (2012) *World Heritage. Benefits beyond Borders*, Cambridge: Cambridge University Press and UNESCO World Heritage Centre.

Galla, A. (1994) Authenticity: rethinking heritage diversity in a pluralistic framework. In Larsen, K. (ed.) *Proceedings of the Nara Conference on Authenticity in relation to the World Heritage Convention,* Japan: UNESCO World Heritage Centre (France), Agency for Cultural Affairs (Japan), ICCROM (Italy) and ICOMOS (France), pp. 315–322.

Gallagher, M. (1995) Taking a stand on hallowed ground, *Planning* 61(1): 10–15.

Garrod, B. and Fyall, A. (2000) Managing heritage tourism, *Annals of Tourism Research* 27(3): 682–708.

Getty Conservation Institute (2014) About the conservation institute. Available at: http://www.getty.edu/conservation (accessed 7 April 2014).

Getz, D. (1989) Special events: defining the product, *Tourism Management* 10(2): 125–137.

Gibson, W. (2012) *Distrust that Particular Flavor*, London: Penguin.

Glastonbury Festival of Contemporary Performing Arts (2014) History. Available at: http://www.glastonburyfestivals.co.uk/history/2001/ (accessed 3 April 2014).

Goodrich, J. N. (1997) Cultural tourism in Europe, *Journal of Travel Research* 35(3): 91.

Goodwin, H. and Santili, R. (2009) *Community Based Tourism: A Success? ICRT Occasional Paper 11.* University of Greenwich, London: International Centre for Responsible Tourism.

Gordin, V. and Matetskaya, M. (2012) Creative tourism in St Petersberg: the state of the art, *Journal of Tourism Consumption and Practice* 4(2): 55–76.

Gordon, R. and Raber, M. (2000). *Industrial Heritage in Northwest Connecticut: A Guide to History and Archaeology*, New Haven, CT: Connecticut Academy of Arts and Sciences.

Griffiths, M. (2011) Those who come to pray and those who come to look: interactions between visitors and congregations, *Journal of Heritage Tourism* 6(1): 63–72.

Gursoy, D., Kim, K. and Uysal, M. (2004) Perceived impacts of festivals and special events by organizers: an extension validation, *Tourism Management* 25(2): 171–181.

Gustafson, P. (2006) Place attachment and mobility. In McIntyre, M., Williams, D. and McHugh, K. (eds), *Multiple Dwelling and Tourism: Negotiating Place, Home and Identity,* Oxford: CABI, pp. 17–31.

Hager, M. and Sung, H. (2012) Local arts agency participation in cultural tourism, *Journal of Heritage Tourism* 7(3): 205–217.

Hale, S. (2010) *Austenland*, New York: Bloomsbury Publishing.

Hall, C. M. (1999) Rethinking collaboration and partnership: a public policy perspective, *Journal of Sustainable Tourism* 7(3&4): 274–289.

Hall, C. M. and Lew, A. (2009) *Understanding and Managing Tourism Impacts: An Integrated Approach*, New York: Routledge.

Hall, C. M. and McArthur, Simon (1998) *Integrated Heritage Management*, London: The Stationery Office.

Hall, C. M. and Piggin, R. (2001) Tourism and World Heritage in OECD countries, *Tourism Recreation Research* 26(1): 103–105.

Hall, C. M. and Weiler, B. (1992) Adventure, sport and health tourism. In Weiler, B. and Hall, C. M. (eds) *Special Interest Tourism*, Sydney: CAB International, pp. 141–158.

Hankey, D. and Brammah, M. (2005) *Management of Urban Cultural Heritage in China: A Sector Overview – Working Paper No. 2*, Beijing: East Asia Infrastructure Department.

Hannabuss, S. (1999) Postmodernism and the heritage experience, *Library Management* 20(5): 295–302.

Hardy, A. (2003) An investigation into the key factors necessary for the development of iconic touring routes, *Journal of Vacation Marketing* 9(4): 314–330.

Harrison, D. and Hitchcock, M. (2005) *The Politics of World Heritage: Negotiating Tourism and Conservation*, Clevedon, OH: Channel View Publications.

Hazen, H. (2008) 'Of outstanding universal value': The challenge of scale in applying the World Heritage Convention at national parks in the US, *Geoforum* 39(1): 252–264.

Hein, G. E. (1998) *Learning in the Museum*, London: Routledge.

Hensel, P., McLaughlin Mitchell, S. and Sowers II, T. (2006) Conflict management of riparian disputes, *Political Geography* 25: 383–411.

Heritage Preservation (2014) Conservation Assessment Progamme. Available at: http://www.heritagepreservation.org/CAP/index.html (accessed 30 April 2014).

Heritage Victoria (2009) Protecting local places. Available at: http://www.dpcd.vic.gov.au/__data/assets/pdf_file/0005/44474/Protecting-Local-Heritage-Places.pdf (accessed 30 April 2014).

Hooper-Greenhill, E. (2007) *Museums and Education: Purpose, Pedagogy, Performance*, London: Routledge.

Hovinen, G. R. (1995) Heritage issues in urban tourism: an assessment of new trends in Lancaster County, *Tourism Management* 16(5): 381–388.

Hsu, C., Killion, L., Brown, G., Gross, M. and Huang, S. (2008) *Tourism Marketing: An Asia Pacific Perspective*, Milton: Wiley.

Hughes, H. L. (2002) Culture and tourism: a framework for further analysis, *Managing Leisure* 7(3): 164–175.

Hughes, H. L. (1998) Theatre in London and the interrelationship with tourism, *Tourism Management* 19(5): 445–452.

Hughes, H. L. and Allen, D. (2005) Cultural tourism in Central and Eastern Europe: the views of induced image formation agents, *Tourism Management* 26(2): 173–183.

Hughes, M. and Carlsen, J. (2010) The business of cultural heritage tourism: critical success factors, *Journal of Heritage Tourism* 59(1): 17–21.

Human, B. (1999) Kodachrome icons: photography, place and the theft of identity, *International Journal of Contemporary Hospitality Management* 11(2/3): 80–84.

ICCROM (2014) Materials and technology. Available at: http://www.iccrom.org/priority-areas/material-science (accessed 10 July 2014).

ICOM (2014a) What we do. Available at: http://icom.museum (accessed 26 March 2014).

ICOM (2014b) Key concepts of museology. Available at: http://icom.museum/professional-standards/key-concepts-of-museology (accessed 7 April 2014).

ICOM (2004) Resolutions adopted by the 21st General Assembly of ICOM, Seoul, Korea. Friday 8 October 2004. Available at: http://icom.museum/resolutions/eres04.html (accessed 24 March 2014).

ICOM Australia (2013) 2013 Awards for International Relations. Available at: http://icom.org.au/site/activitiesiaair2013.php (accessed 8 April 2014).

ICOM Australia (2008) Plans, policies and submissions. Available at: http://icom.org.au/site/policies.php (accessed 8 April 2014).

ICOMOS (2014) *ICOMOS Charter on the Interpretation and Presentation of Cultural Heritage Sites.* Available at http://www.international.icomos.org/charters/interpretation_e.pdf (accessed 10 July 2014).

ICOMOS (2008) *The ICOMOS Charter on Cultural Routes.* Available at: http://www.international.icomos.org/charters/culturalroutes_e.pdf (accessed 30 September 2014).

ICOMOS (2005) Xi'an Declaration on the conservation of the setting of heritage structures, sites and areas. Available at: http://www.international.icomos.org/charters/xian-declaration.pdf (accessed 10 July 2014).

ICOMOS (2004) *International Charters for Conservation and Restoration,* Paris: ICOMOS.

ICOMOS (1999) *Cultural Tourism Charter*, Paris: ICOMOS. Available at: http:/www icomos.org (accessed 14 May 2014).

ICOMOS (1994a) *The Venice Charter*, ICOMOS Scientific Journal Series No. 4. Paris: ICOMOS.

ICOMOS (1994b) *The Nara Document on Authenticity* (The Nara Declaration). Available at: http://www.icomos.org/charters/nara-e.pdf (accessed 10 July 2014).

ICOMOS (1976) *ICOMOS Cultural Tourism Charter* (first version). Paris: ICOMOS.

ICOMOS ICTC (2014) ICOMOS International Cultural Tourism Committee. Available at: http://www.icomos-ictc.org (accessed 7 April 2014).

ICOMOS International Specialised Committee on Cultural Tourism (1993) Cultural tourism. Tourism at World Heritage cultural sites: the site manager's handbook*,* unpublished report to the International Scientific Committee 10th General Assembly, Columbo.

ICOMOS ICTC (2012) ICTC Annual Report 2012. Available at: http://www.icomos-ictc.org (accessed 10 April 2014).

IDCCA (1997) *Illinois Heritage Tourism Program*, Chicago: Illinois Department of Commerce and Community Affairs, Bureau of Tourism.

IFT (2014) Specialist guide for World Heritage sites. Available at: https://www.ift.edu.mo/EN/unesco_specialist_guide/Home/Index/333 (accessed 19 March 2014).

Ito, N. (1994) 'Authenticity' inherent in cultural heritage in Asia and Japan. In Larsen, K. (ed.) *Proceedings of the Nara Conference on Authenticity in relation to the World Heritage Convention,* Nara, Japan: UNESCO World Heritage Centre (France), Agency for Cultural Affairs (Japan), ICCROM (Italy) and ICOMOS (France), pp. 35–46.

Jackson E. and Wong, R. (1982) Perceived conflict between urban cross country skiers and snowmobilers in Alberta, *Journal of Leisure Research* 14(1): 42–62.

Jacob, G. R. and Schreyer, R. T. (1980) Conflict in outdoor recreation: a theoretical perspective, *Journal of Travel Research* 12(4): 368–380.

Jacobs, J. and Gale, F. (1994) *Tourism and the Protection of Aboriginal Cultural Sites*, Special Publication Series No. 10, Canberra: Australian Heritage Commission.

James Madison's Montpelier (2014) Volunteering in archaeology. Available at: http://www.montpelier.org/research-and-collections/archaeology/archaeology-programs/archaeology-volunteer (accessed 8 April 2014).

Jamieson, W. (2000) The challenge of sustainable community cultural heritage tourism. Culture heritage management and tourism: models for co-operation among stakeholders. UNESCO and the Nordic World Heritage Office Conference/Workshop, Bhaktapur, Nepal 8–16 April. Available at: http://www.ucalgary.ca/EV/designresearch/projects/2000/cuc/tp/outreach/Walter%20Nepal.pdf (accessed 13 April 2014).

Jamieson, W. (1995) The use of indicators in monitoring: the economic impact of cultural tourism initiatives, *ICOMOS Canada* 4(3). Available at: http://www.icomos.org/canada/bulletin/vol4_no3_jamieson_e.html (accessed 14 May 2014).

Jansen-Verbeke, M. (1998) Tourismification and historical cities, *Annals of Tourism Research* 25(3): 739–741.

Jansen-Verbeke, M. and Lievois, E. (1999) Analysing heritage resource for urban tourism in European cities. In Pearce, P. and Butler, R. (eds) *Cultural Issues in Tourism Development*, London: CAB International, pp. 81–107.

Jansen-Verbeke, M. and McKercher, B. (2013) Reflections on the myth of tourism preserving 'traditional' agricultural landscapes, *Journal of Resources and Ecology* 4(3): 242–249.

Jansen-Verbeke, M. and Russo, A. P. (2008) Innovative research on the spatial dynamics of cultural tourism. In Jansen-Verbeke, M. and Priestley, G. K. (eds) *Cultural Resources for Tourism, Patterns, Processes and Policies*, New York: Nova Science Publishers, pp. 1–14.

Jennings, G. and Weiler, B. (2006) Mediating meaning: perspectives on brokering quality tourist experiences. In Jennings, G. (ed.) *Quality Tourism Experiences*, Abingdon: Routledge, pp. 57–78.

Johannson, P. and Montagari, R. (1996) The value of travel time: an empirical study using repeated samples of non-business trips, *Tourism Economics* 2(4): 353–368.

Johnson, H. M. (2008) Recontextualizing eisa: transformations in religious, competition, festival and tourism contexts. In Johnson, H. M. and Jaffe, J. (eds) *Performing Japan: Contemporary Expressions of Cultural Identity*, Kent: Global Oriental, pp. 196–220.

Johnson, N. (1999) Framing the past: time, space and the politics of heritage tourism in Ireland, *Political Geography* 18(2): 189–207.

Johnston, C. (1994) *What is Social Value? A Discussion Paper*, Canberra: Australian Heritage Commission.

Jokilehto, J. (1994), Authenticity: a general framework for the concept. In Larsen, K. (ed.) *Proceedings of the Nara Conference on Authenticity in relation to the World Heritage Convention*, Japan: UNESCO World Heritage Centre (France), Agency for Cultural Affairs (Japan), ICCROM (Italy) and ICOMOS (France), pp. 17–36.

Jordan, T. (1999) Back to the future, *Asian Business* 35(6): 23.

Jorgensen, B. S. and Stedman, R. C. (2001) Sense of place as an attitude: lakeshore owners attitudes toward their properties, *Journal of Environmental Psychology* 21(3): 233–248.

Kantanen, T. and Tikkanen, I. (2006) Advertising in low and high involvement cultural tourism attractions: four cases, *Tourism and Hospitality Research* 6(2): 99–110.

Kastenholz, E. Eusébio, C. and Carneiro, M. (2013) Studying factors influencing repeat visitation of cultural tourists, *Journal of Vacation Marketing* 19: 343–358.

Kavanagh, G. (1994) *Museum Provision and Professionalism*, London: Routledge.

Kenderdine, S. (2013) 'Pure land': inhabiting the Mogao Caves at Dunhuang, *Curator – The Museum Journal* 56(2): 199–218.

Kerr, A. (1994) Strange bedfellows: an uneasy alliance between cultural conservation and tourism, *ICOMOS Canada* 3(3). Available at: http://www.icomos.org/canada/bulletin/vol3_no3_kerr_e.html (accessed 14 May 2014).

Kim, H. and Jamal, T. (2007) Touristic quest for existential authenticity, *Annals of Tourism Research* 34(1): 181–201.

Kirshenblatt-Gimblett, B. (2004) Intangible heritage as metacultural production, *Museum International* 56(1/2): 52–65.

Kotler, P. and Armstrong, G. (2003) *Principles of Marketing* (10th Edition), New Jersey, Prentice-Hall.

Kotler, P. and Turner, Ronald E. (1989) *Marketing Management,* Scarborough: Prentice Hall.

Lade, C. (2010) Potential barriers to visitation: a rural cultural heritage museums case, *E-review of Tourism Research* 8(2): 82–94.

Laing, J., Wheeler, F., Reeves, K. and Frost, W. (2014) Assessing the experiential value of heritage assets: a case study of a Chinese heritage precinct, Bendigo, Australia, *Tourism Management* 40: 180–192.

Landorf, C. (2009) Managing for sustainable tourism: a review of six cultural World Heritage sites, *Journal of Sustainable Tourism* 17(1): 53–70.

Larsen, K. (ed.) (1994) *Proceedings of the Nara Conference on Authenticity in relation to the World Heritage Convention,* Nara, Japan: UNESCO World Heritage Centre (France), Agency for Cultural Affairs (Japan), ICCROM (Italy) and ICOMOS (France).

Latvia (2006) Model for cultural heritage objects development. Riga. Available at: http://pilis.lv/a_pnm/files/154_4_Model_development.pdf (accessed 7 March 2014).

Law, E. (1999) Visitor satisfaction at Leeds Castle, Kent. In Leask, A. and Fyall, A. (eds) *Heritage Visitor Attractions*, London: Cassell, pp. 227–291.

Le, D. and Pearce, D. (2011) Segmenting visitors to battlefield sites: international visitors to the former demilitarized zone in Vietnam, *Journal of Travel and Tourism Marketing* 28(4): 451–463.

Leask, A. (2006) World Heritage site designation. In Leask, A. and Fyall, A. (eds) *Managing World Heritage Sites*, Oxford: Elsevier, pp. 5–19.

Leask, A. and Yeoman, I. (1999) *Heritage Visitor Attractions: An Operations Management Perspective*, London: Cassell.

Leiper, N. (2004). *Tourism Management* (3rd Edition), Frenchs Forest, NSW: Pearson Education Australia.

Leiper, N. (1990) Tourist attractions systems, *Annals of Tourism Research* 17(3): 367–384.

Leon, W. and Rosenzweig, R. (1989) *History Museums in the United States. A Critical Assessment*, Chicago: Board of Trustees of the University of Illinois.

Lerkplien, W., Rodhetbhai, C. and Keeratiboorana, Y. (2013) The management style of cultural tourism in the ancient monuments of Lower Central Thailand, *Asian Social Science* 9(1): 112–118.

Levi, D. and Kocher, S. (2013) Perception of sacredness at heritage religious sites, *Environment and Behavior* 45(7): 912–930.

Lewis, R. (1984) Theoretical and practical considerations in research design, *Cornell Hotel Restaurant Administration Quarterly* 24(4): 25–35.

Li, M., Wu, B. and Cai, L. (2008) Tourism development of World Heritage sites in China: a geographic perspective, *Tourism Management* 29: 308–319.

Li, Y. P. and Lo, R. L. B. (2004) Applicability of the Market Appeal – Robusticity Matrix: a case study of heritage tourism, *Tourism Management* 25(6): 789–800.

Litvin, S. and Mouri, N. (2009) A comparative study of the use of 'iconic' versus 'generic' advertising images for destination marketing, *Journal of Travel Research* 48(2): 152–161.

Litvin, S., Goldsmith, R. and Pan, B. (2007) Electronic word-of-mouth in hospitality and tourism management, *Tourism Management* 29: 458–468.

Liu, J. and du Cros, H. (2012) Intangible cultural heritage, education and museums. Focus Issue Seminar 1. Unpublished report to the UNESCO Observatory for Research in Local Cultures and Creativity in Education, Hong Kong.

Liu, T. S. (ed.) (2011) Intangible cultural heritage and local communities in East Asia, *Proceedings of the South China Research Centre, HKUST and the Hong Kong Heritage Museum International Conference in Hong Kong, December 2009*, Hong Kong: HKUST and the Hong Kong Heritage Museum.

Liu, Y. (2013) Image-based segmentation of cultural tourism market: the perceptions of Taiwan's inbound visitors, *Asia Pacific Journal of Tourism Research*, DOI: 10.1080/10941665.2013.833124.

Lord (2002) Creative tourism and cultural development: some trends and observations – Lord Cultural Resources. Available at: www.lord.ca/Media/Creative_Tourism_BK_paper.doc (accessed 7 March 2014).

Lord, G. D. and Lord, B. (1999) *The Manual of Museum Planning* (2nd Edition), London: The Stationery Office.

Lovelock, B. (2004) Tourist-created attractions: the emergence of a unique form of tourist attraction in southern New Zealand tourism geographies, *An International Journal of Tourism Space, Place and Environment* 6(4): 410–433.

Low, S. and Altman. I. (1992) Place attachment: a conceptual inquiry. In I. Altman and Low, S. M. (eds) *Place Attachment*, New York: Plenum Press, pp. 1–12.

Lowenthal, D. (1998) Selfishness in heritage. In Uzzell, David and Ballantyne, Roy (eds) *Contemporary Issues in Heritage and Environmental Interpretation,* London: The Stationery Office, pp. 26–36.

Lowenthal, D. (1994) The changing criteria of authenticity. In Larsen, Knut (ed.) *1994 Proceedings of the Nara Conference on Authenticity in relation to the World Heritage Convention,* Nara, Japan: UNESCO World Heritage Centre (France), Agency for Cultural Affairs (Japan), ICCROM (Italy) and ICOMOS (France), pp. 121–136.

Lowenthal, D. (1985) *The Past is a Foreign Country.* Cambridge: Cambridge University Press.

Lynch, M., Duinker, P., Sheehan, L. and Chute, J. E. (2010) Sustainable Mi'kmaw cultural tourism development in Nova Scotia, Canada: examining cultural tourist and Mi'kmaw perspectives, *Journal of Sustainable Tourism* 18(4): 539–556.

MacCannell, D. (2001) Tourist agency, *Tourist Studies* 1(1): 22–37.

MacDonald, R. and Joliffe, L. (2003) Cultural rural tourism: evidence from Canada, *Annals of Tourism Research* 30(2): 307–322.

Macintosh, A. and Prentice, R. C. (1999) Affirming authenticity: consuming cultural heritage, *Annals of Tourism Research* 26(3): 589–612.

Mack, R. W., Blose, J. E. and Pan, B. (2008) Believe it or not: credibility of blogs in tourism, *Journal of Vacation Marketing* 14(2): 133–144.

Mahon, M. (2007) The changing faces of rural populations, *Journal of Rural Studies* 23(3): 345–356.

Mak, A., Lumbers, M. and Eves, A. (2012) Globalisation and food consumption in tourism, *Annals of Tourism Research* 39(1): 171–196.

Mandala, L. (2013) *The Cultural and Heritage Traveler* (2013 Edition), Alexandria, VA: Mandala Research LLC. Available at: http://mandalaresearch.com/images/stories/free_download_CH_2013.pdf (accessed 4 March 2014).

Mandala, L. (2009) New study reveals popularity of U.S. cultural and heritage travel: large, affluent market focuses on history and tradition. Available at: http://mandalaresearch.com/images/stories/pressreleases/CHT_release_Oct_20.pdf (accessed 24 February 2014).

Mansor, N., Ahmad, W. and Mat, A. (2011) Tourism challenges among the SMEs in state of Terengganu, *International Journal of Business and Social Science* 2(1): 101–112.

Marwick, M. (2001) Tourism and the development of handicraft production in the Maltese Islands, *Tourism Geographies* 3(1): 29–51.

Mason, D. (2011) Escueler taller. A trainer's perspective. In ICOMOS (ed.) *General Assembly*, Paris: ICOMOS, pp. 257–262.

McCool, S. F. and David W. L. (2001) Tourism carrying capacity: tempting fantasy or useful reality?, *Journal of Sustainable Tourism* 9(5): 372–388.

McCormack, R. (2010) The Cultural & Heritage Traveler Study. Mandala Research for the U.S. Cultural & Heritage Tourism Marketing Council. Available at: http://theculturaltraveler.com/media-releases-2008-2012/cat_view/6-white-papers (accessed 4 March 2014).

McDonald, G. F. and Alsford, S. (1989) *Museum for the Global Village. The Canadian Museum of Civilization,* Hull: Canadian Museum of Civilization.

McIntosh, A. J. and Prentice, R. R. C. (1999) Affirming authenticity: consuming cultural heritage, *Annals of Tourism Research* 26(3): 589–612.

McIntosh, R. W. and Goeldner, C. R. (1990) *Tourism Principles, Practices, Philosophies* (6th Edition), New York: John Wiley and Son.

McKean, J., Johnson, D. and Walsh, R. (1995) Valuing time in travel cost demand analysis: an empirical investigation, *Land Economics* 71 (1): 96–105.

McKercher, B. (2003) Adopting a marketing approach to achieve sustainable cultural tourism, *International Journal of Tourism Sciences* 3(1): 129–142.

McKercher, B. (2002) Towards a classification of cultural tourists, *International Journal of Tourism Research* 4: 29–38.

McKercher, B. (2001) Attitudes to a non-viable community-owned heritage tourist attraction, *Journal of Sustainable Tourism* 9(1): 29–43.

McKercher, B. (1998b) The effect of market access on destination choice, *Journal of Travel Research* 37 (August): 39–47.

McKercher, B. (1998c) *The Business of Nature-Based Tourism,* Melbourne: Hospitality Press.

McKercher, B. (1996) Understanding attitudes to tourism in protected areas. In Richins, H. Richardson, J. and Crabtree, A. (eds) *Taking the Next Steps*, Brisbane: The Ecotourism Association of Australia, pp. 229–234.

McKercher B. (1993) Some fundamental truths about tourism: understanding tourism's social and environmental impacts, *Journal of Sustainable Tourism* 1(1): 6–16.

McKercher, B. and Chan, A. (2005) How special is special interest tourism?, *Journal of Travel Research* 44(1): 21–31.

McKercher, B., Chan, A. and Lam, C. (2008) The impact of distance on international tourist movements, *Journal of Travel Research* 47(2): 208–224.

McKercher, B. and Chow, B. (2001) Cultural distance and cultural tourism participation, *Pacific Tourism Review* 5(1/2): 21–30.

McKercher, B. and du Cros, H. (2005) Cultural heritage and visiting attractions. In Buhalis, D. and Costa, C. (eds) *Tourism Business Frontiers: Consumers, Products and Industry,* Butterworth-Heinemann, pp. 211–219.

McKercher B. and du Cros, H. (1999) The fundamental truths of cultural tourism. In Heung V. C. S., Ap, J. and Wong K. K. F. (eds) *Tourism 2000, Asia Pacific's Role in the New Millennium*, Hong Kong: APTA, pp. 272–279.

McKercher, B. and du Cros, H. (1998) I climbed to the top of Ayers Rock and still didn't see Uluru! In Faulkner, D., Tideswell, C. and Weaver, D. (eds) *Progress in Tourism and Hospitality Research 1998*, Canberra: CAUTHE/BTR, pp. 376 – 386.

McKercher B., du Cros, H. and Ho, S. Y. (2004) Attributes of popular cultural tourism attractions, *Annals of Tourism Research* 31(2): 393–407.

McKercher, B. and Ho, P. (2012) Cultural tourism and the enhancement of quality of life. In Uysal, M., Perdue, R. and Sirgy, J. (eds) *Handbook of Tourism and Quality-of-Life Research: Enhancing the Lives of Tourists and Residents of Host Communities*, Dordrecht, The Netherlands: Springer, pp. 341–357.

McKercher, B. and Ho, P. (2006) Assessing the tourism potential of smaller cultural attractions, *Journal of Sustainable Tourism* 14(5): 473–488.

McKercher, B., Ho, S. Y. and du Cros, H. (2005) Relationships between tourism and cultural heritage management, *Tourism Management* 26(4): 539–548.

McKercher, B., Ho, S. Y., du Cros, H. and Chow, B. (2002) Activities based segmentation of the cultural tourism market, *Journal of Travel and Tourism Marketing* 12(1): 23–46.

McKercher, B. and Lau, G. (2007) Understanding the movements of tourists in a destination: testing the importance of markers in the tourist attraction system, *Asian Journal of Tourism and Hospitality Research* 1(1): 39–53.

McKercher, B. and Prideaux, B. (2014) Academic myths of tourism, *Annals of Tourism Research* 46: 16–28.

McKercher, B., Wan, S. M. and Tse, T. (2006) Are short duration cultural festivals tourist attractions?, *Journal of Sustainable Tourism* 14(1): 55–66.

McKercher, B., Weber, H. K. and du Cros, H. (2008) Rationalizing inappropriate behavior at contested sites, *Journal of Sustainable Tourism* 16(4): 369–385.

McNicholas, B. (2004) Arts, culture and business: a relationship transformation, a nascent field, *International Journal of Arts Management* 7(1): 57–68.

Mehmetoglu, M. and Engen, M. (2011) Pine and Gilmore's concept of experience economy and its dimensions: an empirical examination in tourism, *Journal of Quality Assurance in Hospitality and Tourism* 12(4): 237–255.

Messineo, E. (2012) Tourist creative processes and experiences in the European cultural itinerary 'The Phoenicians' Route', *Journal of Tourism Consumption and Practice* 4(2): 41–54.

MICT (2009) *Laos Visitor Etiquette*, pamphlet published by Vientiane Ministry of Information, Culture and Tourism.

Middleton, V. (1994) *Marketing Travel and Tourism* (2nd Edition), Oxford: Butterworth Heinemann.

Mill, R. C. and Morrison, A. (1985) *The Tourism System*, London, Prentice-Hall International.

Miller, J. (1997) Cultural tourism worthy of note, *Hotel and Motel Management* 212: 15–17.

Mkono, M. (2013) African and Western tourists: object authenticity quest?, *Annals of Tourism Research* 41: 195–214.

Möller, A. and Deckert, M. (2009) Project Report – WPA 3.1.1 Market Analysis. Available at: http://www.central2013.eu/fileadmin/user_upload/Downloads/outputlib/CrossCultour_Market_Analysis.pdf (accessed 12 July 2014).

Montgomery, J. (1998) Making a city: urbanity, vitality and urban design, *Journal of Urban Design* 3(1): 93–116.

Morrison, Alison (1998) Small firm co-operative marketing in a peripheral tourism region, *International Journal of Contemporary Hospitality Management* 10(5): 191–197.

MOS (Museum of Sydney) (2014) First Fleet Exhibition, Museum of Sydney. Available at: http://sydneylivingmuseums.com.au/museum-of-sydney (accessed 20 May 2014).

MOS (Museum of Sydney) (2014) About. Available at: http://www.sydneylivingmuseums.com.au (accessed 8 May 2014).

Moscardo, G. (1996) Mindful visitors: creating sustainable links between heritage and tourism. *Annals of Tourism Research* 23(2): 376–387.

Moscardo, G., Morrison, A. L., Pearce, P. L., Lang, C. T. and O'Leary, J. T. (1995) Understanding vacation destination choice through travel motivation and activities, *Journal of Vacation Marketing* 2(2): 109–122.

Moulin, C. and Boniface, P. (2001) Routing heritage for tourism: making heritage and cultural tourism networks for socio-economic development, *International Journal of Heritage Studies* 7(3): 237–48.

MTC (2009) *Ontario Cultural and Heritage Tourism Product Research Paper*, Toronto: Ontario Ministry of Tourism, Culture and Sport. Available at: http://www.mtc.gov.on.ca/en/publications/Ontario_Cultural_and_Heritage_Tourism.pdf (accessed 7 March 2014).

Muller, D. K. and Petterrson, R. (2001) Access to Sami tourism in northern Sweden, *Scandinavian Journal of Hospitality and Tourism* 1(1): 5–18.

Munsters, W. (2012) Malta's candidature for the title of European Capital of Culture 2018: the cultural tourism perspective. Available at: http://www.zuyd.nl/~/media/Files/Onderzoek/Kenniskring%20Toerisme%20en%20Cultuur/Wil%20MunstersMalta%20ECOC%202018.pdf (accessed 7 March 2014).

Muresan, A. (1998) The fortified church of Biertan (Transylvania). In Shackley, Myra (ed.) *Visitor Management. Case Studies from World Heritage Sites*, London: Butterworth-Heinemann, pp. 26–45.

Niemcyzk, N. (2013) Cultural tourists: 'an attempt to classify them', *Tourism Management Perspectives* 5: 24–30.

Nishimura, Yukio (1994) Changing concept of authenticity in the context of Japanese conservation history. In Larsen, Knut (ed.) *1994 Proceedings of the Nara Conference on Authenticity in relation to the World Heritage Convention*, Nara, Japan: UNESCO World Heritage Centre (France), Agency for Cultural Affairs (Japan), ICCROM (Italy) and ICOMOS (France), pp. 175–184.

NPS (2011) *CRM Heritage Stewardship Journal*, National Park Service, USA. Available at: http://www.nps.gov/CRMjournal (accessed 24 March 2014).

NTHP (1999) *Getting Started: How to Succeed in Heritage Tourism,* Washington: National Trust for Heritage Preservation.

Nyaupane, G., White, D. and Budruk, M. (2006) Motive-based tourist market segmentation: an application to Native American cultural heritage sites in Arizona, USA, *Journal of Heritage Tourism* 1(2): 81–99.

Nyiri, P. (2006) *Scenic Spots. Chinese Tourism, the State and Cultural Authority*, Pullman, WA: Washington State University Press.

Olsen, D. H. (2006) Management issues for religious heritage attractions. In Timothy, D. and Olsen, D. H. (eds) *Tourism Religion and Spiritual Journeys,* Abingdon: Routledge, pp. 104–118.

Olsson, A. (2010) A tourist attraction's members: their motivations, relations and roles, *Scandinavian Journal of Hospitality and Tourism* 10(4): 411–429.

O'Sullivan, D. and Jackson, M. J. (2002) Festival tourism: a contributor to sustainable local economic development?, *Journal of Sustainable Tourism* 10(4): 325–342.

Özel, C. and Kozak, N. (2012) Motive based segmentation of the cultural tourism market: a study of Turkish domestic tourists, *Journal of Quality Assurance in Hospitality and Tourism* 13(3): 165–186.

Palmer, C. (1999) Tourism and the symbols of identity, *Tourism Management* 20(3): 313–321.

Palmer, M. (2000) Signposts and gatekeepers: tourist information and holiday experience in the Dominican Republic. Available at: http://kiskeya-alternative.org/publica/palmer/signs.html (accessed 15 March 2014).

Pan, B., MacLaurin, T. and Crotts, J. (2007) Travel blogs and the implications for destination marketing, *Journal of Travel Research* 46: 35–45.

Pan, S. and Ryan, C. (2007) Analysing printed media travelogues: means and purposes with reference to framing destination image, *Tourism, Culture and Communication* 7: 85–97.

Past Preservers (2014) Digging starts on the Tutankhamun Tomb Replica Project. Available at: http://networkedblogs.com/Thmh0 (accessed 10 April 2014).

Patuelli, R., Mussoni, M. and Candela, G. (2013) The effects of World Heritage sites on domestic tourism: a spatial interaction model for Italy, *Journal of Geographical Systems* 15(3): 369–402.

Pearce, D. (1989) *Tourism Development* (2nd Edition), London: Longman.

Pearce, P. L. and Lee, U. I. (2005) Developing the travel career approach to tourist motivation, *Journal of Travel Research* 43: 226–237.

Pearson, M. and Sullivan, S. (1995) *Looking after Heritage Places. The Basics of Heritage Planning for Managers, Landowners and Administrators.* Melbourne: Melbourne University Press.

Pedersen, A. (2002) Managing tourism at World Heritage sites: a practical manual for World Heritage site managers. Available at: http://whc.unesco.org/uploads/activities/documents/activity-113-2.pdf (accessed 14 July 2014).

Pedrotti, F. (2012) Concept design – an innovative approach to learning: the case of Saint James' Way as a playground for meaningful learning experiences, *Journal of Tourism Consumption and Practice* 4(2): 25–40.

Peleggi, M. (1996) National heritage and global tourism in Thailand, *Annals of Tourism Research* 23(2): 432–448.

Perrottet, T. (2002) *Route 66 AD: On the Trail of Ancient Roman Tourists*, Sydney: Random House.

Petroman, I., Petroman, C., Marin, D., Ciolac, R., Văduva, L. and Pandur, I. (2013) Types of cultural tourism, *Scientific Papers: Animal Science and Biotechnologies* 46(1): 385–388.

Petzet, M. (1994) 'In the full richness of their authenticity' – the test of authenticity and the new cult of monuments. In Larsen, Knut (ed.) *1994 Proceedings of the Nara Conference on Authenticity in relation to the World Heritage Convention*, Nara, Japan: UNESCO World Heritage Centre (France), Agency for Cultural Affairs (Japan), ICCROM (Italy) and ICOMOS (France), pp. 85–100.

Pine, J. and Gilmore, J. (1999) *The Experience Economy*, Boston: Harvard Business School Press.

Piscitelli, M. (2011) Preservation of paths for a sustainable tourism in the Amalfi coast, *Journal of Heritage and Sustainable Development* 1(1): 41–48.

Pocock, C., Stell, M., Frost, L., Crozier, J. and Ancher, S. (2010) *Living Memory and the Interpretation of Heritage. Developing a Multimedia Interactive to Record and Store Personal Stories for Use in Heritage Interpretation and Research*, Goldcoast, Australia: Sustainable Tourism CRC.

Poon, A. (1988) Innovation and the future of Caribbean tourism, *Tourism Management* 9(3): 213–220.

Poon, A. (1994) The 'new tourism' revolution, *Tourism Management* 15(2): 91–92.

Popp, M. (2012) Positive and negative urban tourist crowding: Florence, Italy, *Tourism Geographies: An International Journal of Tourism Space, Place and Environment*, 14(1): 50–72.

Prentice, R. C. (1993) *Tourism and Heritage Attractions,* London: Routledge.

Prideaux, B. and Kininmont, L.J. (1999) Tourism and heritage are not strangers: a study of opportunities for rural heritage museums to maximize tourism visitation, *Journal of Travel Research* 37 (Feburary): 299–303.

Quinn, B. (2006) Problematising 'festival tourism': arts festivals and sustainable development in Ireland, *Journal of Sustainable Tourism* 14(3): 288–306.

QVB (Queen Victoria Building) (2014) About QVB. Available at: http://www.qvb.com.au/about-qvb (accessed 25 March 2014).

Ramsey, D. and Everitt, J. (2008) If you dig it, they will come!: Archaeology heritage sites and tourism development in Belize, *Central America Tourism Management* 29(5): 909–916.

Rátz, T. and Puczkó, L. (2003) A World Heritage industry? Tourism at Hungarian World Heritage sites. In Gravari-Barbas, M. and Guichard-Anguis, S. (eds) *Regards croisés sur le patrimoine dans le monde à l'aube du XXIe siècle*, Paris: Presses de l'Université de Paris-Sorbonne, pp. 467–481. Available at: http://www.ratztamara.com/holloko.pdf (accessed 11 May 2009).

Richards, G. (2011) Cultural tourism trends in Europe: a context for the development of cultural routes. In Khovanova-Rubicondo, K. (ed.) *Impact of European Cultural Routes on SMEs' Innovation and Competitiveness*, Strasbourg: Council of Europe Publishing, pp. 21–39.

Richards, G. (1996) *Cultural Tourism in Europe,* Oxford: CAB International.

Richards, G. and Marques, L. (2012) Exploring creative tourism, *Journal of Tourism Consumption and Practice* 4(2): 1–11.

Richards, G. and Raymond, C. (2000) Creative tourism, *Atlas News* 1: 23.

Richardson, John I. (1996) *Marketing Australian Travel and Tourism: Principles and Practice*, Melbourne: Hospitality Press.

Robinson, M. (1999) Collaboration and cultural consent: refocussing sustainable tourism, *Journal of Sustainable Tourism* 7(3 &4): 379–397.

Rosenbaum, Alvin (1995a) Cultural resources and sustainable tourism: the end of tourism as we know it. Lecture for the International Institute of Tourism Studies, George Washington University,Washington, DC. Available at: http://www.al.net/endtourism.html (accessed 6 June 2000).

Rosenbaum, Alvin (1995b) *A Regional Development Strategy: National Heritage Tour Routes,* Paper prepared for the Pennsylvania's Heritage Partnerships Conference, Pittsburgh. Available at: http://www.al.net/Strategy.html (accessed 6 June 2000).

Rössler, M. (2006) World Heritage cultural landscapes: a UNESCO flagship programme 1992–2006, *Landscape Research* 31(4): 333–353.

Rössler, M. (1994) Cultural landscapes, itineraries and canals for the World Heritage list. In ICOMOS and Ministry of Culture, Spain (eds) *Routes as Part of our Cultural Heritage*, Madrid: Meeting of Experts, ICOMOS and Ministry of Culture, pp. 59–70.

Roura, R. (2009) The polar cultural heritage as a tourism attraction: a case study of the airship mooring mast at Ny-Ålesund, Svalbard, *Teoros* 28(1): 29–38.

Rudd, M. A. and Davis, J. A. (1998) Industrial heritage tourism as Bingham Canyon Copper Mine, *Journal of Travel Research* 36(3): 85–89.

Russo, A. P. (2002) The 'vicious cycle' of tourism development in heritage cities, *Annals of Tourism Research* 29(1): 165–182.

Russell, Roslyn and Faulkner, Bill (1999) Movers and shakers: chaos makers in tourism development, *Tourism Management* 20(4): 411–423.

Ryan, Chris (2000) Tourist experiences, phenomenographic analysis, post-positivism and neural network software, *International Journal of Tourism Research* 2(2): 119–132.

Ryan, C. and Dewar, K. (1995) Evaluating the communication process between interpreter and visitor, *Tourism Management* 16(4): 295–303.

Sakharchuk, E., Kharitonova, T., Krivosheeva, T. and Ilkevich, S. (2013) The study of the present state and prospects of cultural tourism in the Russian Federation (exemplifying the Moscow region), *World Applied Sciences Journal* 27: 309–314.

Salazar, N. (2012) Community-based cultural tourism: issues, threats and opportunities, *Journal of Sustainable Tourism* 20(1): 9–22.

Salazar, N. (2005) Tourism and glocalization: 'local' tour guiding, *Annals of Tourism Research* 32(3): 628–646.

Sandhusen, R. (2008) *Marketing* (4th Edition), Hauppauge, NY: Barrons.

Sangpikul, A. (2010) Marketing ecotourism through the internet: a case of ecotourism business in Thailand, *International Journal of Hospitality and Tourism Administration* 11(2): 107–137.

Santana, G. (2003) Tourism development in coastal areas – Brazil: economic, demand and environmental issues, *Journal of Coastal Research* 19: 85–93.

Santos, C., Bekhassen, Y. and Caton, K. (2008) Reimagining Chinatown: an analysis of tourism discourse, *Tourism Management* 29(5): 1002–1012.

Schmiechen, J., James, D. and Tremblay, P. (2010) *Learning Markets and Indigeneous Tourism: Action Research Pilot of Developing a Learning Markets Cluster and Sample Itinerary in Central Australia,*Canberra: CRC for Sustainable Tourism. Available at: http://www.crctourism.com.au/wms/upload/resources/100025%20Learning%20Markets%20WEB.pdf (accessed 14 April 2014).

Schweitzer, C. (1999) The hot ticket to cool meetings, *Association Management* 51(8): 121–130.

Sculptures by the Sea (2013) History/Frequently Asked Questions/Tactile Tours. Available at: http://www.sculpturebythesea.com/Home.aspx (accessed 4 April 2014).

Seaton, A. V. and Bennett, M. (1996) *The Marketing of Tourism Products: Concepts, Issues and Cases*, Boston: International Thompson Business Press.

Secretary of Culture (2014) *Museum of Portuguese Language in São Paulo*. Available at: http://www. museulinguaportuguesa.org.br/info_ingles.php (accessed 8 April 2014).

Shackley, M. (ed.) (1998) *Visitor Management: A Strategic Focus*, London: Focal Press.

Sharda, N. and Ponnada, M. (2008) Tourism blog visualiser for better tour planning, *Journal of Vacation Marketing* 14(2): 157–167.

Sharples, L., Yeoman, I. and Leask, A. (1999) Operations management. In Leask, A. and Yeoman, I. (eds) *Heritage Visitor Attractions. An Operations Management Perspective*, London: Cassell, pp. 22–38.

Sharpley, Richard (2000) The consumption of tourism revisited. In Robinson, Mike, Long, Philip, Evans, Nigel, Sharpley, Richard and Swarbrooke, John (eds) *Motivations, Behaviours and Tourist Types*, Leeds: Centre for Travel and Tourism/Business Education Publishers, pp. 381–392.

Shoval, N. and Raveh, A. (2004) The categorization of tourist attractions: the modeling of tourist cities based on a new method of multivariate analysis, *Tourism Management* 25(6): 741–750.

Silapacharanan, S. and Dupuy, J. J. (2011) The impacts of enhancing value of traditional architecture on regional development. In ICOMOS (ed.) *General Assembly*, Paris: ICOMOS, pp. 306–311.

Silberberg, T. (1995). Cultural tourism and business opportunities for museums and heritage sites, *Tourism Management* 16(5): 361–365.

Sintas, J. L. and Alvarez, G. (2005) Four characters on the stage playing three games: performing arts consumption in Spain, *Journal of Business Research* 58: 1446–1455.

Sizer, S. R. (1999) The ethical challenges of managing pilgrimages to the Holy Land, *International Journal of Contemporary Hospitality Management* 11(2/3): 85–90.

Sjogren, T. and Brannas, K. (1996) Recreational travel time conditional on supply, work travel time and income, *Tourism Economics* 2(3): 268–275.

Sletvold, O. (1996) Viking heritage: contexts and commodification. In Robinson, M., Evans, N. and Callaghan, P. (eds) *Tourism and Culture: Image, Identity and Marketing*, Sunderland, UK: The Centre for Travel and Tourism/British Education Publishers, pp. 217–230.

Smith, M. (2003) *Issues in Cultural Tourism Studies*, London: Routledge.

Snepenger, D., Meged, K., Snelling, M. and Worrall, K. (1990) Information search strategies by destination naïve tourists, *Journal of Travel Research* 29(1): 13–16.

Snowden, D. (2008) *Heritage Tourism in Australia: A Guide for Historical Societies*, Canberra: Federation of Australian Historical Societies Inc. Available at: http://www.history.org.au/Documents/Heritage_Tourism_in_Australia.pdf (accessed 14 May 2014).

Sofield, T. and Li, S. (1998) Tourism development and cultural policies in China, *Annals of Tourism Research* 25(2): 362–392.

Sokchea, M. and Di Certo, B. (2012) Angkor corruption alleged [Sok Kong sued for stealing revenue from Angkor Wat] *Phnom Phen Post*, 12 March 2012. Available at: http://khmerization.blogspot.hk/2012/03/angkor-corruption-alleged-sok-kong-sued.html (accessed 12 March 2014).

Sollner, A. and Rese, M. (2001) Market segmentation and the structure of competition: applicability of the strategic group concept for an improved market segmentation on industrial markets, *Journal of Business Research* 51: 25–36.

Solomon, P. (1997). Conversation in information-seeking contexts: a test of an analytical framework, *Library and Information Science Research* 19(3): 217–248.

Soontayatron, S. (2013) Thais' coping with sociocultural impacts of tourism development, *Asia Pacific Journal of Tourism Research*, DOI: 10.1080/10941665.2013.839458.

Spearritt, P. (1991) Money, taste and industrial heritage. In Richard, J. and Spearritt, P. (eds) *Packaging the Past? Public Histories*, Melbourne: Melbourne University Press and Australian Historical Studies, pp. 33–45.

Staiff, R. and Bushell, R. (2013) Mobility and modernity in Luang Prabang, Laos: re-thinking heritage and tourism, *International Journal of Heritage Studies* 19(1): 98–113.

Stalker, P. (1984) Visions of poverty, visions of wealth, *New Internationalist* December: 7–9.

Stamenkovic, I. and Jaksic, S. (2013) Tourism potential of the old town centre in Sambor, based on the Hilary Du Cros Model, *European Research* 53(6–2): 1746–1754.

Stebbins, R. A. (1996) Cultural tourism as serious leisure, *Annals of Tourism Research* 23: 948–950.

Steiner, C. J. and Reisinger, Y. (2006) Understanding existential authenticity, *Annals of Tourism Research* 33(2): 299–318.

Stewart, S. I. and Vogt, C. A. (1999) A case-based approach to understanding vacation planning, *Leisure Sciences* 21: 79–95.

Stocks, J. (1996) Heritage and tourism in the Irish Republic – towards a giant theme park. In Robinson, M., Evans, N. and Callaghan, P. (eds) *Tourism and Culture: Image, Identity and Marketing*, Sunderland, UK: The Centre for Travel and Tourism/British Education Publishers, pp. 251–260.

Stoddard, J., Pollard, C. and Evans, M. (2012) The triple bottom line: a framework for sustainable tourism development, *International Journal of Hospitality and Tourism Administration* 13(3): 233–258.

Stovel, H. (1998) *Risk Preparedness: A Management Manual for World Cultural Heritage*, Rome: ICCROM.

Suitman.org (2012) Public Fair No. 1. Available at: http://suitman.org/news.php?cid=32&feature=0 (accessed 20 May 2014).

Theerapappisit, P. (2009) Pro-poor ethnic tourism in the Mekong: a study of three approaches in northern Thailand, *Asia Pacific Journal of Tourism Research* 14(2): 201–221.

Thevenot, G. (2007) Blogging as a social media, *Tourism and Hospitality Research* 7(3/4): 287–289.

Thorne, S. (2012) Canada's cultural tourism industry: the numbers shouldn't surprise us, Economic Development.org. Available at: http://economicdevelopment.org/2012/11/canadas-cultural-tourism-economy-8-billion-and-counting (accessed 24 February 2014).

Thorne, S. (2008) Place as product: a place-based approach to cultural tourism. Available at: http://ttracanada-torc.ca/torc/downs1/Place-Based%20Cultural%20Tourism.pdf (accessed 7 March 2014).

Tides Institute and Museum of Art (2012) ARTSIPELAGO works to increase vibrancy in Passamaquoddy Region thanks to ArtPlace grant. Available at: http://www.tidesinstitute.org/artplace.html (accessed 20 May 2014).

Tighe, A. J. (1986) The Arts/Tourism Partnership, *Journal of Travel Research,* 24 (3): 2–5.

Tilden, F. (1977) *Interpreting Our Heritage* (3rd Edition), Chapel Hill: University of North Carolina Press.

Timothy, D. J. (1997) Tourism and the personal heritage experience, *Annals of Tourism Research* 24(3): 751–754.

TQ (nd) Cultural tourism. Brisbane: Tourism Queensland. Available at: http://www.tq.com.au/fms/tq_corporate/research/fact_sheets/cultural_tourism.pdf (accessed 7 March 2014).

Tracy, B. (2004) The 7 Ps of marketing: take charge of your marketing efforts and beat the competition with this simple formula. Available at: http://www.entrepreneur.com/article/70824 (accessed 25 March 2014).

Tufts, S. and Milne, S. (1999) Museums: a supply-side perspective, *Annals of Tourism Research* 26(3): 613–631.

Tunbridge, J. E. and Ashworth, G. (1996) *Dissonant Heritage: The Management of the Past as a Resource in Conflict*, Chichester: John Wiley and Sons.

TV (2013) *Cultural Tourism Market Profile Year Ending June 2013*, Melbourne: Tourism Victoria.

Tweed, C. (2005) Taxonomy of cultural attractors. Deliverable D8. PICTURE (pro-active management of the impact of cultural tourism upon urban resources and economies). Available at: http://www.culture-routes.lu/picture/IMG/pdf/225_long_en.pdf (accessed 28 March 2014).

Twigger-Ross, C. L. and Uzzell, D. L. (1996) Place and identity processes, *Journal of Environmental Psychology* 16(3): 205–220.

Uluru-Kata Tjuta National Park (2010) Management Plan 2010–2020. Available at: http://www.environment.gov.au/resource/management-plan-2010-2020-uluru-kata-tjuta-national-park (accessed 8 April 2014).

UM (2012) Cultural heritage travelers. University of Minnesota Tourism Centre. Available at: http://www.tourism.umn.edu/ResearchReports/MarketSegments/CulturalHeritage/index.htm (accessed 24 February 2014).

UNESCO (2014) Intangible heritage. Available at: http://portal.unesco.org/culture/en/ev.php-hURL_ID=34325&URL_DO=DO_TOPIC&URL_SECTION=201.html (accessed 8 April 2014).

UNESCO (2013) Cultural tourism definition. Available at: http://culent.com/2013/03/25/unesco-cultural-tourism/ (accessed 24 February 2014).

UNESCO (2008) *World Heritage Information Kit*, Paris: UNESCO.

UNESCO (2007) Frontiers of the Roman Empire World Heritage Site Hadrian's Wall Management Plan 2008–2014. Available at: http://www.visithadrianswall.co.uk/dbimgs/3_%20Hadrian's%20Wall%20 2008-2014%20-%20Greyscale%20text%20%26%20appendices.pdf (accessed 15 March 2014).

UNESCO (2006) International Conference on the Safeguarding of Tangible and Intangible Cultural Heritage: Towards an Integrated Approach, *Proceedings of the UNESCO General Conference in Nara, Japan, October 2004*, Tokyo, Japan: UNESCO and the Ministry of Culture, Japan.

UNESCO (2003) UNESCO Convention for the Safeguarding of the Intangible Cultural Heritage. Available at: http://www.unesco.org/culture/ich/index.php?lg=en&pg=00006 (accessed 31 January 2014).

UNESCO (2000) Levuka, Fiji Action Plan. Forum conducted at UNESCO Culture Heritage Management and Tourism: Models for Co-operation among Stakeholders Conference/Workshop, Bhaktapur, Nepal 8–16 April 2000.

UNESCO (1999) *Interim Report on the Project Concerning the Proclamation by UNESCO of Masterpieces of Oral and Intangible Heritage of Humanity*, Paris: UNESCO.

UNESCO (1998) *Draft Decisions Recommended by the Program and External Relations Commission 155th Session of the Executive Board 2/11/1998 Resolution 3.5.5*, Paris: UNESCO.

UNESCO and Nordic World Heritage Office (1999) *Sustainable Tourism and Cultural Heritage. A Review of Development Assistance and Its Potential to Promote Sustainability*, Nordic World Heritage Office and UNESCO, Norway.

UNESCO Bangkok (2014) UNESCO Asia-Pacific Awards for Cultural Heritage Conservation. Available at: http://www.unescobkk.org/culture/wh/asia-pacific-heritage-awards (accessed 7 April 2014).

UNESCO Creative Cities Network (2006) Towards Sustainable Strategies for Creative Tourism, Santa Fe, NM, October 2006.

UNESCO/HarperCollins (2014) *The World's Heritage. A Guide to All 981 UNESCO World Heritage Sites*, Paris: UNESCO Publishing/HarperCollins.

UNESCO Intangible Cultural Heritage (2014) Safeguarding without freezing. Available at: http://www. unesco.org/culture/ich/index.php?lg=en&pg=00012 (accessed 7 May 2014).

UNESCO, Nara, Japan (2006) *International Conference on the Safeguarding of Tangible and Intangible Cultural Heritage: Towards an Integrated Approach,* Nara, Japan: UNESCO.

UNESCO Observatory RLCCE (2012) Intangible Cultural Heritage, Education and Museums. RLCCE Focus Issue Seminar 1. UNESCO Observatory for Research in Local Cultures and Creativity in Education, Hong Kong.

UNESCO WHC (2014a) World Heritage. Available at: http://whc.unesco.org (accessed 2 April 2014).

UNESCO WHC (2014b) Managing Cultural World Heritage (Resource Manual). Available at: http:// whc.unesco.org/en/resourcemanuals (accessed 2 April 2014).

UNESCO WHC (2014c) World Heritage Convention. Available at: http://whc.unesco.org/en/convention/ (accessed 7 April 2014).

UNESCO WHC (2014d) World Heritage and Sustainable Tourism Programme – The Five Programme Objectives. Available at: http://whc.unesco.org/en/tourism/(accessed 9 July 2014).

UNESCO WHC (2013) Convention Operational Guidelines – World Heritage Convention. Available at: http://whc.unesco.org/pg.cfm?cid=57 (accessed 9 July 2014).

UNESCO WHC (2002) Minutes of Budapest World Heritage Committee Meeting. Available at: http:// unesdoc.unesco.org/images/0012/001257/125796e.pdf (accessed 2 April 2014).

UNESCO WHC News (2014) Director-General opens international conference in Bergen on UNESCO culture conventions. Available at: http://whc.unesco.org/en/news/1115 (accessed 2 April 2014).

UNESCO WHC News (2012) Vigan, Philippines recognized for best practice in World Heritage site management. Available at: http://whc.unesco.org/en/news/948 (accessed 2 April 2014).

UNESCO WHC, ICOMOS, ICCROM and IUCN (2013) *Managing Cultural World Heritage*. Paris: UNESCO Resource Manual Series. Available at: http://whc.unesco.org/en/managing-cultural-world-heritage (accessed 26 March 2014).

UNESCO WHC, ICOMOS, ICCROM and IUCN (2010) *Managing Disaster Risks for World Heritage*. Paris: UNESCO. Available at: http://whc.unesco.org/en/managing-disaster-risks (accessed 26 March 2014).

UNWTO (2014) Vietnam hosts first international conference on spiritual tourism. Available at: http:// media.unwto.org/news/2013-11-29/viet-nam-hosts-1st-international-conference-spiritual-tourism (accessed 7 May 2014).

UNWTO (2012) *Tourism and Intangible Cultural Heritage*, Madrid: UNWTO (Hilary du Cros: principal author).

UNWTO (2008a) *International Conference on Tourism, Religion and Dialogue of Cultures, Cordoba, Spain*, Madrid: UNWTO.

UNWTO (2008b), '*Tourism and Handicrafts*', A Report on the International Conference on Tourism and Handicrafts, Madrid: UNWTO.

UNWTO (2006a) *Cultural Tourism and Poverty Alleviation: The Asian Perspective*, Madrid: UN World Tourism Organization. Available at: http://www.wtoelibrary.org/content/l3163r/fulltext.pdf (accessed 24 February 2014).

UNWTO (2006b) *Poverty Alleviation through Tourism, a Compilation of Good Practices*, Madrid: UNWTO.

UNWTO (2006c) *A Report on the International Conference on 'Cultural Tourism and Local Communities' Yogyakarta, Indonesia 8–10 February 2006*, Madrid: World Tourism Organization.

UNWTO (2004a) *Indicators of Sustainable Development for Tourism Destinations: A Guidebook*, Madrid, UNWTO.

UNWTO (2004b) *Tourism Congestion Management at Natural and Cultural Sites*, Madrid: World Tourism Organization.

UNWTO (2002) *Tourism Market Trends: World Overview and Tourism Topics*, Madrid: World Tourism Organization.

UNWTO (2001) *Yunnan Province Tourism Development Master Plan*, Madrid: National Tourism Administration of the People's Republic of China, Yunnan Provincial Tourism Administration and United Nations World Tourism Organization.

Urban Splash (2014) Mills Bakery, Royal William Yard Plymouth, UK. Photos available at: http://www.urbansplash.co.uk/gallery/mills-bakery (accessed 25 March 2014).

Urry, J. (2002) *The Tourist Gaze*, Second edition, London: Sage.

US ICOMOS (1996) *The ICOMOS International Committee on Cultural Tourism*, US/ICOMOS Newsletter Number 6 (Special Edition), Chicago, IL: US ICOMOS.

van der Ark, A. and Richards, G. (2006) Attractiveness of cultural activities in European cities: a latent class approach, *Tourism Management* 27(6): 1408–1413.

VB (Visit Britain) (2010) *Culture and Heritage Topic Profile*. London: Visit Britain. Available at: http://www.visitbritain.org/Images/Culture%20%26%20Heritage%20Topic%20Profile%20Full_tcm29-14711.pdf (accessed 7 March 2014).

Ventacachellum, I. (2004) Crafts and tourism. Available at: http://www.craftrevival.org/AHTML/Tourism.htm (accessed 10 April 2005).

Vogt, C. A., Kah, A., Chang, H. and Leonard, S. (2008) Sharing the heritage of Kodiak Island with tourists: views from the hosts. In Prideaux, B., Timothy, D. and Chon, K. (eds) *Cultural and Heritage Tourism in Asia and the Pacific*, Abingdon: Routledge, pp. 118–133.

Vong, F. (2013a) Application of cultural tourist typology in a gaming destination – Macao, *Current Issues in Tourism*, DOI: 10.1080/13683500.2013.842543

Vong, F. (2013b) Relationships among perception of heritage management, satisfaction and destination cultural image, *Journal of Tourism and Cultural Change* 11(3): 287–301.

VW (Visit Wales) (2009) Cultural tourism research – Cardiff: visit Wales and the Arts Council of Wales. Available at: www.artswales.org/3060.file.dld (accessed 7 March 2014).

Walle, A. H. (1993) Tourism and traditional people: forging equitable strategies, *Journal of Travel Research* 31(3): 14–19.

Wang, N. (1999) Rethinking authenticity in tourism experience, *Annals of Tourism Research* 26(2): 349–370.

Wantanabe, K. (2006) The history of Japan's system for the protection of cultural property. In UNESCO (ed.) *International Conference on The Safeguarding of Tangible and Intangible Cultural Heritage: Towards an Integrated Approach. Proceedings of the UNESCO General Conference in Nara, Japan, October, 2004*, Nara, Japan: UNESCO and the Ministry of Culture, Japan, pp. 79–84.

Welgemoed, Marietha (1996) The tourist guide as culture broker: a South African scenario. In Robinson, Mike, Evans, Nigel and Callaghan, Paul (eds) *Tourism and Culture: Image, Identity and Marketing*, Sunderland, UK: The Centre for Travel and Tourism/British Education Publishers, pp. 297–302.

Wenger, A. (2008) Analysis of travel bloggers' characteristics and their communication about Austria as a tourism destination, *Journal of Vacation Marketing* 14(2): 169–176.

Whitfield, S. (2009) Stein's Silk Road legacy, *Asian Affairs* 40(2): 224–242.

Whyte, B., Hood, T. and White, B. (eds) (2012) *Cultural and Heritage Tourism: A Handbook for Community Champions*, Ottawa: Federal Provincial Territorial Ministers of Culture and Heritage. Available at: http://www.tpr.alberta.ca/tourism/tourismdevelopment/pdf/CulturalHeritageTourismHandbook.pdf (accessed 24 February 2014).

Whytock, J. K. (1999) National historic sites and national parks in Canadian heritage tourism presentation made to the International Conference on Heritage and Tourism, Hong Kong.

Williams, D. R. and McIntyre, N. (2012) Place affinities, lifestyle mobilities, and quality-of-life, In Uysal, M., Perdue, R. and Siggy, M. (eds) *Handbook of Tourism and Quality-of-life Research*, The Netherlands: Springer, pp. 209–231.

Williams, P. (2010) Cultural tourism and the UK City of Culture. Tourism insights. Visit Britain. Available at: http://www.insights.org.uk/articleitem.aspx?title=Cultural+Tourism+and+the+UK+City+of+Culture (accessed 7 March 2014).

Williams, P. and Stewart, J. (1997) Canadian aboriginal tourism development: assessing latent demand from France, *Journal of Tourism Studies* 8(1): 25–41.

Winter, T. (2002) Angkor meets Tomb Raider. Setting the scene, *International Journal of Heritage Studies* 8(4): 524–539.

Winter, T., Teo, P. and Chang, T. (2009) Introduction. In Winter, T., Teo, P. and Chang, T. (eds) *Asia on Tour: Exploring the Rise of Asian Tourism*, London and New York: Routledge, pp. 1–18.

Wong, C. (2013) The sanitization of colonial history: authenticity, heritage interpretation and the case of Macau's tour guides, *Journal of Sustainable Tourism* 21(6): 915–931.

Wong, C. and McKercher, B. (2013) Web markers for various tour products: the case of Hong Kong, *Tourism Management Perspectives* 8: 126–130.

Wong, C. and McKercher, B. (2010) Tourist information centre staff as knowledge brokers: the case of Macau, Annals of Tourism Research 38(2): 481–498.

World Monuments Fund (2014) World Monuments Fund Sustainable Tourism Pledge. Available at: http://www.wmf.org/content/sign-our-pledge (accessed 7 April 2014).

Xie, P. F. (2006) Developing industrial heritage tourism: a case study of the proposed Jeep Museum in Toledo, Ohio, *Tourism Management* 27: 1312–1330.

Xie, P., Osumare, H. and Ibrahim, A. (2007) Gazing the hood: hip-hop as tourism attraction, *Tourism Management* 28(2): 452 – 460.

Xu, K., Yan, T. and Zhu, X. (2013) Commodification of Chinese heritage villages, *Annals of Tourism Research* 40: 419–422.

Yale, P. (1998) *From Tourist Attractions to Heritage Tourism* (2nd Edition), Huntingdon: Elm Publications.

Yan, C. and Morrison, A. (2007) The influence of visitors' awareness of World Heritage Listings: a case study of Huangshan, Xidi and Hongcun in Southern Anhui, China, *Journal of Heritage Tourism* 2(3): 1–14.

Yan, L. and McKercher, B. (2013) Travel culture in Eastern Jin China (317–420 AD): the emergence of a travel culture of landscape appreciation, *Annals of Tourism Research* 43: 20–36.

Yang, L. (2011) Ethnic tourism and cultural representation, *Annals of Tourism Research* 38(2): 561–585.

Yang, L. and Wall, G. (2009) Ethnic tourism: a framework and an application, *Tourism Management* 30(4): 559–570.

Zeppel, H. (1992) *Cultural Tourism in Australia: A Growing Travel Trend,* Townsville, Australia: Material Culture Unit/Department of Tourism, James Cook University.

Zeppel, H. and Hall, C. M. (1991) Selling art and history: cultural heritage and tourism, *Journal of Tourism Studies* 2(10): 29–45.

Zheng, X. and Gretzel, U. (2010) Role of social media in online travel information search, *Tourism Management* 31: 179–188.

Index